Aging in Twentieth-Century Britain

BERKELEY SERIES IN BRITISH STUDIES

Edited by Mark Bevir and James Vernon

1. *The Peculiarities of Liberal Modernity in Imperial Britain,* edited by Simon Gunn and James Vernon
2. *Dilemmas of Decline: British Intellectuals and World Politics, 1945–1975,* by Ian Hall
3. *The Savage Visit: New World People and Popular Imperial Culture in Britain, 1710–1795,* by Kate Fullagar
4. *The Afterlife of Empire,* by Jordanna Bailkin
5. *Smyrna's Ashes: Humanitarianism, Genocide, and the Birth of the Middle East,* by Michelle Tusan
6. *Pathological Bodies: Medicine and Political Culture,* by Corinna Wagner
7. *A Problem of Great Importance: Population, Race, and Power in the British Empire, 1918–1973,* by Karl Ittmann
8. *Liberalism in Empire: An Alternative History,* by Andrew Sartori
9. *Distant Strangers: How Britain Became Modern,* by James Vernon
10. *Edmund Burke and the Conservative Logic of Empire,* by Daniel I. O'Neill
11. *Governing Systems: Modernity and the Making of Public Health in England, 1830–1910,* by Tom Crook
12. *Aging in Twentieth-Century Britain,* by Charlotte Greenhalgh

Aging in Twentieth-Century Britain

Charlotte Greenhalgh

UNIVERSITY OF CALIFORNIA PRESS

University of California Press, one of the most
distinguished university presses in the United States,
enriches lives around the world by advancing scholarship
in the humanities, social sciences, and natural sciences. Its
activities are supported by the UC Press Foundation and
by philanthropic contributions from individuals and
institutions. For more information, visit www.ucpress.edu.

University of California Press
Oakland, California

© 2018 by Charlotte Greenhalgh

Library of Congress Cataloging-in-Publication Data

Names: Greenhalgh, Charlotte, 1983– author.
Title: Aging in twentieth-century Britain / Charlotte
  Greenhalgh.
Description: Oakland, California : University of
  California Press, [2018] | Series: Berkeley Series in
  British Studies ; 12 | Includes bibliographical
  references and index. |
Identifiers: LCCN 2018002049 (print) |
  LCCN 2018005555 (ebook) | ISBN 9780520970809 (Pub) |
  ISBN 9780520298781 (cloth : alk. paper) |
  ISBN 9780520298798 (pbk. : alk. paper)
Subjects: LCSH: Older people—Great Britain.
Classification: LCC HQ1064.G7 (ebook) | LCC HQ1064.G7
  G736 2018 (print) | DDC 305.260941—dc23
LC record available at https://lccn.loc.gov/2018002049

Manufactured in the United States of America

26 25 24 23 22 21 20 19 18
10 9 8 7 6 5 4 3 2 1

*Dedicated to Penelope's grandparents,
Vicki and Geoff Burgess
and Laurel and Rodney Greenhalgh*

CONTENTS

List of Illustrations ix
Acknowledgments xi

Introduction: Aging and Twentieth-Century Britain 1

1. Experts and the Elderly: Social Research on Old Age 18

2. Talking with Peter Townsend: Elderly Britons at Home 46

3. Into the Institution: Residential Care for the Aged 77

4. "Making the Best of My Appearance": Grooming in Old Age 103

5. Games with Time: Autobiography and Aging 133

Epilogue 156

Notes 173
Bibliography 219
Index 241

ILLUSTRATIONS

1. "Stepney Stories" summaries 25
2. "Stepney Stories" key 26
3. "Features of ageing" questionnaire 35
4. Questionnaire from *Old and Alone*, by Jeremy Tunstall 37
5. Sheet from Charles Booth's poverty map of London 50
6. Old people's bungalows 52
7. Front cover illustration for *Elderly Housebound*, by Douglas R. Snellgrove 54
8. Photographs from *Old People*, by Seebohm B. Rowntree 55
9. "Grandfather and Baby" 57
10. "Man in Doorway" 59
11. "Woman in Apron" 60
12. Corridor in a former workhouse, Wolverhampton 85
13. Voluntary home, Liverpool 86
14. Local authority home, London 87
15. Local authority institution, Norfolk 88
16. "Smart for Your Age," British *Vogue*, 1938 110

17. November 1950 cover of British *Vogue* featuring Mrs. Exeter *112*
18. Mrs. Exeter's suit, British *Vogue*, 1957 *113*
19. Mrs. Exeter at dinner, British *Vogue*, 1959 *114*
20. Mrs. Exeter's black dress, British *Vogue*, 1953 *115*
21. Barbara Goalen, British *Vogue*, 1956 *116*
22. "Clothes with No Age Tag," British *Vogue*, 1957 *118*
23. Older man in British *Vogue*, 1954 *120*
24. Front cover illustration for *Between High Walls: A London Childhood*, by Grace Foakes *151*
25. Back cover illustrations for *Between High Walls: A London Childhood*, Grace Foakes *152*

ACKNOWLEDGEMENTS

My professional life has been transformed by generous mentors, and I am deeply grateful to each of them. Caroline Daley gave me the confidence and skills that I needed to get started as an academic. Matt Houlbrook turned his intelligence and creativity to the task of graduate supervision with focus and endless energy. Clare Corbould showed me how to approach academic life with vision and strategy. James Vernon has provided constant encouragement and guidance since he first heard me speak about this project in 2012. His collaborative approach to editing transformed the experience of being a first-time book author and made it enjoyable.

While writing this book, I benefited from the insights and generosity of friends and colleagues at the University of Auckland, the University of Oxford, and Monash University. I am grateful to Christopher Hilliard for his recommendations for supervisors and mentors in Britain and Australia. My warmest thanks go to my colleagues at Monash for supporting the publication of this book and for sharing their smarts. Bain Attwood, Branka Bogdan, Megan Cassidy-Welch, Adam Clulow, Daniella Doron, Scott Dunbar, Kat Ellinghaus, David Garrioch, Michael Hau, Carolyn Holbrook, Peter Howard, Carolyn James, Diana Jeske, Julie Kalman, Ernest Koh, Paula Michaels, Ruth Morgan, Kate Murphy, Kathleen

Neal, Seamus O'Hanlon, Susie Protschky, Noah Shenker, Agnieszka Sobocinska, Taylor Spence, Claire Spivakovsky, Rachel Standfield, Al Thomson, and Christina Twomey, you taught me much about writing. Josh Specht, thank you for sharing the book-writing journey and for your enthusiasm and empathy. Genevieve de Pont, thank you for the pots of tea, for letting me work at your dining room table for so many hours, and for the inspiring conversations. I offer my wholehearted thanks to Toby Harper, Deborah Montgomerie, Matt Houlbrook, Erika Hanna, and Clare Corbould, who each read the full manuscript of this book and equipped me to write the final version (and the final final version). Jonathan Burgess, thank you for the meticulous proofreading; your attention to detail when reading footnotes is just one of your excellent qualities as a sibling. My thanks also go to Sarah-Ann Burger, Anne Holloway, and Mel Thorn, who solved last-minute dilemmas born of distance.

The research for this project was made possible by funding from the Commonwealth Scholarship Commission. Green Templeton College at the University of Oxford and the Center for British Studies at the University of California, Berkeley, provided additional financial support. A grant from the School of Philosophical, Historical, and International Studies at Monash University subsidized publication of the book's images.

My thanks go to the archivists at the University of Sussex, the University of Essex, and the United Kingdom Data Archive, who helped me source the archival material that is at the heart of this project. I would like to give special thanks to Nigel Cochrane from the University of Essex and to Bethany Morgan from the United Kingdom Data Archive for their generous and knowledgeable assistance. I am grateful to Condé Nast Publications, the Norman Parkinson Archive, and others for allowing me to publish the images in this book. I thank Baroness Jean Corston for her generous permission to use photographs that were taken by Peter Townsend. I thank Emma Gleadhill for her determined work arranging image permissions and Bethany White for locating images in *Woman's Own* and *Women's Weekly*.

I am fortunate to have been able to present versions of this research at conferences and seminars at the Max Planck Institute of Human Development, the University of Melbourne, the University of Waikato, the Institute of Historical Research at the University of London, the University of Auckland, the University of Birmingham, the North American Conference on British Studies, the University of Queensland, the University of Brighton, the University of Manchester, Monash University, the University of Oxford, and the University of California, Berkeley. My thanks go to the organizers, participants, and audiences at these wonderful events. I am grateful for visiting fellowships at the Max Planck Institute of Human Development and the University of Oxford.

Selina Todd and Michael Roper were among the first to advise me about publishing this research. Kate Fisher, Claire Langhamer, and Jon Lawrence were generous readers of the manuscript. I give my sincere thanks to Bradley Depew, Niels Hooper, Dore Brown, Genevieve Thurston, Victoria Baker, and the rest of the team at the University of California Press. I have relished the chance to work with you.

My daughter, Penelope, was five months old when I signed the contract for this book. I finished the manuscript thanks to a huge amount of support from my family. I am grateful to Scott for parenting our baby while I wrote. Penelope's grandparents provided countless hours of childcare. My heartfelt thanks go to Vicki and Geoff Burgess and to Laurel and Rodney Greenhalgh. This book is dedicated to you.

INTRODUCTION

Aging and Twentieth-Century Britain

We all wish to grow old. If we are fortunate enough to make it into our advanced years, our ideas about what it means to age will very likely have changed during the course of our lives. This book charts the way elderly people in Britain experienced and narrated their own lives in the twentieth century. It focuses on the 1930s to 1970s but takes account of the entire century. Over this period, the circumstances of old age transformed, but people continued to look to their individual life histories to understand what it meant to be aged.

Between the 1930s and the 1970s, older people spoke to the British public in new ways. During those momentous midcentury decades, Britain, like other Western nations, developed a welfare state that was stronger than any seen previously. Politicians and policymakers relied to an unprecedented degree on the data and recommendations of social researchers. These investigators were better funded than ever before to seek out the experiences and views of the population groups for whom governments were making policy. In doing so, the researchers left behind a mountain of material documenting the ideas of old people. These sources included elderly Britons' grooming habits, their notions of what made a dwelling into a "home," their thoughts about health, love, and loneliness, and much else besides.

But to what extent did social researchers take into account those testimonies they so carefully gathered, recorded, analyzed, and stored? In other words, what impact did old people's ideas about themselves have on government policy? This book answers this question. It shows that even in the heyday of social research, when social movements worldwide were bringing voices of the previously marginalized to the fore, the force of old people's testimony was blunted by political exigencies and a continuing tendency to assume that younger people knew best. To come to this conclusion, this book considers the voices of old people that I have been able to recover from the data that significant researchers left behind. Other materials, such as autobiographies and beauty magazines, provide further insight into the lives and minds of elderly British people in the mid-twentieth century. Even photographs taken by researchers, many of which were never published, can be interpreted as expressions of selfhood. Comparing all of these data to the policies they generated allows me to ascertain the extent to which old people's voices were heard in the twentieth century.

VOICES OF THE AGED

A range of elderly Britons who were the subjects of midcentury social research revealed a common desire to represent their own lives. Since the 1930s, social researchers had sought out the views of "ordinary people"—commonly defined as nonexperts—as they turned their attention from social "problems" to everyday life and argued that gathering first-person evidence provided new insights for social scientists.[1] A section of the British public embraced the chance to take part in social science research. The research organization Mass Observation, for example, appealed for participants in the pages of the *New Statesman* in 1937 and 1947.[2] Around three thousand Britons had participated in the organization's national panel of volunteer writers by 1955. Some had a passing interest in social research that led them to contribute a single month of diary entries. Others, however, diligently submitted their personal diaries for decades.

These volunteers were likely to be middle class, but their most common characteristic was sympathy for the project of social research, which complemented their progressive politics and enjoyment of writing.[3] After 1945, the expanding welfare state required "a constant flow" of this kind of information in order to design and monitor its redistributive efforts.[4] For example, hundreds of elderly Britons who had moved to residential homes during the late 1950s spoke to researcher Peter Townsend as part of his assessment of 1948 legislation that claimed to transform care for the aged.[5]

Unlike the volunteers for Mass Observation's panel, the participants in Townsend's projects were selected by the researcher as part of his construction of representative samples. The 203 elderly interviewees who contributed to Townsend's study of family life, for example, were chosen at random from the lists of patients held by doctors in the borough of Bethnal Green in East London.[6] Given the invitation, however, most of the elderly residents of Bethnal Green relished the chance to speak at length about their lives. A majority agreed to talk with Townsend on multiple occasions, for up to an hour at a time. Many of the interviewees and their relatives turned Townsend's unstructured interviews to their own ends by boasting, cracking jokes, and rehearsing well-worn family tales. Participants who faced new adversities in late life demonstrated their stoicism and strength and highlighted the continuities of aging. According to the testimonies of these individuals, families remained close and working lives were long. Britons remembered their dead. It was common for older people to talk about their lives at midcentury, but the presence of a listening social researcher, notebook in hand, was a novel feature of this storytelling scene.

A number of elderly interviewees disputed the optimistic views that social researchers held about welfare services for the aged, including that these services should be more widely available. When he spoke with a sociologist during the 1960s, elderly interviewee Mr. Thomas was ambivalent about Meals on Wheels (he was concerned that he might let hot food go to waste), home care (he wanted home help, but he believed that nothing would be done to organize this), and old people's clubs (he argued with the interviewer's claim that affordable clubs existed, where tea was served instead of alcohol).[7] Aging interviewees were just as likely to reject the dire diagnoses of medical experts as they were to doubt the apparent promise of welfare policies for the aged. This pattern confused researchers, who recorded the frequency with which people who appeared to them to be "almost dying on their feet" insisted that they "mustn't grumble" or that their health was "fair."[8] Doctors were no more popular, it seemed, than social scientists. A number of interviewees said that their "strong constitution" was the result of personal discipline, which they displayed through "clean living" and resisting the temptation to "let themselves go."[9] Similarly, recovery from illness was framed by elderly people as "perseverance" that took medical professionals by surprise.[10] Elderly interviewees frequently took control of their conversations with experts. A number of bereaved people drew a veil over feelings that they did not wish to share with others, controlling their exchanges with researchers by, for example, reciting stoic sentiments such as, "You never get anywhere if you stay and brood," and perhaps the death of a loved one was "for the best."[11]

The most vulnerable older people—those who were older, poorer, and more isolated than their peers—were likely to live in residential institutions and were often housed in public homes that still resembled workhouses at midcentury. A number of them were vocal about the turn their lives had taken. Many residents of these old-age institutions screamed or grumbled about their discomforts.[12] Almost five hundred among them gave interviews when Townsend's research team visited residential homes around England and Wales during the late 1950s. Social researchers completed questionnaires and read case files in the attempt to understand the lives of elderly residents. Townsend even moved into a residential home and lived there for several days. Residents of some institutions, however, stayed silent for fear of offending workers and administrators who had the power to exact punishments. Social scientists replicated aspects of Townsend's study in 2005 and 2006 to bring the record he created of life inside residential homes up to the twenty-first century.[13] Even fifty years later, residents spoke about the failures of policymakers to act on the testimony of the aged.

For some aging Britons, it was just as important to be seen as it was to be heard. Older people with the resources and the inclination to be fashionable wielded tools of grooming and style, donning well-cut suits, charming accessories, or a touch of rouge. Those who looked to fashion magazines like British *Vogue* for inspiration found that aging bodies were prominent in their pages. However, fashion-conscious elderly people typically had a flexible approach to the latest fads. They understood that the ability to discern clothes that were age appropriate, or "just right," was itself the height of fashion.[14] In so doing, elegant elderly Britons made "the best" of their appearances and delivered visual cues about their character and social status.[15] The care they took to continually fine-tune their grooming habits demonstrated the ability of older people with health and resources to adjust to physical aging with time. Careful grooming was a way for Britons of a certain class to meet the challenges of later life and to claim pleasures from aging bodies, but this was denied to many of their less well-off peers.

The driving ambition of older Britons to speak in public about their lives is chronicled in their published autobiographies. Aging authors had diverse aims. Some celebrated their professional successes. Others aimed to solve a family mystery or settle an old score.[16] The older autobiographers who published such varied stories during the mid- to late twentieth century had a common interest in portraying the immense social changes of that century. As one writer put it, the stories of "those who have lived through the last sixty or seventy years" were virtually guaranteed to be fascinating.[17] Aged autobiographers wrote about how they had been "helped or hindered, according to their capacity and temperament, by the far-reaching changes of that period."[18] Local history groups and community presses that flourished starting in the late 1960s made the same assessment of writers born at the turn of the century. Community presses took advantage of new and inexpensive printing techniques to publish the life stories of elderly working-class authors. Such writers regarded the years of their childhoods across a chasm of time that contained a depression, two world wars, and the construction of the postwar welfare state. These authors were awed by the speed of social change; they experienced the uncanniness of living through disparate times and wrote about the bittersweet melding of family memories with social injustices of the past. The renowned wisdom of the aged was tempered, at least in the telling of older autobiographers, by distrust of memories that sometimes seemed too rosy.

OLD AGE IN BRITISH HISTORY

Compared to other periods in the life cycle, the category of old age is particularly broad and unhelpful for understanding the experiences of individuals. Old age encompasses a much longer period than childhood or adolescence: it can last up to forty years, sometimes more. Many of the characteristics that are associated with old age occur across the life cycle. Ill health, for example, can strike at any age. Diseases such as Alzheimer's are not, however, an inevitable part of aging.[19] Medical researchers in the 1950s showed that some cases of "mental degeneracy" in old age were caused by malnutrition, highlighting the importance of changing material circumstance to the nature of aging.[20] Social researchers at midcentury demonstrated that social isolation was not a function of old age, as had been widely believed, but was usually the consequence of the breakup of families earlier in life, perhaps due to violence or desertion.[21] It is for these reasons that scholars have suggested dividing the category of old age into third and fourth ages, or "young" old age and "old" old age.[22] But these categories run into the same problem, that people of similar ages are quite different. For historians, the category of old age best identifies the interactions of older people and the state, which have frequently been determined by chronological age. Aging Britons, though, usually did not see themselves as "old" in the way that policymakers and social researchers conceived the category. Instead, Britons experienced growing older over time and in the course of their own lives. Aging, therefore, was a process that was relative, subjective, and virtually lifelong.

The life expectancy of Britons has increased dramatically since the late nineteenth century. In the nineteenth century, average life expectancy was around forty to forty-five years. Men and women born in 1851, for example, could expect to live to forty and forty-three, respectively.[23] Men born fifty years later, in 1901, could expect to live to fifty-one, and women to fifty-eight. Life expectancy continued to rise steadily over the twentieth century. Men and women born in 1991 can expect to live to seventy-six and eighty, respectively. Most of these gains in years have been the result of improved chances of survival beyond infancy and childhood. In the late nineteenth century, a dramatic drop in the number of deaths among babies and children occurred at the same time that the birth rate began to fall.[24] In addition, starting in the 1970s, developed countries, including Britain, have slowly and steadily added to life expectancy by improving the health of older people.[25] As a result, the proportion of the British population aged over sixty-five increased during the past century from one in twenty people to one in six.[26] News coverage of Britain's "aging population" in the 1930s to the 1970s, and up to today, has repeated the misguided notion that it was uncommon to reach old age before the twentieth century. In fact, people who survived their hazardous early years could reasonably expect to live for sixty years or more, even in the preindustrial past.[27] The elderly were a sizeable and visible group in past societies. Between 6 and 10 percent of European and North American populations were aged over sixty between the early modern period and the early twentieth century.[28]

In Europe, old age has been the subject of increasing levels of legal and bureaucratic management since the Middle Ages. In its earliest versions, this took a passive form: people over the age of sixty or seventy were exempted from certain public duties, such as military service, compulsory labor, or the payment of taxes.[29] The specter of destitution in old age informed subsequent efforts to manage it. From the seventeenth century, the practices of "discriminating relief" that judged individuals to be deserving, or not deserving, of charity shaped the lives of the large proportion of elderly who lived in poverty.[30] These practices generated new records of life in old age by logging the details of work, family, and moral character that were believed to justify the provision or denial of relief. Recognizably "modern" ways of dealing with old age, such as public service pensions and specialist medicine, began in the eighteenth century.[31] During this period, states that were growing in size and influence introduced the first public service pensions and were influenced by early texts in political arithmetic, public administration, and statistics.[32] Each of these fields offered new ways of thinking about old age, often in quantitative and bureaucratic forms that encouraged increased activity by the state.

The British state has refined and formalized the boundary of old age. The institutions of old age expanded in the nineteenth century in response to industrialization, urbanization, and population growth.[33] Poor Law Commissioners set sixty as the marker of old age in 1834.[34] Sixty-five was the first official pension age in 1898.[35] The state pension, introduced by the Liberal government in 1908, had a powerful effect on Edwardian poverty despite its limited aim to provide below-subsistence level support for "the very old, the very poor, and the very respectable."[36] Due to the destitution of many older Britons, state pensions were taken up in huge numbers.[37] Pensions and retirement would become a mass experience under the twentieth-century welfare state. By midcentury, it was popularly accepted that old age began at the state pension age of sixty or sixty-five (for women and men, respectively). Historians have argued that this definition has informed people's expectations of both state activity and personal experiences in later life.[38]

There is a particular history of old age among women. Women have had longer life expectancy than men since 1837, when the government began keeping records of births and deaths in England.[39] Women have historically been more likely to survive into old age, but as studies from the 1940s until the 1990s have shown, they have done so in poorer health.[40] In the 1930s, researchers observed that working-class women "put their own health, and food, needs after those of their husbands and children," with the result that many of these women were malnourished.[41] A study in the late 1940s found that older women were more likely than older men to be housebound or otherwise restricted in mobility and that they were affected in old age by the symptoms of having given birth in adverse conditions.[42] Women have been more likely to be poor in old age, in part because they have had shorter and more sporadic working lives.[43] In the twentieth century, women were typically dismissed from their jobs earlier than men on account of being "too old" to work, and they commonly left paid employment to care for aging parents and other relatives.[44] However, women continued to do domestic work until very late ages. Until the 1940s, women had access to pensions only if they were widows or the wives of insured men.[45] Despite this patchy coverage, almost two-thirds of the 490,000 people who qualified for the first pensions in Britain on January 1, 1909, were women, and this was because of their high level of poverty.[46] Until the 1970s, women's access to benefits depended on their marital status, while men's qualification depended on employment.[47]

The humane treatment of the elderly had particular symbolic significance in the postwar period due to the claim that the British welfare state now provided for its citizens from the cradle to the grave. Starting in the middle of the twentieth century, health and welfare professionals, local authorities, and voluntary organizations offered a patchwork of new services—including home care, Meals on Wheels, residential care, and housing—to improve the lives of elderly people with the greatest needs.[48] The introduction of universal healthcare in 1948 had wider effects. Older people were the particular beneficiaries of services designed to treat the general population, including the provision of spectacles and false teeth. From the 1970s, the aged enjoyed the advantages of technological advancements such as hip replacements and pacemaker technology.[49] In the final decades of the twentieth century, such improvements lengthened later life. Many older Britons responded to such developments in state welfare along generational lines. By midcentury, for example, many elderly people celebrated state pensions and viewed them as a right of citizenship, saying, "It's a wonderful thing since they came in."[50] They were more doubtful about the health and domiciliary services that had been introduced since 1945. As Townsend pointed out, the new definitions of "public responsibility," "need," and "respect" that he thought should inform care for the aged could be taught to the young in schools and universities.[51] Older Britons, however, had been "brought up to treat these terms very differently" from the young.

The meaning and experience of old age in the twentieth century have been bound up with the history of the British welfare state. But histories of the welfare state have changed in recent decades as historians have shown how contested and uneven forms of welfare provision were, as well as how they remained nested in local, voluntary, and imperial structures.[52] For all its claims to provide Britons with universal coverage, the welfare state remained organized by gender, race, class, and age. Built on these unequal foundations, the British state excluded many from its social protections.[53] Both poverty and welfare were features of old age throughout the twentieth century, and there was persistent inequality among older generations.[54] Just as Charles Booth had found in late nineteenth-century London, the European Commission Observatory on Ageing and Old People reported in 1992 that 30 percent of the British elderly lived below the poverty line.[55] Social class governed people's access to material and emotional comforts in late life. Class also helped determine who was asked to speak about aging and in what venues they were heard. Researchers, for example, conducted interviews differently depending on whether they were speaking to working-class elderly people in Bethnal Green or to residents of old-age institutions. And middle-class volunteers for Mass Observation wrote about topics ranging from personal grooming to international affairs, subjects that were never raised with working-class or institutionalized interviewees. The treatment of older people by social scientists offers an account of the ways that social class and access to resources shaped the experience of aging throughout the twentieth century.

· · ·

Old age is a qualitatively distinct period of life that has not often been explored by modern British historians. Scholars across the disciplines of psychology, economics, sociology, gerontology, geography, and history have placed age alongside gender, race, region, religion, and class as "a crucial determinant of economic, social and cultural life."[56] Yet most historians have been reluctant to give age the analytical primacy they have afforded to class, race, and gender.

Twentieth-century transformations in the public treatment of old age established many elements of the theory, policy, and infrastructure that we associate with later life today. The pattern of lengthening life expectancy and lower birth rates and the concomitant "dramatic long-run increase in the proportion of older people" in Britain began in the late nineteenth century and turned into a source of social anxiety when the "aging population" became statistically apparent in the 1920s and 1930s.[57] During the first half of the twentieth century, doctors and psychiatrists introduced the idea that old people required particular medical attention and the services of specialists who understood the physiology of aging and could develop treatments and technologies for associated health problems. Geriatric medicine was invented around the time of World War I and was practiced by innovative physicians led by Marjory Warren in Britain and William Ferguson Anderson in Scotland from 1935, although the professional status and official reforms sought by geriatricians came much later.[58] Geriatric medicine argued that aging and disease were distinct from each other, and it introduced treatments for the maladies of late life. Starting in the mid-1940s, psychiatrists began to make similar distinctions between the process of aging, diseases such as Alzheimer's, and the manifestations of mental health problems in the elderly.[59] However, the sluggish spread of their diagnostic tools meant that Britons frequently lacked the language to describe mental health issues in old age, as opposed to psychological neuroses, until late in the century.

A number of twentieth-century British historians, notably Pat Thane, have been intrigued by these important changes and have looked closely at some of the intellectual and political shifts underpinning them.[60] These scholars have sought to interrogate the claims made by midcentury experts and reformers about what difference they would make in the lives of old people. Historians have assessed the successes and failures of efforts to improve standards of life for the aged. In the postwar period, for example, both conservative and progressive politicians made claims about the newly humane treatment of the elderly, but they simultaneously undermined the redistribution of wealth to this population.[61] Echoing the findings of midcentury social surveys such as those authored by Townsend, Joseph Sheldon, and Michael Young—and particularly their "rediscovery" of poverty in the 1960s—historians have pointed to the intransigence of poverty in old age over the twentieth century.[62] In doing so, they have described "parallel" histories of old age in the twentieth century that track advances in medical knowledge and citizenship rights but also the consistent failure of governments to transfer an equitable share of the nation's wealth to the old.[63]

When historians of old age chart increasing interventions by the British state and technical innovations such as the advent of geriatric medicine, they sometimes reflect the priorities of policymakers and professionals rather than the lives of the elderly. For example, historians who have relied on research publications and other official sources have created a closed-circuit discussion between midcentury experts, who diagnosed and treated the "problems" of old age, and historical accounts of their increasingly humane treatment of aging Britons. Yet the public treatment of old age does not provide a proxy for personal experiences of aging. As Thane has written, postwar medical researchers had "little evidence" to support their claim that retirement caused sickness and even death.[64] Sociologists of the period who were "fixated" on the notion that "occupation rather than income conferred status and dignity" saw "gloom" in retirement that was not always shared by older people.[65] In the 1970s, researchers showed that the "minority of genuinely sad cases" that came to the attention of psychologists during previous decades had been "represented as the norm" of aging.[66] Elderly people have a history that is intertwined with the work of experts who have written about them, but ultimately these are separate stories. The intellectual and political priorities of researchers did not determine how older Britons felt about aging.

At first look, it seems that the "affective turn" in history writing would open up the history of the private lives of the aged.[67] Recent scholarship has argued that historians are well equipped to discuss the interior world. Emotions, as Monique Scheer has demonstrated, leave material traces that can be identified through archival research.[68] Scholars in the field of the history of emotions have long worked to establish public norms of feeling in the past.[69] This has established that emotions are not universal but rather change over time. As historians have shown, affective life both has a history and creates broader change.[70] The behaviors of families who have kept or revealed their secrets, for example, have shaped public norms, even if historians mostly track social changes as if they always began with public life.[71] Scholars have started to examine the connection between state activity and self-identity, too, most famously in Carolyn Steedman's analysis of "orange juice and milk and dinners at school" and what they taught her about her personal value and "right to exist."[72]

Historians of old age have been slow to adopt insights from histories of subjectivity and emotion. They have not responded, for example, to W. Andrew Achenbaum's call that historians should "probe the inner lives" of their aging subjects.[73] Evidence for personal experiences of old age has come mostly from the narrow records of well-known "articulate old women" and "powerful old men," such as Octavia Hill, Beatrice Webb, and William Gladstone.[74] Scholars who have pored over letters and diaries in search of descriptions of aging have declared the topic rarely discussed.[75] Historians Selina Todd and Claire Langhamer have used youthful experiences to demonstrate that the life cycle has determined historical meanings of work, gender, and family life, but their insights have not been applied to later life.[76] And the history of emotions has so far upheld a particular focus on the experiences of the young. Histories of trauma, for example, are more likely to consider soldiers in the trenches than people with chronic illness.[77] Likewise, histories of love and sexuality lavish attention on courtship, wedding days, and first childbearing.[78] Even in the midst of an affective turn, historians are mostly silent on the inner lives of the elderly.

• • •

This book seeks out the voices of older people in the fields of social science, state welfare, commerce, and literature. In particular, it tells the story of how twentieth-century social researchers worked to harness and expand the authority of the aged. Their efforts yielded invaluable material for the investigation of the lives of older Britons in the past. British people sent Mass Observation their testimony in such quantity that archivists, historians, and a digitization project have taken almost fifty years to make it readily accessible to the historically minded public.[79] Peter Townsend archived his reports of multiple sets of interviews with just over 200 East Londoners and their families, as well as records of conversations with the residents and staff of 173 old-age institutions and additional research data ranging from questionnaires and diaries to photographs. These sources record what older people said on their doorsteps and in institutions during face-to-face conversations with the experts of their day.

Archivists have long called for historians to ask fresh questions of raw research data and thus provide "secondary" analysis of it.[80] The archives contain the fruits of immersive and exhaustive research techniques that were employed from the 1940s to the 1970s, but these studies would be difficult to repeat today, mostly due to cost. Historians have successfully used secondary analysis to reassess historical narratives about class identity and social disadvantage, the topics that midcentury research frequently investigated. In his examination of interviews that were conducted during the early 1960s in Luton, for example, Mike Savage has paid new attention to the ways that interviewees hesitated when they were asked questions about social class. Savage's analysis reveals that workers in Luton did not define classes as "clusters of occupational groups" in the way sociologists did but rather saw the working classes as "normal, authentic people, largely devoid of social distinction."[81] Savage has shown that the different views held by social researchers and their subjects skewed the famous conclusions of researchers about working-class experiences of postwar affluence. Selina Todd has used a similarly critical reading of interview notes to argue that social researchers in Liverpool missed evidence of deprivation and financial insecurity among working people during the 1950s and 1960s.[82] Jon Lawrence examined the ways that the class identities of interviewers and interviewees affected how social research questions about status were asked and answered and how this led researchers to underestimate the social ambitions of working-class men.[83] These historians have reassessed the findings of twentieth-century social researchers and identified the roots of significant narratives of modern British history such as postwar affluence and its effects on working-class culture.

The purposes of my secondary analysis of social research data are to recover unpublished evidence of the lived experiences of aging and to reposition researchers and other professionals within scenes of fieldwork. Midcentury social researchers intended to record the lives of the old in order to affect policymaking, but I show that they changed the experience of old age from the moment they knocked on the doors of the elderly. Exchanges between interviewers and interviewees, like those between residents and workers in old-age institutions, became meeting points for public and private ideas about aging. Each participant in these interviews was able to learn new things about aging from the interaction. Sometimes the methods of such conversations taught its participants more about the shifting social status of older people than the words that were spoken. New health and welfare services also helped to change Britons' ideas about and experiences of old age. This reading of the sources diverges from the political and intellectual priorities that directed the attention of twentieth-century researchers, which provide important context for the collection of older people's narratives. I use social research data to identify when older people spoke about their lives, which audiences they addressed, and to what ends. The long history of invoking old age in order to consider the meaning of life, death, and morality has created enduring ideas about the wisdom and the folly of older people that are primarily symbolic.[84] I argue that Britons revealed more about aging when they discussed topics apart from late life. This provides a good reason to listen to elderly people when they long for lost loved ones and gossip about family gatherings.

In an unpublished essay from January 1946, a railway draughtsman who was a contributor to the social research organization Mass Observation wrote, "I was 70 yesterday, so personally I feel I am now 'elderly' and need not feel so rigidly that I must be always BUSY. I wonder whether we shall have visitors, and how they will affect our lives. I shall no doubt be busy in the garden, and in fetching boughs from the woods and chopping; I am not too old for any of these activities."[85] This writer proclaimed that reaching the age of seventy had made him "elderly," but he disowned its connotations of dependence and debility by presenting the term inside scare quotes. In particular, he was careful to differentiate his feeling that he need not always be "busy" in old age from his active social, physical, and home life. The man was "not too old" to cut firewood or debate the state of contemporary religious faith and international relations, as he went on to do in the essay. The aging process had delivered personal gains to offset its costs. "Now that I am 70," the man wrote, "life is calm and peaceful; I enjoy many simple pleasures, and look forward to old age with interest." Within one letter, he described himself as "elderly," "not too old," and looking forward to old age. This man's shifting identification with the concept of old age related to his social and household obligations more than his physical capabilities, and it had even less to do with the number of years he had lived. He queried public categories of old age almost forty years after state pensions had helped formalize them. His approach to aging would have been familiar to many of the older Britons who are discussed in this book. Their views are at the heart of its story.

CHAPTER ONE

Experts and the Elderly

Social Research on Old Age

In 1861, journalist and reformer Henry Mayhew described visiting a woman of around sixty who was so "broken up with age, want, and infirmity" that he thought she scarcely seemed human.[1] To Mayhew, peering into a dark and bare apartment in East London, the woman looked like "a bundle of rags and filth stretched out on some dirty straw in the corner." He asked for her story. After giving an account of her life and of the deaths of her husband and eight children, the woman revealed that in old age she had nothing, earned only a little money collecting dog feces for a tanner, and was lying down because of the "dizziness in my head." A century later, social researcher Peter Townsend witnessed a very different East London scene. Living in neat terraced cottages with gardens and pets, family photos on the wall, and furniture that had been received as gifts or inheritance, the older people who spoke to Townsend "drew attention to their unimpaired faculties, to their individuality and to the compensations they recognized for things they had lost."[2] The twentieth century offered these residents of East London a new kind of old age.

Over the first half of the twentieth century, the material lives of the elderly were transformed by a degree of state activity that had been unimaginable in Mayhew's London. Depictions of the aged in public life changed too, although vignettes from the pages of Mayhew and

Townsend were part of a tradition of seeking out the stories of the elderly. By the time of Townsend's visits to East London, the state had relieved the elderly of abject poverty. Yet the elderly hardly credited this to state welfare or the classification of old age pensioner that made them eligible for the state's services. Instead, Townsend wrote, they "thought of themselves, first as members of families and workgroups, as grandmothers, aunts or housewives, as grandfathers, uncles and cabinet-makers, and only second as individuals old in years."[3] Much of the history of old age has reversed Townsend's formulation by focusing on the development of old age as a political category and an object of policy. This work has produced excellent knowledge of improvements in the material conditions of old age that occurred during the twentieth century but has not often examined the new forms of affective and social life that resulted.

During the twentieth century, social research delineated old age as an object of study and state intervention. Expert attention was drawn to old age in the 1890s because of the particular poverty of elderly people. Social research and social reform went hand-in-hand at this time, and they would continue to do so throughout the twentieth century. The research methods, findings, and advocacy of social surveyor Charles Booth, for example, helped spur the introduction of state pensions in 1908. From this period on, social researchers contributed to political debates about the expansion of welfare services for older Britons. As Jordanna Bailkin has written, the welfare state "required a constant flow of information" and relied on "an army of experts" to monitor its projects.[4] As well as developing new ideas about the public treatment of old age, scholars began to investigate the private lives of the elderly using the methods of psychology and the social sciences. Since the 1950s, historians have used the resulting publications to discuss new patterns of social life, such as widespread retirement and family support between households.[5] But to what extent did researchers pay attention to the voices of older people in their work? What drove social researchers to listen more closely to the stories of individual elderly people over the course of the twentieth century? And why were they so much more likely to ask older people about household chores than about childhood memories?

This chapter tracks the development of knowledge about aging individuals between the 1890s and the 1960s through poverty research, psychology, policymaking, and the social sciences. Elderly individuals became increasingly visible over time as twentieth-century social researchers observed their neighborhoods, mapped their streets, and collated the case files of charitable institutions. From the 1940s, aging subjects answered medical and social questionnaires that became the basis for statistics that researchers calculated about the conditions of old age. By the 1950s, older people spent hours conversing with researchers after being chosen as subjects of case studies and interviews. During the postwar period, such direct evidence from research subjects acquired intellectual authority and high political stakes as researchers and policymakers debated the achievements and priorities of the expanding welfare state. There was double motivation for researchers to seek out the voices of the elderly, and yet in subsequent stages of the research process—including recording, analysis, authorship, and publication—experts consistently wrote over the testimony of the old. The secondary analysis of historic data, however, refocuses attention on stories that were told by elderly Britons and remain in the archives.

OLD AGE AND POVERTY RESEARCH

Around 1900, older people came to the attention of social surveyors because of their poverty. By the late nineteenth century, London in particular was buzzing with revelations about the poverty that existed within its boundaries. A series of harsh winters, outbreaks of cholera, and the collapse of the Thames shipbuilding industry drew attention to London's "great poverty in the midst of plenty" and heightened fears of social unrest in London's East End.[6] The 1880s was a decade of intellectual upheaval, including the debate over the ideas of New Liberalism, the establishment of the Fabian Society in 1884, and discussion of collectivist solutions to social problems.[7] Journalistic exposés such as those authored by George Sims (*How the Poor Live*, 1883) and Andrew Mearns ("The Bitter Cry of Outcast London," 1883) told the stories of individuals struggling to survive in the city.[8] Religious works such as *Into Darkest England*, written by General Booth of the Salvation Army (1890), shared many of the same concerns.[9] Newspapers drew public attention to the problems of poverty by adopting these themes and employing sensationalist reporting styles, beginning with articles by W. T. Stead in the *Pall Mall Gazette*.[10]

Departing from the perspective of earlier Victorians, who claimed that destitution was evidence of a failure of moral will on the part of the poor, late nineteenth-century writers began to explain poverty as a cycle that was governed by environmental or biological factors. Once poor, they argued, individuals were likely to remain so due to the conditions in which they lived and worked. Wealthy individuals and political leaders championed new technologies to measure the problem. In 1884, Henry Hyndman, founder of the Social Democratic Foundation, claimed that over 25 percent of London's workers lived in extreme financial hardship.[11] In the same year, the mayor of London asked the city's Statistical Society to determine which methods of assistance were most beneficial to the poor and should therefore be employed by the Relief Fund that year.[12] Civic leaders were optimistic that more data would reveal the correct actions to take to improve social conditions.[13] The intervention of "heroic investigators and reformers" appeared to be necessary to break the cycle of poverty.[14]

Charles Booth was the first to personally investigate the causes and extent of poverty rather than relying on census figures.[15] The scale of his statistical survey of London was far greater than previous investigations and is likely the largest private research project ever undertaken in Britain.[16] The survey was completed over seventeen years (1886–1903) and was published in three series—on poverty, industry, and religion, respectively—each with multiple volumes. The poverty series collated, categorized, and mapped the reports of school board visitors about the extent of poverty in households in East London and in the streets of all other areas of London, describing about 3,400 streets, or 180,000 households.[17] Booth calculated that around 30 percent of London's population lived in poverty, showing that it was a greater problem than others had been able to discern.[18]

Booth's social research made him into a social reformer for the aged, despite his earlier commitment to presenting facts about social problems rather than to devising their solutions.[19] After finding significant numbers of elderly among the poor, Booth wrote that "poverty is essentially a trouble of old age."[20] He concluded that the introduction of a universal, noncontributory old-age pension would ameliorate the "gravest sector of misery" that he had encountered.[21] Booth's subsequent work aimed to present a "systematic empirical case" for the introduction of state pensions.[22] Seebohm Rowntree supported Booth's claims when he studied York and found that poverty was determined by the lifecycle because of changes to family earnings and expenses.[23] Young people could save a little money in their initial working years, but their wages failed to accommodate the needs of a family beyond the support of a few children. This desperate need eased when adult children began to contribute wages to the household economy, only to return when aging parents were unable to secure steady employment for themselves. The statistical analysis presented in these studies and subsequent social surveys unsettled earlier portrayals of poor individuals as "masters of their fate" and suggested that poverty was the outcome of a series of problems that governments could conceivably compensate for, including the "problem" of old age.[24]

In his study, Booth combined the testimony of working people with statements by figures of professional authority to draw attention to the lives of individual Britons.[25] Workers, trade union leaders, and employers contributed to Booth's industry series, for example, by completing questionnaires and being interviewed for the study.[26] Ministers and local government officials returned questionnaires for the religion series, and 1,800 people gave personal interviews.[27] The reading public found this level of detail about the lives of ordinary Britons both original and compelling.[28]

When Booth used the records of workhouses, though, he reproduced only elderly people's interactions with local authorities, not a full account of their lives. For example, he relied on the judgments officials made about the causes of the predicaments elderly individuals found themselves in, which included ostensible neglect, adultery, and drunkenness.[29] At the end of the nineteenth century, working people commonly made applications to charity. Household budgets were so tight that a small amount of money made the difference between independence and indigence. For this reason, Alison Light has written that if working-class families have an "ancestral home," it is the workhouse.[30] The records of workhouses, though, were skewed first by the efforts of these institutions to dissuade applications to charity and second by their requirement that applicants perform a particular version of their life stories to secure help.[31] Inside workhouses, families were separated, personal possessions were confiscated, and people were disciplined with physical labor, such as picking oakum. The workhouse was the object of universal hatred and fear among the working classes, especially after unions restricted the provision of alternative forms of relief from the mid-1860s in an effort to standardize Poor Law practices and thus treat poverty more "scientifically."[32] Historian Peter Mandler has shown that working people knew how to present themselves to get help by using narratives that were distinct from the ways they actually used charity to get by.[33]

Booth's 1892 study of old age presented cases of older people who had been admitted to the workhouses in Stepney, St Pancras, and Ashby-de-la-Zouch because of their extreme poverty.[34] His "Stepney Stories," for example, were summaries of the lives of elderly paupers in a few short lines (figure 1). There were feelings coded into these narratives, but the repertoire was limited to pity, shame, and hopelessness. Like the relieving officers of the local unions, Booth was more interested in categorizing the causes of poverty than in learning about the lives of individuals. The researcher used a key to label each person's story with the main culprit of their destitution: the label *D*, for example, stood for *drink* (figure 2). Rather than celebrating personal testimony, Booth wrote that there were "few stories that cannot be forcibly expressed by marital condition, age, and three letters."[35] Early social research such as this was not generous to the old. Researchers carefully excised "the mental, moral, and social side of human nature" from their methodology.[36] Their stringent recommendations downgraded the requirements of Britons just because they were old. In 1901, for example, Rowntree assumed that older people could get by on two-thirds of the income of younger adults.[37] As late as 1930, *The New Survey of London* asserted that old people needed to eat only 60 percent of the calories consumed by an active adult male.[38] During the early decades of the century, researchers aimed to calculate the absolute minimum amount of money that an older person would need to pay for food, clothing, rent, and heating.

Booth helped create the social scientific category of old age by arguing that older people shared the experience of poverty due to their age rather than to their individual characteristics. His subsequent aim was to release older people from both poverty and the Poor Law. Booth argued that pensions should be universal and compulsory and therefore easily distinguished from the stigmatizing system of charitable relief. He suggested that the elderly over the age of sixty-five be given tax-funded payments of five shillings per week, rising to seven shillings per week after they reached the age of seventy.[39] However, long-standing judgments of poverty as a moral affliction coexisted with innovative arguments in both research and reform. Booth's proposal was notably different from campaigns for a state pension scheme that would be limited to the "thrifty"—that is, those who belonged to friendly societies.[40] Yet Booth himself remained an advocate of "discriminatory relief" for the young. He argued that Poor Law institutions could better discipline the able-bodied once they were freed from taking care of the aged poor.

Politicians and policymakers were less generous to the old than researchers recommended, yet the introduction of state pensions transformed the lives of many elderly people who lived in extreme poverty.

No.	Sex.	Condition.	Age.	Occupation.	Cause of Pauperism.	Years Chargeable.	Story.	Known Pauper Relatives.
*518	(*Infirm*) Male	(*contd.*) Widow'r	70	Blacksmith	(*Old Age* contd.) Z e u See p. 61.	10	Early applications for wife, who died (1885) in Sick Asylum. Work irregular; lived well at times, starved at others.	...
*519	,,	Married	68	Carman	Z e s See p. 61.	5	In same place 12 years, 21s. a week; would not pay 6d. a week to yard club. Came to parish for medicine.	...
*520	Female	Widow	80	Boot-closer	Z q See p. 63.	9	Had relief at husband's death (1866). Sons do not like to keep her.	...
521	Male	Widow'r	65	Baker (journeyman)	Z q See p. 63.	6 m	35 years in England. Not able to work at trade for 6 years; been in tea warehouse. Lived with son.	Brother-in-law, X.
*522	Male	Widow'r	87	Shopkeeper (formerly Seaman)	Z q	13	In timber department of docks for 40 years. Hard-working, but quarrels and drinks. Admitted with wife, who died in 1886.	...
523	,,	Married	69	Cigar-maker and Dock Labourer	Z i	6	Admitted in 1883; not seen wife for 8 years. Out for 7 months in 1885; lived by begging.	...
524	,,	Widow'r	61	Labourer	Z i	1 m	Lost his speech and cannot get work. Lived 6 years in Peabody Buildings.	...
525	,,	,,	72	Coal-whipper	Z i	11½	Re-admitted in 1882. Sons promised an allowance, but did not pay it, so he preferred the workhouse.	...
526	,,	,,	70	,,	Z i	10	Lived with daughter, but she cannot keep him. Has not been out since 1884. Injured eye.	Daughter, S. Sister-in-law, S w. Sister-in-law, No. 272. Nephew, No. 1115. Nephew, S e.
527	Female	Single	73	Nurse	Z i	8	Been chargeable to Poplar 5 years. Could not keep her situations.	...
*528	Male	Widow'r	80	Carpenter	Z i See p. 69.	6	Disabled. Had not worked for 11 months, when daughter got him admitted (1883). She had kept him.	...
529	,,	,,	66	Labourer (formerly Seaman)	Z i	3	Wife died in asylum (1880). Man gave up the sea through failing sight. Comfortable home then: in 1886 he is homeless — walked streets for two nights.	...
530	,,	Single	63	General Labourer	Z i	4	Stays at common lodging-houses when out. Runs errands.	Brother, S u.

Figure 1. The records of workhouses took up huge sections of Booth's pamphlets on old age. This page of "Stepney Stories" judged ostensible causes of poverty among older Britons to include old age, extravagant living, unemployment, a queer temper, sickness, and incapacity. Charles Booth, *Pauperism, a Picture; And Endowment of Old Age, an Argument* (London: Macmillan, 1892), 288.

APPENDIX B

STEPNEY PAUPERISM

The method adopted for tabulating the causes of poverty was as follows. To each cause I affixed an alphabetical symbol, using a capital letter where the cause given is the principal one, and a small letter where it is contributory, thus:

Cause.	Principal.	Contributory.	Father or Husband.	Mother or Wife.	Both.
Crime	C	c	c^1	c^2	c^3
Vice	V	v	v^1	v^2	v^3
Drink	D	d	d^1	d^2	d^3
Laziness	L	l	l^1	l^2	l^3
Pauper association	P	p	p^1	p^2	p^3
Heredity	H	h	h^1	h^2	h^3
Mental disease	M	m	m^1	m^2	m^3
Temper (queer)	Q	q	q^1	q^2	q^3
Incapacity	I	i	i^1	i^2	i^3
Early marriage (girl)	G	g	g^1	g^2	g^3
Large family	F	f			
Extravagance	E	e	e^1	e^2	e^3
Lack of work (unemployed)	U	u	u^1	u^2	u^3
Trade misfortune	T	t	t^1	t^2	t^3
Restlessness, roving, tramp	R	r	r^1	r^2	r^3
No relations	N	n			
Death of husband	W	w			
Desertion (abandoned)	A	a			
Death of father or mother (orphan)	O	o	o^1	o^2	o^3
Sickness	S	s	s^1	s^2	s^3
Accident	X	x	x^1	x^2	x^3
Ill luck	Y	y			
Old age	Z	z	z^1	z^2	z^3

Figure 2. The key describing the reasons for pauperism that accompanied Booth's tables. Charles Booth, *Pauperism, a Picture; And Endowment of Old Age, an Argument* (London: Macmillan, 1892), 250.

The research of Booth and others dovetailed with a political debate that had begun when Joseph Chamberlain made pensions an election issue in 1882. At that time, every suggested scheme was voluntary and inaccessible to the poorest Britons, and pensions that redistributed wealth to the most disadvantaged were not discussed.[41] In 1886, the Conservative government appointed a committee to investigate the question of pensions, which prioritized encouraging thrifty behavior over ending poverty in old age.[42] Set at five shillings for people aged over seventy, the 1908 state pension offered less money at an older age than Booth had advised. Instead of freeing the elderly from means tests, the scheme offered a sliding scale of payments that was based on income. Those who had received relief under the Poor Law were disqualified. The effects of the introduction of a state pension varied according to the degree of poverty in different areas of Britain: up to 90 percent of people over seventy qualified in Ireland, compared to 40 percent of that group in England and Wales and 50 percent in Scotland.[43] At the same time, private pensions that were developed for civil servants and white-collar workers changed the lives of middle-class people by creating a predictable age of retirement, after which pensioners could enjoy a secure, if low, income and a stage of life free from work.[44]

THE PSYCHOLOGY OF AGING

During the 1920s and 1930s, psychologists considered the inner lives of the elderly and helped popularize a new vision of old age.[45] In 1922, American psychologist Granville Stanley Hall tried to chart the psychic experience of aging and establish the meaning of old age. Older people were perfect subjects for such an investigation because, Hall argued, people became "hyperindividualized" over lengthy lifespans.[46] The author had lofty goals for his subjects. "We need prophets with vision," he wrote, "who can inspire and also castigate" their compatriots.[47] Yet, during Hall's research, the American elderly disappointed him. When Hall distributed questionnaires in homes for the aged, for example, he found the responses by residents to be "trivial, tediously and irrelevantly reminiscent, or else descriptive."[48] Their emotional tenor was not what he had hoped for either. "There was pathos and pessimism galore," he commented, "while disciplined tranquility and serenity" were scarce. Exasperated with his subjects, Hall turned instead to correspondence with "eminent" and "distinguished" older people. In his 1925 publication *Middle and Old Age*, British physician Leonard Williams also looked to the internal lives of the old as he attempted to describe the physical, mental, and spiritual habits of longevity or, as he put it, "the best means of arriving at Old Age."[49] Williams did not share Hall's high expectations of the elderly. Rather, he wrote that people's survival to late ages was sufficient evidence of their wisdom.[50] In fact, Williams observed a "blunting" of the senses and emotions over time.[51] Still, Williams suggested that late life was ideal for intellectual and spiritual achievements, and he believed that the old could enjoy a "peaceful and fruitful" mental life.[52]

The psychology of the old took on further significance in the 1930s and 1940s in the context of European fascism and total war. From 1937, Mass Observation focused on discovering the private opinions of British people by using an array of methods from anthropology, social psychology, surrealism, literary criticism, and sociology.[53] Mass Observation's interest in the "collective subconscious" of modern Britain emerged from interwar anxieties about the spread of fascism and political instability, and the fears of the project's founders, Charles Madge and Tom Harrisson, about the potential of mass media and popular culture to manipulate and misrepresent public views.[54] Madge and Harrisson initially pursued two lines of research. In London, Madge set up a national panel of volunteers who wrote diaries and answered monthly questionnaires. At the same time, Harrisson led a project of anthropological immersion in the local culture of Bolton. Each of these methods represented a unique version of emerging intellectual interest in everyday life, the subconscious, and emotions. After 1939, the conditions of total war made such interest in civilian morale mainstream. Wartime governments were keen to measure popular opinion because the ability of Britons to cope with aerial bombardment had not been tested.

Mass Observation helped the government carry out this task by working with the Ministry of Information (from 1940 to 1941) and the Admiralty (from 1941 to 1942), and some of its members joined the more structured governmental projects of the Wartime Survey and its subsequent postwar Social Survey. Harrisson argued pessimistically that "popular morale was more fragile and changeable" than was popularly assumed.[55]

Participation in Mass Observation's research fit the contemporary aims of antifascists and progressives.[56] Many of the three-thousand-odd Britons who contributed to the national panel between 1939 and 1955 identified strongly with aspects of progressive politics and felt that their written contributions to the project were a democratic service. However, this did not mean that the Mass Observation panel members thought of themselves as "ordinary." Rather, participants "tended to see themselves as unusual people," distinguished by their engagement with high culture, science, and technology.[57] Their defining feature, however, was their readiness to volunteer the time and effort that was required to respond to the organization's "probing" questionnaires.[58] Mass Observation collated a staggering number of accounts of opinions, feelings, ambitions, and even dreams through the voluntary participation of Britons in diary writing, street interviews, and questionnaires and, famously, their involuntary role in Mass Observation's recording of street life and commercial entertainments. The desire to contribute did not end with the war. In 1947, Mass Observation published an appeal in the *New Statesman* for volunteers and received more than twice as many responses as they had garnered in the first appeal for potential participants in 1937.[59] By requiring participants to examine themselves and write about their lives, Mass Observation encouraged and recorded practices of self-reflection that would transform social research on old age.

SOCIAL WELFARE

Like Mass Observation, advocacy groups for the elderly benefited from wartime funding. The population first became a visible wartime problem in 1939, when 140,000 people were discharged from hospitals over the course of two days to make room for civilian victims of bombing.[60] Voluntary groups worried about how the elderly infirm could care for themselves at home, and officials were concerned that the old and sick might cause epidemics in bomb shelters.[61] The National Old People's Welfare Committee was formed in 1940 to advocate for better provision for elderly evacuees, arrange visiting services for isolated and struggling individuals, and collate and communicate information about wartime provisions for the old.[62] The National Corporation for the Care of Old People was set up in 1947 with funding from the wartime Lord Mayor's Air Raid Distress Fund and the Nuffield Foundation to address hardships in housing and health and coordinate and provide grants to voluntary organizations working with elderly people.[63] During the same period, Britons were witnessing the successful implementations of government planning and control in aspects of everyday life such as rationing and manpower.[64] National associations for the old began to advocate for a broad range of government services for the old within postwar reconstruction.

The 1942 Beveridge Report popularized the notion of universal state pensions as part of a comprehensive social safety net. William Beveridge had been asked to review existing social insurance schemes, which offered a confusing range of arrangements for workers to gain compensation for sickness, going blind, disability, and industrial injuries through seven different government departments.[65] Beveridge surprised the government by suggesting radical change in the creation of a system of national insurance.[66] He argued that the government should intervene to guarantee its citizens the basic means to live rather than relying on the free market, self-help, and applications to charity by those who suffered misfortune. Part of his plan was the provision of subsistence-level incomes for all pensioners.[67] Popular reception of the report was euphoric, and the first 635,000 published copies quickly sold out.[68] This popularity ended discussion of alternative pension schemes by Labour or Conservative politicians.[69] There was opposition to universal social insurance in the Conservative Party, for example, but politicians did not want to criticize the suggested changes in the face of their strong public support. Even by giving muted approval of Beveridge's plan, Conservatives helped Labour to a decisive victory in the 1945 election.

The National Insurance Act 1946, introduced in July 1948, was celebrated as insuring the British population against all risks, from the cradle to the grave. British employers and workers made compulsory payments to secure cover for unemployment, sickness, maternity and widows' benefits, and old age pensions, with governments funding the balance. Following Beveridge's recommendation, Britons received flat-rate benefits in return for their flat-rate contributions.[70] The arrangement proved long lasting. The Conservative Party preferred targeted benefits to universal pensions, but public opinion prohibited changes to the scheme.[71] Instead, Conservative governments required workers and employers to make higher payments to lessen the cost to the state. In 1957, the Labour Party argued that the rate of contributions and payments should be linked to earnings so that the payments made by higher earners would subsidize the pensions of poorer people.[72] Once in power, however, Labour governments chose to increase pension payments rather than changing the system to make it more redistributive. By 1948, when the first payments were made, state pensions were insufficient for subsistence living.[73] The costs of basic commodities increased by 50 percent between 1946 and 1957.[74] The value of pensions, however, was reviewed only every five years. Increasing numbers of pensioners relied on means-tested National Assistance benefits to survive. While the philosophy of a universal social safety net was popular, the inconsistent delivery of national insurance guaranteed continued commercial and charitable activity.

As well as arguing for greater financial support for older people, postwar reformers were fighting to improve the inner lives of the aged. Marjory Warren, who was advocating the creation of the medical specialty of geriatrics, argued in the 1940s that services for the elderly should go far beyond medical treatment. They should keep older Britons "not merely alive, but also important, useful, healthy and happy, and with as much enjoyment of mind and body as was physically possible to them."[75] The topic of discussion at the 1946 conference of the National Old People's Welfare Committee was how to provide "not just a living but a real life for the ageing population."[76] Speakers at the 1950 conference emphasized the importance of providing the elderly a "dignified, creative and comfortable" existence.[77] Care for the elderly realized a new set of social values and approaches to citizenship that Mathew Thomson has termed "a kind of secular, human-centred spirituality."[78]

In the postwar welfare state, these ambitious goals for life in old age were described as the collective responsibility of all Britons. As Minister of Health Aneurin Bevan proclaimed, the "care of the old was not a family or individual problem but a social problem," and this common goal would be realized through the work of the welfare state.[79] Yet the incomplete delivery of welfare meant that commercial and voluntary organizations needed to step in to fulfill government objectives. Welfare services for the elderly, for example, were provided largely by volunteers because local authorities were focused on residential care for older people.[80] Such services, it was believed, delivered particularly desirable changes to the affective lives of the aged. Hot meals, delivered to the elderly directly in their homes by the Women's Voluntary Service or in luncheon clubs, were understood to deliver emotional and social goods that were as important as the food's nutritional value.[81] Home helps cooked, cleaned, and shopped for older people; they also provided sociability and conversation and supported self-esteem by enabling the elderly to live in their own homes.[82] Volunteers organized social visiting and clubs to combat the perceived loneliness and boredom of older Britons.[83] However, there were limits to such voluntary work. Volunteer organizations were typically unable to deliver meals in urban areas or on weekends and holidays. In response, the National Assistance (Amendment) Act allowed local authorities to provide meal services in 1962.[84] Originally part of a program designed to assist older people during influenza epidemics, domestic helpers were an exception to the pattern of voluntary efforts for the old, as they were provided by local authorities.[85] By the mid-1950s, 3 percent of older people received such domiciliary services, and this figure rose to 6 percent in the working-class borough of Bethnal Green.[86] In 1961, there were 250,000 families receiving domestic help for a family member who was elderly or chronically ill.[87] Families were expected to cover part of the cost of this service, and local authorities each set their own charges.[88]

SOCIAL SCIENCES

Postwar Britain has been called the age of the expert due to its burgeoning network of professional groups, new forms of career training, and belief in social planning.[89] Plate-glass universities of the 1950s championed the social sciences as the best way to understand the problems of modern life.[90] Training schemes and syllabi that featured sociology and psychoanalytically oriented casework taught new ethics to professional welfare workers. Education had particular influence on the delivery of welfare after the explosion of training in the 1960s, when the number of students completing degrees in social work increased almost fivefold.[91] By the end of the decade, the National Council of Social Services decided that even those who wanted to volunteer their time to help the elderly needed to be trained.[92] Between the 1950s and the 1970s, the social sciences received increased government funding, the Home Office financed social work training, university-based social science faculties expanded, and the Social Science Research Council was established to support research in the field.[93] The elevated status of the social sciences aligned with midcentury enthusiasm for scientific knowledge and technical skill in multiple fields.[94]

In line with these developments, the body of literature that described the everyday and affective lives of the elderly in Britain expanded exponentially from the 1950s. National organizations for the elderly collated the messages that were delivered by government ministers, medical practitioners, health and welfare professionals, voluntary organizations, and business owners and published them in conference proceedings and guidelines for working with the elderly.[95] Authors extended the medical and social surveying of the elderly to different regions of the United Kingdom.[96] Others updated the literature on pensioners and poverty.[97] In studies of old age that included sociological and sociomedical research, writers popularized the theories of anomie and disengagement that originated in the work of American researchers.[98] Social researchers also began to assess the welfare services that were newly available to the aged.[99] Some narrowed their focus to groups that were the particular targets of welfare, such as older people who lived alone, were housebound, or lived in institutions.[100] British social researchers contributed to the international comparison of the social and medical problems of old age.[101] In each of these fields, whether through direct investigation or recommendations, researchers were engaged in discussions of both inner lives of the elderly and social policy for old age.

By the 1960s, assessments of affective life in old age were regularly tied to the provision of welfare and medical services. Herbert Miller's 1963 sociomedical study of the elderly in his practice in the West Midlands, *The Ageing Countryman*, for example, responded to a set of concerns about the delivery of health and welfare services to older people living in rural areas, where both population and infrastructure were sparse.[102] The first half of the study described the "countryside and community" of Miller's practice, while the second half was written for the "medical man" and operated as a textbook about the medical afflictions of old age.[103] Some elements of the expert observation of earlier social surveys remained in the study, but the information in Miller's study was gathered in direct contact with elderly Britons through a questionnaire and medical examinations. In his four-page questionnaire, Miller included questions about the physiological, mental, and emotional aspects of old age. The possible answers to Miller's questions, which were laid out in a series of boxes, drew a line between experiences of old age and their management by health and welfare services (figure 3).

FEATURES OF AGEING

Mobility	Unlimited	Limited*			
		Goes out	Confined to house	Confined to room	Confined to bed

* ……………………………

Feet	No complaint of pain	No treatment required	Complaint of pain*			
			Chiropody required		Surgery required	
			Not rec'd	Rec'd	Not rec'd	Rec'd

* ……………………………

Varicose Veins	Absent	Present		Vertigo	No	Yes*
		Without symptoms	With symptoms			
			Without ulcer	With ulcer	Falls	No	Yes*

* ……………………………
* ……………………………

Vision (with glasses if worn)	Good	Fair	Poor	Very Poor or Blind	Hearing (with aid if used)	Good	Fair	Poor	Very Poor or Stone Deaf

Glasses	Not needed	Needed	
		Not owned	Owned*

*Source ……………………………

Hearing aid	Not needed	Needed	
		Not owned	Owned*

*Source and type ……………………………

State of Teeth	Good	Fair	Bad	False Teeth	Not Needed	Needed	
						Not owned	Owned

Micturition	Normal	Frequency		Occasional incontinence
		Diurnal	Nocturnal ( )	

Memory	Good	Fair*	Poor*	Very Poor*

* ……………………………

Emotional adjustment to old age	Good*	Average	Bad*

* ……………………………

Mental state	No abnormal features	Abnormal features* requiring		
		No Supervision	Intermittent Supervision	Constant Supervision

* ……………………………

Personality	Robust	Adequate	Inadequate

Sleep	Good	Disturbed*

* ……………………………

Figure 3. Identifying the "features of ageing" was no longer treated as a subtopic of poverty research but took in the physiological, mental, and emotional aspects of old age. Herbert Crossley Miller, *The Ageing Countryman: A Socio-Medical Report on Old Age in a Country Practice* (London: National Corporation for the Care of Old People, 1963), 151.

His inquiry about older people's ability to leave their house, room, or bed—that is, their mobility—was also a measurement of their loneliness and social isolation. The next question asked about a body part that had particular symbolic value for expert understandings of old age: feet. Here, the admission of a physical complaint triggered a set of queries about medical and social services, in this case podiatry (chiropody) and surgery. Speaking at the National Old People's Committee conference in October 1950, a podiatrist described how older people who lived alone had difficulty caring for their feet and therefore suffered from painful ingrown toenails, which made walking difficult or impossible.[104] The speaker asserted that this "crippling" effect of age caused many old people to "give up" on life and become a "burden" to the state. In contrast, at a small cost to local authorities or voluntary organizations, a session of podiatry would keep older men and women "on their own two feet" and support their physical and emotional independence, avoiding the cost of residential care.[105] For the social researcher and the podiatrist alike, the strength of an old person's feet quantified the extent of his or her self-reliance and consequently the state of his or her self-esteem.

During the 1960s, elderly individuals became increasingly visible to readers of sociological case studies. Jeremy Tunstall's 1966 research, published under the title *Old and Alone*, on elderly people who were single, recently widowed, or housebound, shared Miller's focus on mobility, grooming, and social isolation (figure 4).[106] Tunstall wrote that he was interested in taking an expansive view of old age. He used case studies and published his interview reports to keep sight of "the old person as a whole."[107] Tunstall seemed to create revealing portraits of older subjects. Take, for instance, Mr. Thomas, who, Tunstall wrote, "can get out of doors, but he can only walk slowly and has to stop frequently. He stands at the top of the street quite often. He has difficulty with climbing stairs and at present is sleeping on the ground floor—he has a bed in the front room. He admits he is short winded.... Cutting his toe-nails takes him a long time; when cutting them he is afraid of having a dizzy bout."[108]

Questionnaires

TO ALL

17) Here are some things that quite a few people over 65 have difficulty in doing without help.

	No difficulty	Difficulty	IF DIFFICULTY	
Do you or would you have difficulty in:			Can you do it on your own, even with diff? Yes No	Do you usually have someone to help you with it? (Who?)
(1) Going out of doors on own				
(2) Going up and down stairs on your own				
(3) Getting about house on your own				
(4) Getting in and out of bed				
(5) Washing or bathing yourself				
(6) Dressing yourself and putting on your shoes				
(7) Cutting own toenails				

Figure 4. Questionnaires about domestic tasks and physical limitations produced a dispiriting picture of aging. Jeremy Tunstall, *Old and Alone: A Sociological Study of Old People* (London: Routledge and Kegan Paul, 1966), 321.

Mr. Thomas, however, had not directed this intimate version of his life. Rather, the content and structure of the paragraphs were determined by Tunstall's questionnaire, down to the matching order of sentences in the case study to questions in the researcher's survey. This approach turned sociological observation of the older man's life to policy ends. Tunstall recorded the domestic routines of Britons like Mr. Thomas to identify potential points of outside intervention, such as help with getting out of the house, navigating stairs, or bathing. In doing so, he depicted old age as slow moving and monotonous and portrayed the lives of his subjects as cycles of household drudgery. When older Britons gained the ability to direct the narratives of their lives, they told a different story.

INTERVIEWING THE ELDERLY

Peter Townsend aimed to contribute a more balanced account of the lives of older Britons, one that recognized their personal strengths and the contributions they made to social life. To do so, the researcher interviewed 203 older people in Bethnal Green, East London, between October 1954 and November 1955. Before the mid-twentieth century, interviews had been used by doctors, clergy, social workers, and welfare officials to assess people's rights to claim the benefits of "medical treatment, welfare, or moral salvation."[109] Social researchers had commonly sought out the judgments and records of these "cultivated" observers as the best way to understand British social life. Starting in the 1950s, however, researchers began to argue that "direct" evidence—such as the words of their subjects—was superior to judgments made by experts.[110] Social scientists turned interviewing to new purposes, and by the 1960s, "informal interviewing" was widely used by researchers to collect "story-like narratives" from subjects and advance research careers.[111] This method of interviewing contributed to a shift of the attention of social researchers away from examining populations and toward studying the lives of individuals.[112]

Townsend's research methods involved lengthy exchanges with elderly Britons, and this has made the researcher himself part of the archival record of old age in Britain. Townsend said that his curiosity about the family lives of the elderly originated from his own biography. Townsend was born in 1928. When he was two years old, his parents separated and he and his mother moved in with his grandmother.[113] His experiences as a single child, Townsend said, led to his "enormous interest in family relations and extended family life."[114] His first major study at the Institute of Community Studies concentrated on working-class elderly people in the borough of Bethnal Green, nearby the institute. Townsend's interest in working-class culture was also born of his biography. He celebrated what he called his "mixed-class background" in the North of England and his grandmother, who was "thoroughly working class."[115] The researcher later reflected that his enthusiasm about working-class culture had perhaps blinded him to its "oppressive" qualities, including violence and male domination.[116]

Townsend's research was framed by, and contributed to, debates between the main political parties of his day. He said that he was aware "from the beginning" of "the connections between research and action," and he remarked, "Some of my work naturally affected political decisions."[117] While social science has no single party affiliation, during the postwar period the Labour Party in particular supported greater funding for the social sciences and argued that "the scientific method could be usefully applied to social and political issues and eliminate Britain's problems in a planned society."[118] Both Clement Attlee, leader of the Labour Party from 1935 to 1955 and prime minister from 1945 to 1951, and William Beveridge held posts at the London School of Economics. Harold Wilson, the Labour prime minister from 1964 to 1970 and again from 1974 to 1976, was a statistician trained by Beveridge. These scholar-politicians, as Bailkin has written, shared "great faith in the transformative power of their fields" of social science and demography.[119] Townsend's first research post was at Political and Economic Planning, a research organization that was "open to points of view from all political perspectives."[120] In his next job, at the Institute of Community Studies, he learned more about "the relationship between politics and science" from Michael Young, who had helped draft the Labour Party's manifesto in 1945.[121] In the 1950s, Townsend "became immersed with Richard Titmuss in the back room work of the Labour Party," where he contributed to the Labour Party plan on pensions.[122] He continued to work with Labour Party committees until the late 1980s.

Townsend's commitment to "distributional justice for all, not welfare for a few," made him a prominent critic of both political parties.[123] Even in his earliest publications, the researcher argued that the welfare state had not ended poverty and that much more should be done for disadvantaged Britons. His project *The Last Refuge* (1962) was designed to test the degree to which life had improved for older people in residential care since the Labour government announced its reforms in 1946. Townsend described how his "shocking" first visit to a residential institution shook the faith he had felt as an "aware, young and hopeful" believer in the postwar project of "building a bright new social Jerusalem and the Welfare State."[124] Subsequently, he advocated research about "the life of the poorest and most handicapped members of society" and established his special interest in the fields of old age, disability, and health inequality.[125] This included participation in the Child Poverty Action Group's "The poor get poorer under Labour" campaign, which has been cited as one reason Labour lost the 1970 election.

Townsend's methods of interviewing expressed his egalitarian commitment to the worth of individuals. His technique involved more than "merely ticking off the questionnaire"; he would talk with his subjects, sometimes for hours.[126] Townsend used an open interview schedule that, he said, gave older people the freedom to decide which stories they wanted to tell. This gave researchers the "sense of priorities as people regard them" and afforded interviewees the power to influence the direction of the research.[127] Townsend's method of interviewing was inspired by social anthropology, which he had encountered through the work of Meyer Fortes, a professor of anthropology at the University of

Cambridge.[128] Aiming for a version of anthropological immersion in the community, Townsend visited most of his elderly subjects on multiple occasions and insisted that their views mattered to social science. Other parts of Townsend's method, though, amplified his own analyses over the contributions of his research subjects. Ultimately, he used the stories of his subjects to inform government policy on old age. To do so, Townsend converted the varied stories told by 203 individuals into averages and case studies. In its published form, each section of *The Family Life of Old People* (1957) concluded with policy recommendations for employment, pensions, or housing. This required streamlining the stories of the elderly. The researcher later regretted this emphasis, writing that his research "tended to be a little too biased" toward developing policy at the expense of recording more about older people's lives.[129]

The primacy of Townsend's voice was established long before he wrote up policy proposals. Townsend used the technology of tape recording only in follow-up interviews with a dozen of "the most interesting people" he visited.[130] He preferred to rely on his memory to generate the record of an interview. To aid him in recalling, Townsend wrote notes during interviews. To make sure that his elderly interviewees felt comfortable, the researcher would ask, "You don't mind if I take a note? I have to do this, because I forget things." Afterward, he typed a full account of each interview.[131] To Townsend's mind, an advantage of this system was the ability to "select and order" his data as he went "in a way which would easily be accessible afterwards." At the same time, he explained that he would "iron out the hesitations, and the blurs, and the half finished sentences," aiming to "recapture" the way that people spoke. Even forty years later, when he was interviewed by Paul Thompson in 1997, the researcher had few regrets about this method of note taking and celebrated its efficiency in analyzing and organizing data. His strategy highlights some of the ways that hierarchy coexisted with egalitarianism in midcentury social research projects. The keen attention researchers paid to individuals was balanced by the investment of social scientists in large-scale solutions to the problems of old age.

The Last Refuge expressed the tensions that were inherent to midcentury social research in different ways, because its interviews took place inside institutions. Townsend and other researchers who worked on this project devoted more time to interviews with professionals working in aged care, for example, than they spent talking with older people themselves. The "first step" that Townsend and his small team of researchers took in each locality was to visit the chief welfare officer of the area and "cross examine him, interview him … to hear his side of the developments that were taking place, and what progress was being made" in residential care.[132] These interviews with chief welfare officers, who were mostly men, were similar to the open interviews that Townsend had completed in Bethnal Green and took, on average, a little over two hours.[133] The researchers also interviewed 489 older people who had moved to residential homes during the preceding four months and who were thus likely to have the clear memories of the reasons for their admission. But Townsend developed a questionnaire for these residents that took less time, around thirty-five minutes, to complete.[134] He later regretted the brevity of these exchanges. In hindsight, Townsend wished he had "looked more at individual people and the families and the localities they came from."[135] Such biographical detail, he said, would also give health and welfare workers "better means of engaging with the past of the people they're treating," leading to improved care for the aged. Townsend later advised other researchers to leave plenty of time for "spontaneity" to make the most of just these kinds of "chances that will never be repeated."[136]

Social scientific depictions of old age were jointly created by social researchers and their subjects. Interviews were conversations, and many elderly people were eager for the chance to speak about their lives and have their stories published. Interviews that took place in older people's homes recorded the interactions of elderly Britons with their families and neighbors. Discussions that occurred inside residential homes captured exchanges between elderly people and home managers, owners, and workers. Townsend reflected that a key strength of *The Last Refuge* study was the "roundedness" of the depictions, which was a result of "trying to put together the testimony of different people" in this way. He heard from older people who were "at the sharp end of things," as well as the people who were "managing their lives."[137] In Bethnal Green, listening audiences chimed in during interviews to support the anecdotes that elderly people told. In residential homes, however, welfare workers were more likely to interrupt and restrict the storytelling of elderly people than to embellish it. The conditions of these interviews revealed as much about the lives of older people as their testimony did.

The Last Refuge project was the last time that Townsend would conduct in-depth fieldwork. In 1963, he became founding professor of sociology at the University of Essex. The researcher's next major study, *Poverty in the United Kingdom* (1979), was team researched, and Townsend's primary contributions were interpreting its statistics and writing up the findings.[138] Although he would not conduct another large interviewing project, Townsend was himself interviewed by sociologist and oral historian Paul Thompson eight times between June 1997 and February 1999. In their final discussion, Thompson asked the seventy-year-old Townsend to reflect again on the topic of old age. From the perspective of late life, Townsend presented a more personal narrative of aging than he had done previously and described the lifelong process of growing older. In response to Thompson's question, he asked, "Well, what about my twenties, my thirties, my forties, my fifties, sixties and seventies?"[139] Townsend was given more than enough time to remember each of the phases of his life: Thompson's interviews with him lasted for over twenty hours and are the longest in the Pioneers of Social Research archive. Still, Townsend now saw some of the shortcomings of the interview format, and he protested, saying, "No doubt I would do a better job if I sat down quietly and recollected it in tranquility."[140] Like Townsend, elderly Britons had mixed experiences during social science interviews. Many older women and men enjoyed telling Townsend about their lives. Although a handful among them refused to speak, it was more common for interviewees to debate the questions that social researchers asked and to take control of the conversation. To his frustration, and sometimes to his embarrassment, Townsend's interviews were full of tensions that were caused by the dual priorities of mid-twentieth-century research, which aimed to honor the words of individuals to improve the lives of the many.

• • •

By 1970, it seemed that an army of professional and voluntary workers anticipated every need of the elderly. "Today," wrote Nesta Roberts, the ill were "cared for at home by doctor and district nurse."[141] Roberts went on to describe the way that handrails and ramps supported the gait of unsteady feet. Physiotherapists and podiatrists drove the immobile to their appointments. Library vans delivered large-print books to the doors of the curious. Churchgoers supplied tape recordings of services to the devout. A "squad of schoolboys" tidied neglected gardens.[142] Volunteers delivered hot meals to the hungry five days a week. It appeared there was no problem of old age without a solution. The only shortcomings of this system, according to Roberts, were those created by inadequate staff numbers and funding. It was for these reasons that general practitioners and district nurses were overburdened and that the false teeth they supplied might fit only "approximately."[143] But, these issues aside, Roberts, in a history of the National Old People's Welfare Council that was published on the group's thirtieth anniversary, outlined the increasingly humane treatment of older generations in twentieth-century Britain.

Roberts listed the fruits of twentieth-century research on the lives of the elderly. By 1970, experts had quantified many of the difficulties of old age, from sore feet to stairs. Roberts highlighted the fact that state and voluntary organizations had established services to address each previously unmet need. The reassuring structure of Roberts's book, in which each ailment or frustration was matched by its remedy, suggested that fears of growing old were unfounded, because a sound safety net would afford individuals security and self-respect as they grew older. Her formula was a popular way of explaining how the older generation was faring in the postwar period, and the outline of the book was repeated in histories of twentieth-century Britain that chart the expansion of welfare and medical services over the period, although these volumes pay greater attention to the limitations of this "overburdened" system.[144]

Yet the extension of the welfare state did not end inequality and exclusion in old age. Poverty and welfare were twin features of old age throughout much of the twentieth century, and these issues came under expert scrutiny multiple times. While the problems of age did not disappear, the fields of expertise that Roberts referenced—particularly those of psychology, social science, and the welfare professions—shaped understandings of the lives of the elderly that were distinctive to the twentieth century. These conceptions of old age explored the ideas that material comfort and emotional satisfactions might be viewed as rights of citizenship in late life in the same way as the financial contributions of state pensions. Along the way, social researchers engaged older Britons in their research, transforming public representations and archival records of old age.

CHAPTER TWO

Talking with Peter Townsend

Elderly Britons at Home

Early one morning in 1954, Peter Townsend knocked on the door of 284 Willmot Street, which had been the home of Rose and Charles Ellwood for the past twenty years.[1] After "much rasping of bolts," the door opened only three inches, where a stout chain held it. Mrs. Ellwood spoke through the narrow gap. "What use is it to us?" she demanded of Townsend's project on the family lives of the elderly. Townsend supplied the "rather hopeful answer" that an interview with the couple would help him understand the problems of the aged and contribute to the development of old age policy. Rose, however, doubted the usefulness of his project. "I suppose we'll all be dead and buried by then," she replied.

Townsend returned to Willmot Street on the evening of June 15 to speak with Charles Ellwood, whose name the researcher had drawn in his random sample of older people from doctors' lists for Bethnal Green. After agreeing to talk, the seventy-one-year-old man stood on the threshold rather than inviting the researcher into the flat. He threw "anxious, almost scared, glances" over his shoulder at the door leading to the room where his wife sat. This was not a promising beginning, and yet, as their conversation evolved, Townsend grew fascinated by the views of the older man. He visited Mr. Ellwood several more times, and each time they spoke about the man's life for between thirty minutes and over an hour. Charles was a laborer on the railway who earned around £4 per week, and he also did most of the housekeeping, shopping, and cooking because Rose had been "very poorly" since fracturing her leg and spine several years before. Charles was fiercely determined to keep working. He insisted that in retirement he would be "worse off in every way." The couple led a quiet life and had no children. Rose had miscarried three years into their marriage, and they had not been able to conceive again after that. Most of their siblings were dead, and their only family contact was with a niece, Emmie, who visited Mrs. Ellwood every morning and sometimes stayed at the flat for up to eight hours.

The interviewer and interviewee gradually developed a rapport. Townsend later described how he achieved this with larger families, where there were always visitors who were "getting mugs of tea, with sterilized milk," and "slabs of bread pudding, given from the oven."[2] The crowds meant that Townsend could never conduct his interviews "in a kind of formal, officious way." Instead, the researcher explained, he would establish "a joking relationship" that entailed everybody present making "great mocking fun of almost every question I asked." In his conversation with Charles, the scene was quieter and the conversations more intimate. Townsend wrote that his visits to the Ellwoods were especially "revealing" about the older man's fears of retirement and about his home life with Rose. In one interview, the researcher even raised the "delicate" question of sex, a topic that rarely featured in old age research at the time. Charles answered, describing his view that "decent women" did not "want too much of it" and that men who were strong enough could wait for three or four months at a time.

In the mid-twentieth century, the home was newly imagined as a place of familial privacy, but it was also the site of increasing intrusions by experts and bureaucracy.[3] The interlopers included social researchers who pried into matters as personal as one's sex life. Townsend's introduction to Bethnal Green reworked early twentieth-century social scientific observations of working-class neighborhoods and, through greater attention to the psychic importance of home, reversed the conclusion these earlier observations had drawn about life in the "London slums."[4] He wrote that the terraced cottages of the East London borough displayed "neatness and dignity" and that their "small back-yards and gardens" showed that privacy was sacred to the inhabitants.[5] Household possessions revealed the diversity of emotional lives that were played out inside these cottages: photos indicated the size of families, incorrect clocks were a sign of isolation and "weary resignation," furniture had frequently been gifted by or inherited from loved ones, and radios and televisions were a sign of connection to the outside world.[6] Townsend's interviewees told him that the worst loneliness was caused by private tragedies, such as lost contact with grandchildren or the death of a spouse or child, which revealed the limitations of the measurement of household organization as a means for understanding emotions in old age.[7] Townsend highlighted the difference that growing older made to domestic lives. For the older residents of Bethnal Green, who had been living in the same house for, on average, twenty-four years, home "embodied a thousand memories and held promise of a thousand contentments."[8] In old age, the household was "an extension of personality" and "a symbol of family unity and tradition."

To match these psychological insights, Townsend quantified the function of home and family for old people. He calculated that, on average, his research subjects had thirteen family members living within a mile of their home.[9] Eighty-five percent of his subjects had children living within a mile, and half of them had children living on the same street, in the same block of flats, or just around the corner. On average, his subjects met one of their relatives each day.[10] Experimenting with how to communicate these social facts, Townsend presented older people's primary social connections in "kinship maps" that arranged marriages, births, and visiting patterns in visual format.[11] These maps built on the quantitative evidence he gathered about the density of families within this East London neighborhood. The diagrams conveyed the richness of social life through their crowdedness and webs of connections and adopted the appearance of a logical and scientific arrangement of knowledge in their key, signs, and straight lines. While Townsend used his interviews to devise these charts, older people and their families used sociological interviews to tell personal stories about aging, claim admired character traits, and take control of the discussions they had within their homes. Aging interviewees informed Townsend that, from their perspective, social researchers had usually gotten old age wrong. Townsend collected and archived hundreds of their tales but published only a small proportion of them in what would become classic sociological texts on old age. Thus, more than his famous studies, Townsend's unpublished papers reveal older people's desire to represent their lives.[12]

AT HOME IN THE WELFARE STATE

By the mid-twentieth century, social researchers had been using households to investigate the material circumstances of Britons for over fifty years. The visibility and measurability of houses were key to Booth's project to create a "moral topography" of poverty and a clear basis for political action on old age pensions.[13] Booth's investigators measured privation street by street. Their assessments resulted in Booth's maps of London, which categorized each street by its level of poverty, producing a visual display of degrees of hardship (figure 5). In the pages of early twentieth-century studies, urban streets set the scene for discussions of poverty and opened windows on to its social effects. According to the theories of physical environmentalism, the state of the homes and neighborhoods of London revealed the moral qualities of the city's inhabitants. A. L. Bowley and Alexander Robert Burnett-Hurst cataloged poverty through the occupation of space by families, which they measured by the rent they paid, the number of rooms they used, and the heights of their ground floors.[14] The presence of unacceptably cramped, dark, and damp houses asserted the "real volume of poverty" against the naysayers who judged earlier descriptions of such conditions merely "the fruit of

Figure 5. One sheet of Charles Booth's map of London, which famously quantified the city's poverty street by street and in visual form. "Map Descriptive of London Poverty, 1898–9," Booth/E/1, Charles Booth's London: Poverty Maps and Police Notebooks, Charles Booth Archive, London School of Economics Library, London School of Economics.

an overheated imagination."[15] For Seebohm Rowntree and other physical environmentalists, the high walls, narrow streets, and overcrowding in slum neighborhoods bred a "jaded and spiritless" population.[16]

Interwar and postwar commentators and architects contributed to the conceptual shift from Victorian liberalism to greater social planning when they designed special housing for the elderly (figure 6). In 1935, for example, the think tank Political and Economic Planning claimed that the happiness of retired people depended on "the comfort and pleasantness of their homes."[17] According to the organization, the elderly should ideally live in "small, inexpensive and easily run" houses with spaces for age-appropriate leisure activities that were envisaged to take place in "garden plots, allotments, old people's clubs, and rest rooms." This ambitious vision of specially designed homes for the aged did not gain much political traction at a time when homebuilding was focused on the needs of returned soldiers. In the postwar years, new champions of homes planned for the aged emerged, such as occupational therapists. Local authorities took the lead in housing policy from the 1960s by building greater numbers of small units deemed suitable for older inhabitants.[18]

In the postwar period, domestic arrangements in the home attracted fresh political concern. A decisive shift in household makeup had occurred after World War I, when the real value of the pension rose and older people were able to retain the independence of their households and avoid imposing on their children.[19] Greater numbers of the elderly were living alone. The organization of their households became part of debates over the ethics and efficacy of social welfare. Harvard sociologist Talcott Parsons made the influential assertion that the increased mobility of younger people caused the social isolation of the old.[20] This encouraged British commentators to worry anew about the corrosive influence of industrialization, urbanization, and welfare services on family bonds. The argument took on economic dimensions as governments accepted more of the financial burden of caring for the old. Geoffrey King, for example, who was permanent secretary at the Ministry of Pensions and National Insurance, thought that the

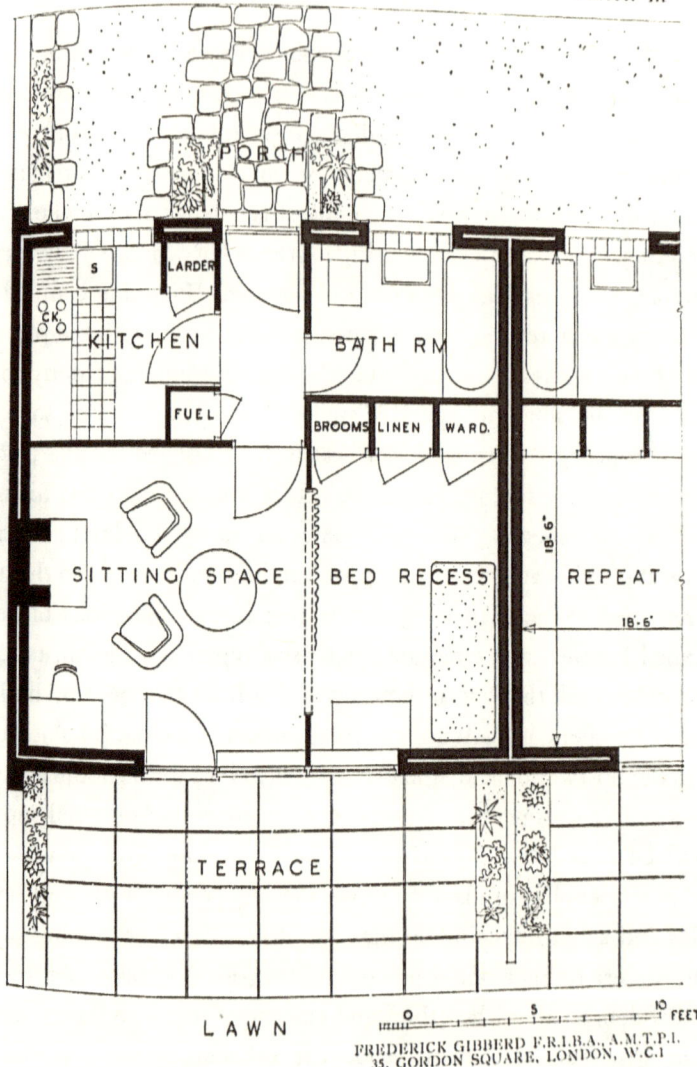

Figure 6. In the postwar period, the environment inhabited by older people was imagined as an ideal bungalow, such as this one in Hackney, designed by architect and town planner Frederick Gibberd. National Old People's Welfare Committee, *Age Is Opportunity: A New Guide to Practical Work for the Welfare of Old People* (London: National Council of Social Service, 1949), following p. 56.

government faced a problem of provision for the aged "largely because of the loosening of family ties and insistence on individual rights and privileges to the exclusion of obligations and duties which has developed so markedly in recent years."[21] Along with many high-profile commentators, King argued that the state's provision of welfare damaged the character of the British people. To calculate the potential financial costs of welfare for the aged, researchers needed to establish the likelihood that adult children would support their aging parents, a question that framed the keen interest of social scientists in the state of family life in postwar Britain.

Researchers conceived of living alone as a problem because, they claimed, older Britons were lonely (figure 7). This argument underlined expert concern with domestic arrangements and supported particular kinds of interventions in the lives of the elderly. Loneliness was believed to have serious consequences for health. Physician Trevor Howell wrote in 1953 that loneliness was among "the greatest enemies" of the elderly and linked solitary existence to senility and "rapid deterioration."[22] In 1960, gerontologist Kenneth Hazell wrote that loneliness caused physical illness, poor diet, and "mental illness in the way of apathy, indifference, depression or even dementia."[23] Researchers suggested that the problem of loneliness could be identified when older people stopped attempting to meet behavioral norms and that it could be alleviated by social contact with others, particularly in clubs or through visits by volunteers. Both the domestic realm and informal communal areas such as parks, however, were portrayed as isolating in the absence of interventions by health and welfare workers. According to both researchers and welfare professionals, social contact was properly supplied through community services, such as the Grandfathers' Club shown in figure 8, and not by unofficial means.

Concerns about the domestic lives of the elderly shaped the sociomedical research of the 1940s. From this time, researchers focused their studies on the ability of older Britons to complete a set of daily domestic tasks. The physician Joseph Sheldon, for example, calculated the percentages

Figure 7. Although this older woman sat in physical comfort, her lone figure and the gaze she cast at the outside world communicated her apparent loneliness. Douglas R. Snellgrove, *Elderly Housebound: A Report on Elderly People Who Are Incapacitated* (Luton: White Crescent, 1963), front cover.

of elderly in his survey who had difficulty with stairs or queues, who fell over because of vertigo or because they had difficulty seeing in the dark, and who were confined to their bed, house, or district.[24] Sheldon presented a wealth of statistics on the physical limitations of old age and their remedies, such as false teeth and spectacles.[25] He identified domestic difficulties that had broad significance and produced what he called "a comprehensive picture of the present pattern of old age in society."[26] Using these precise measurements of domestic life, Sheldon argued that commentators had it wrong. Whether an elderly person lived alone did not predict the degree of familial support or social interaction they enjoyed.

VII. *Games-room of Grandfathers' Club, Poplar. This club, attached to Trinity Congregational Church, provides a daily hot meal and opportunities of social intercourse for lonely old men in the neighbourhood*

VIII. *Loneliness: nothing to do, nowhere to go*

Figure 8. According to the captions for these images, older men who did not belong to a social club had "nothing to do, nowhere to go." Seebohm B. Rowntree, *Old People: Report of a Survey Committee on the Problems of Ageing and the Care of Old People* (London: Oxford University Press, 1947), following p. 76.

Sheldon's research described the close relations between generations living in different houses, who were "independent in health and cooperative in illness."[27] His research demonstrated that the boundaries of households were frequently crossed during family life, including to care for older relatives. Sheldon judged that elderly individuals lived near to family members when a hot meal could be carried from door to door without needing to be reheated.[28] His statistics and diagrams demonstrated the important role played in the lives of the elderly by relatives, whose contributions were far greater than Parsons, King, and other commentators had acknowledged.

Sheldon warned that the incorrect ideas held by civil servants about the elderly would lead to ineffective policy.[29] He therefore applauded Townsend's *The Family Life of Old People*, published nine years after his own study, for uncovering a "wealth of facts" about the family lives of the elderly, which until that moment had been largely "the province of opinion." Townsend rejected Parsons's influential theory that extended families had been broken up in urban industrial society and replaced by isolated conjugal families.[30] Likewise, he dismissed the fears of British civil servants that families could no longer care for the elderly and that the responsibility and expense would instead fall to the state. Townsend uncovered a system of family life that was invisible in official statistics, such as the census, that were based on nuclear families.[31] Instead of "disintegrating," he wrote, families were adjusting to new facts of work and living arrangements.[32] "To the old person as much as to the young," Townsend observed of the postwar world, the extended family was "the supreme comfort and support," and its "central purpose is as strong as ever." Townsend explained that family life provided "self-fulfillment and expression" as Britons moved through the lifecycle from child to parent to grandparent. In fact, the generation gap had reduced from thirty years in the late nineteenth century to twenty-three years in the 1950s, so it was more likely for grandparents to care for their grandchildren and for adult children to care for their parents during their own middle age and early old age (figure 9).[33] Townsend argued that extensive systems of

Figure 9. Peter Townsend's research drew attention to the involvement of grandparents in childcare, as did his photographs. "Grandfather and Baby," box 35, file B9, Photographs, SN 4723 The Family Life of Old People 1865–1955, Peter Townsend Collection, National Social Policy and Social Change Archive, Albert Sloman Library, University of Essex, Colchester. Copyright Baroness Jean Corston.

familial care meant that the ability of relatives to live near one another underwrote the financial health of the state.[34] Housing plans needed to change, he insisted, to allow generations to live close together and provide this care in "institutions without walls."[35]

The Family Life of Old People drew attention to the active roles played by older Britons in working-class family life. To this end, Townsend selected thirteen photographs to appear in the book that depicted a range of family relationships and occasions.[36] His photographs featured lively scenes set against the brick walls and narrow lanes of East London (figures 10 and 11). Townsend took close-up portraits to give the viewer the sensation of standing in a circle of relatives in a doorway. Some of the images capture his subjects laughing into the camera.[37] The photographs displayed the intimacy of family life and highlighted the social connections of the elderly. Writing to the chairman of his publishing company, Routledge and Kegan Paul, Townsend argued that his images were necessary to explain family lives in Bethnal Green to readers who lived outside of London, in line with the aim of British scholars to apply anthropological perspectives to their home communities.[38] Discerning that the expense of including the photographs was the sticking point for his publishers, Townsend offered to fund some of the cost of publication out of his own pocket.[39] However, he failed to convince them. It was not until the publication of *The Last Refuge* that Townsend was able to express his arguments about the lives of the old in photographs.

Townsend talked enthusiastically about visiting the busy household of Sarah and Robert Agombar as late as his interviews with Paul Thompson in 1997.[40] After Townsend's first visit to the couple, Robert had "pressed" him to visit again, which he did, at least eleven more times.[41] The Agombar household was bursting with family. Sarah and Robert had eight children and twenty-one grandchildren. During one of Townsend's visits, the couple also welcomed their daughter-in-law, their son John, their grandson Christopher, and their youngest daughter, Martha.[42] Martha lived only a few minutes' walk away, and the couple's youngest son, also named Robert, lived even closer by, in the same block

Figure 10. Photographic portraits of individuals that were included in Townsend's research recorded intimate scenes of later life. "Man in Doorway," box 35, file B9, Photographs, SN 4723 The Family Life of Old People 1865–1955, Peter Townsend Collection, National Social Policy and Social Change Archive, Albert Sloman Library, University of Essex, Colchester. Copyright Baroness Jean Corston.

Figure 11. "Woman in Apron," box 35, file B9, Photographs, SN 4723 The Family Life of Old People 1865–1955, Peter Townsend Collection, National Social Policy and Social Change Archive, Albert Sloman Library, University of Essex, Colchester. Copyright Baroness Jean Corston.

of flats. The unity of the family was displayed on the walls of the living room, where Townsend counted thirty-seven photographs, including large wedding photographs that Sarah had paid for in weekly installments over many years. Robert described the emotional intensity of the bond between Sarah and her children. He pointed out a picture of his son Ben, who had been killed in war. To illustrate their loss, Robert said, "If his mother's little finger ached, he'd be in pain all over his body."

The couple's living and visiting arrangements relied on the close confines of urban boroughs. Such midcentury social arrangements were on the brink of changes as a result of slum clearance, suburbanization, and the building of council estates on the edges of cities. Under the postwar program of slum clearance, authorities demolished 1.2 million substandard houses and moved over 3 million people in England and Wales.[43] Working-class families made pragmatic decisions when they were offered a choice between the comfort, space, and privacy of council housing and "the poor housing, mutuality and familiarity of the older districts," usually finding the latter to be the inferior option.[44] Organized on a points system, council housing allocation "did not and could not take into account" the location of kin.[45] According to historian Ben Jones, higher quality housing may have been the greatest improvement the state made to working-class life in the twentieth century.[46] Yet older Britons were overrepresented among the minority of people in midcentury surveys who were against the idea of moving to council housing.[47] A number of Townsend's interviewees said that they wanted to die in their houses and be "carried out." Florence Parsons, for example, was determined not to move. "If you gave her Buckingham Palace she wouldn't take it," said her daughter.[48] Florence may well have gotten her wish. To be allocated council housing, it was usually necessary to belong to a "nuclear family, preferably intact and not too large," and without elderly relatives.[49]

Despite their preference for staying put, many of the elderly residents of Bethnal Green lived in cottages that were scheduled for demolition. Some had already been shifted out and had moved into ground-floor flats. Townsend's discussions with the Agombar family often became a chorus of complaints about just such a move, with mother, father, daughter, and son all speaking at once.[50] Sarah and Robert were sad to see children playing in the streets instead of in the yards of terraced houses, where their own children had played. Robert wanted to have a garden and to breed chickens and rabbits. No such hobbies were on offer amid the "bricks and windows" of 1950s London, said his wife. The older couple did not sympathize with the council's objectives to create public space between blocks of flats, seeing this instead as "waste ground." "You could build a row of little cottages in between these blocks," suggested Robert, imagining exactly the type of housing that had long been judged unsanitary and was the specific target of the clearances.

From the mid-1950s, researchers investigated the social effects of slum clearance in a series of social surveys.[51] They argued that slum clearance and the move to council estates destroyed working-class urban life, which relied on tight-knit groups of kin living in close proximity.[52] The Agombars, for example, had seen some of their children move out of the city to obtain better housing. The farther-flung offspring visited twice a month, significantly less than the parents were used to. Council estates themselves were short on public spaces like shops and pubs. And as working-class families moved out of poverty, thanks to full employment, rising wages, and the expanding welfare state, social researchers noted the decline of the interdependence that they judged characteristic of "traditional" working-class lives.[53] The council estates that replaced slum housing came to symbolize the newfound "affluence" of working people in Britain.[54]

All of this reinforced public concern that dispersed families would no longer be able to provide care for the elderly, making old people socially isolated and a burden on the state. Yet, as later research would show, the communality of "traditional" neighborhoods was overplayed, and there was significant continuity in social patterns throughout the twentieth century.[55] Subsequent research projects uncovered the persistence of working-class patterns of socializing and family support on council estates late in the century.⁵⁶ In Brighton, for example, neighbors were rehoused on the same estates. The ongoing poverty of many residents meant that they continued to borrow from and lend to one another to get by.⁵⁷ By the early 1970s, some Brighton estates were home to several generations of the same families, supporting daily contact of the kind that the Agombars enjoyed in the 1950s.⁵⁸ Social researchers therefore contributed to the downplaying of ongoing disadvantage and the overstatement of cultural changes at midcentury. The lives of many older Britons were shaped by poverty, welfare, and family, and this was true before, during, and after the expansion of state welfare and the widespread clearance of slums. In their interviews, though, aging Britons were keen to stress continuities of their own characters above the persistence of challenging circumstances. Their desire to do so reshaped the substance of social scientific interviews at midcentury.

LONG WORKING LIVES

Townsend was primarily interested in talking with Charles Ellwood because of the older man's dread of retirement. At midcentury, retirement was widespread among working people for the first time. A fixed retirement age helped formalize a chronological point of entry to old age and propagate a simplistic public account of the nature of aging.⁵⁹ These ideas built on a long history of anxiety over joblessness in the twentieth century. During the Depression, for example, commentators had worried that the unstructured free time of the unemployed would lead to hopelessness and even immoral and criminal behavior.⁶⁰ The popular stages theory proposed that unemployed workers would pass through four phases: the unbroken, the resigned, the distressed, and the apathetic. The theory seemed to explain the findings of famous social surveys of unemployment, such as the study of the Austrian textile village of Marienthal that was carried out under the direction of Paul Lazarsfeld in 1933.⁶¹ Social scientists understood unemployment to be the most urgent social problem of their day, and contemporary novels, such as Walter Greenwood's *Love on the Dole* (1933) and Walter Brierley's *Means Test Man* (1935), portrayed for a popular audience the unhappy effects of idleness on marriages and families.[62] In the context of economic depression and uncertain labor markets during the interwar years, governments had encouraged the employment of younger people, in part by lowering the retirement age from seventy to sixty-five in 1925.[63]

Older people were more likely to take the view that formal employment was only one face of work. Retired men and women and housewives who wrote for Mass Observation in 1948, for example, treated a question about their "present occupation" little differently from older people who were employed in the formal labor market. A retired farmer from Essex made a typical claim when he stated, "Being retired and able to choose my own jobs, I have no complaints."[64] A ninety-year-old woman wrote, "[As] my own mistress (housewife, children all grown up) I can do pretty well as I like."[65] Although she did not have "a large enough income to do *all* I'd like," she articulated a set of ambitious dreams: "I want to study languages, travel." A few years earlier, however, in the world of industrial warfare, powered by home front workers, retirement was experienced by some as exclusion from the world of usefulness and full citizenship. In 1943, a number of older men and women bluntly explained that they had no job or declined to answer questions about work.[66] Others listed problems and gripes that were heightened by the feeling that individuals should contribute to the war effort: they felt frustrated to have been rejected from useful positions or reported tension in their workplaces.[67]

World War II rearranged assumptions about participation in the workforce in a number of ways. The wartime industries created full employment, and commentators no longer worried about the effects of unemployment. Instead, public discussions emphasized the fact that all workers could play a part in the war effort, especially in industrial production. Some older people objected to arbitrary age limits to their ability to make high-status or helpful contributions to the war effort. After the war, in the context of labor shortages, academic and governmental publications reframed the psychological problem of retirement and encouraged older workers to stay in employment.[68] The authors of these publications argued that work conferred mental stimulation and feelings of worth, which led to good psychological health.[69] In the postwar period, the psychological sciences revealed that older workers benefited from their range of abilities and experiences, even though they might be slower at performing certain repetitive tasks.[70] Yet businesses preferred to employ younger workers long after the experts highlighted the contributions of the aged.[71] Commentators continued to imagine retirement as a time of social disconnection that should be limited to shorter periods of time and more advanced ages. Townsend agreed that retirement was a "tragic event for men."[72] He pointed out that, for older men, the approach of retirement "threatened many of the long-standing associations of their lives."[73] Retirement, Townsend wrote, "reminded them of their failing strength and skill and that their period of usefulness to others was coming to an end."

The older men who spoke to Townsend clearly articulated the importance of paid work to masculine identity and self-worth. Yet in their telling, the connection was not broken by shorter hours or leaving the workplace. Instead, older men and their kin described men's industriousness as an internal attribute and provided evidence taken from the long histories of their working lives. Harriet Allen, for example, described her sixty-nine-year-old husband's attitude toward his work for building firms: "[He] wants to keep on as long as he can. He's a man who's always been out. He can't content himself at home."[74] Harriet felt that her husband was a certain kind of man—one who had "always been out"—and that he would remain so, regardless of his employment status. Likewise, it was common for men to continue to display pride in their abilities as younger men after departing the workplace.[75] During interviews, former garbage man John Regelous lifted his retirement certificate, which recognized thirty-four years of "loyal service" to the borough of Bethnal Green, down from the wall of his flat and boasted of gold, silver, and bronze medals that he had won for driving his garbage truck.[76] Robert Agombar, who had been a street sweeper and garbage man for Bethnal Green for close to four decades, did the same thing with his retirement certificate. Robert's wife and son nudged and winked at each other behind his back, gently making fun of the older man, who had once kept the document hanging over his bed. Telling and retelling these stories was a shared pastime within families and their repetition an occasion for affectionate humor.

Beyond the borders of Bethnal Green, the goals held by older Britons were varied and ambitious. In August 1944, a group of older people recorded their aims in life for Mass Observation.[77] None of their plans fit with the narrow image of old age that was depicted in much contemporary social research. One seventy-seven-year-old man hoped to publish a book titled "Scientific Paradoxes and Problems."[78] A sixty-nine-year-old widow planned to pen weekly letters to an invalided acquaintance.[79] At sixty-eight, a recently married man was interested in propagating vegetarianism, socialism, temperance, and a host of "other –isms" and planned to father children.[80] A sixty-four-year-old woman just wanted to die "suddenly" and "without nuisance"—so long as she got to "see Hitler get his, before I go."[81] The aging process was employed differently across these answers, providing incentive for one writer to "justify my existence" and making others feel that "ambitions and aims" belonged to the past.[82] Like the aging inhabitants of Bethnal Green, however, these writers assumed they would lead an active later life and make particular contributions to their families.

Especially among working-class families, both men and women experienced periods of unemployment, and this trend intensified with age. Older women were especially likely to be sacked, and their marginal employment status was rarely well measured.[83] When in work, women typically carried the "double load" of formal employment and household labor, and these domestic responsibilities continued after retirement.[84] In their conversations with Townsend, older women were careful to balance descriptions of physical aging with proof of their continued performance of vital roles in the household. Ellen Nash said that her husband "mucks in, especially if I don't feel too well," by washing dishes and carrying coal.[85] But she then seemed to quickly rethink the claim. After an "embarrassed silence," she added that normally, "by the time he gets home there's nothing left for him to do." The daughter of Florence Parsons insisted that even when her mother was ill, you couldn't get her to bed.[86] Instead, the younger woman teased the researcher for asking whether Florence was assisted in her chores by her adult children. "Help her with the shopping?" she asked in jest. "Don't put those ideas into her head. I want her to keep getting *mine*." Older men who took on domestic tasks after retirement described their contributions in ways that preserved the unique roles of their wives. A seventy-three-year-old retired schoolmaster, for example, gradually began to help his wife after he stopped working, starting with "rougher or less skilled types of house work: washing up, helping with bed-making, polishing floors, preparation of vegetables."[87] After his wife had an accident, though, the man took on the responsibility of cooking, too, and found that he enjoyed it. The man's deliberate reference to his wife's mishap made their situation seem temporary, but in fact, the blurring of gender roles is a necessary feature of many marriages in later life.[88]

Rather than exploring the ways that older people adjusted and shared their domestic duties, Townsend focused on the segregation of roles between elderly couples, which he explained as an extension of traditional working-class family arrangements. He wrote that husbands had great authority as the heads of households but that they helped little with housekeeping.[89] Instead of relying on a spouse's assistance, older women formed close relationships with female relatives, especially adult daughters, so that both work and leisure were segregated by sex. In Townsend's view, the unhelpful and intrusive presence of men in the home after they retired only caused friction between couples. This description of marital relations complemented Townsend's account of the attachment between older Britons and their adult children and strengthened his book's argument that younger family members did the real work of caring for the aged. However, Townsend failed to fully examine the depth of feeling that sometimes existed within long-established marriages. Even within their large and tight-knit family, for example, Sarah and Robert Agombar claimed a particular connection for themselves. After Robert retired at the age of sixty following an accident, the couple appreciated spending more time together in the home. "We play with our two selves now," said Sarah. In return, Robert volunteered, "I get the hump when she goes out." Retirement may have done more to support the midcentury ideal of companionate marriage than the commercial leisure activities that were enjoyed by younger couples.[90]

Women were in the foreground of Townsend's studies in a number of ways.[91] They outnumbered men among interviewees for *The Family Life of Old People* as well as among the oldest residents in his study of residential homes *The Last Refuge*. Most of the staff of residential homes Townsend investigated were women, too.[92] Townsend dedicated *The Family Life of Old People* to his mother and grandmother. *The Last Refuge*, was dedicated to his first wife, Ruth Townsend (née Pearce), who worked as a researcher on the project. In making the point that care was reciprocal between generations, Townsend mostly described the work of women, and especially the work of grandmothers. Social research was itself gendered. In the 1950s, twenty-two thousand social workers were the "routine ground troops" of social research, and 95 percent of them were women.[93] However, most academic positions in universities and social research institutions were held by men.[94] In his studies, Townsend did not consider the costs to older women of their unpaid work in the home or of their employment in residential care, which offered low wages and inconvenient early morning, evening, and weekend hours.[95] Instead, he assumed that many women were altruistic and benefited from doing care work.[96] Townsend later regretted that he had not been "more systematically on the look-out for family strains and tensions" in his research.[97] The violence and psychological and sexual abuse that was experienced in homes across the social classes, for example, would be uncovered by later researchers. In line with his view of female attributes, Townsend's recommendation to improve care of the aged was that the state should support families—meaning daughters and wives—in caring for the elderly in their homes.

ILL HEALTH AND BEREAVEMENT

In *The Family Life of Old People,* Townsend described in detail the difficulties that were caused by physical aging, especially for the 30 percent of older women and 22 percent of older men among his sample who were infirm or bedridden.[98] Townsend pointed out that once people were confined to the home, they were unable to take part in social activities and relied even more on family, especially on adult daughters.[99] One-fifth of the older people in the survey, however, were single, childless, or had relatives who were unable to help.[100] Even the well connected were keenly aware of the heavy burden they added to family life when relatives gave up paid employment or faced dual obligations to aging parents and their own children.[101] The emotional drama was clear. Yet there were aspects of older people's behavior that seemed confusing to Townsend. He recorded common refrains such as: "I'm not ill in myself. It's just the growth"; "I'm fairly good in myself, but it's my eyes what worries me"; and, "As far as general health it's good. But I've got arthritis badly."[102] He was baffled by the tendency of interviewees to demarcate their true state—represented by the phrase "in myself"—from many of their ailments.

To older men and women, good health typically meant the ability to meet their responsibilities and demonstrate character. The important distinction was between "difficulties of immobility, pain or breathing," which were common and expected parts of old age, and "acute sickness," like fever or exhaustion, which might be more disruptive of social roles.[103] Many older Britons met the former with stoicism and the latter with distress. Illness and operations were the favorite topic of conversation among the retired men and women who sat together and chatted in Victoria Park Square, beside the Bethnal Green public library.[104] These discussions allowed people to evaluate their own ability to cope in comparison with that of others.[105] Interactions with experts could work in the same way. Andrew Holborn, who had been in Bethnal Green hospital for six weeks after breaking his spine, told Townsend that a doctor commended his resolve when speaking to other patients: "You be like this one, it's will-power that's getting him right."[106] Andrew's wife, Florence, supported his story: "I heard all about him from others there. He was always laughing and cracking a joke." Andrew even satirized the kind of maudlin behavior that he had avoided. "Well, it's no use lying there with a face like that," he said as he gave what Townsend described as "a very long and hideous" expression. After Andrew had successfully impressed his doctor with his determination and good humor, he and his wife employed the same technique in conversation with the visiting social researcher.

In their stories, Townsend's interviewees made clear that the physical manifestations of aging had not interrupted the most meaningful aspects of their lives. In fact, the aging bodies of their parents gave some adult children the chance to prove their affections and recognize the lifelong dedication of their mothers in particular. When Mary Pheby found herself unable to get out of bed, for instance, her daughter took time off work to care for her and run errands on her behalf.[107] In Mary's telling of it, these actions recompensed her good character. She said of another child, "If my son thought I wasn't well he'd give me the top brick off the house. He always says 'a good heart never wants for long.'" Similarly dedicated, Marion Kempley had been lifting and dressing her mother, Lilian, since the elderly woman found herself unable to walk after suffering a stroke.[108] At the time of the interview with Townsend, Marion could no longer manage to move her mother from her armchair, where Lilian lived and slept. Social researchers worried that such infirmity was inseparable from isolation and loneliness, but Lilian contradicted that claim: "If I was lonely I could have plenty here. They think I'm a wonderful mother. They think I'm wonderful not to grumble." The woman's aging body restricted her to an armchair but also invited the care and admiration of her family. Lilian saw the help she received from her children as a tribute to her stoicism and a reward for services rendered. Age may have wearied her, but Lilian's essential self was intact.

Townsend's interviewees spoke about health problems that caused sudden disruptions to family life in somber tones. Sarah Agombar, for example, described becoming unwell at the age of seventy-six as a dramatic event: "Last January I collapsed in bed. It was as if I had a black-out. I was there ten weeks. It's the first illness I'd ever had."[109] The actions of relatives confirmed the significance of the episode. Sarah reported, "My Sarah Ann put her coat on and came straight down here from Yarmouth, she said what a shock she'd had." Other family members, too, came "rushing up," as "they'd never heard of Mum being ill in bed before." Despite her seventy-six years and the fact that she no longer felt fit enough to climb the stairs of the flat at the time of her interview, Sarah presented her temporary confinement to bed as a shocking event in the life of the Agombar clan. A skilled storyteller, Sarah interwove the tales of her collapse and the panicked responses of relatives in ways that emphasized her own centrality to the family's life.

Commentators at the time and since have interpreted the medical treatment of older people in the twentieth century as the cause of disengagement and "social death" among the aged.[110] They claimed that the elderly were being removed in increasing numbers from care in their local communities to die in hospitals and other institutions, where they were cut off from the social bonds they had formed over a lifetime.[111] The small proportion of older people who lived in institutions were likely to experience this separation from the outside world, and widowed men in particular had increased chances of isolation, yet the relationship between affective life and death often worked the other way around. Older people did not usually express strong emotions about death itself. Rather, the focus of their concern was the fate of those they would leave behind. The elderly volunteers writing for Mass Observation speculated about how many—or more often how few—years they might yet live. These aging Britons did not report morbid fears over the approach of their demise. Instead, they expressed a sense of regret over the trouble it might cause others and sadness about the loss of close relationships. Even the widespread fear of dying, which was carefully distinguished from the experience of death itself, was felt mostly on behalf of others. In the words of one sixty-year-old woman, "I do very greatly fear being ill enough to die, for myself, and still more for those whom I love."[112] A sixty-five-year-old married man felt brave: "I have reached the age (65) when death cannot be very far off.... I am ready for it, and not afraid of it and in some minds welcome the idea of it." His only dread was for his younger wife, who would "be very 'lost' and lonely if I went, and would also be very poor."[113] The chief regret of the aged was that death would end their emotional and financial support of loved ones. This was the opposite conclusion about aging to that drawn by sociologists, who thought that "social death" occurred as "biological death" drew near.[114]

Widowerhood cast a reflective light on love and marriage in old age, and this view persisted over time. Nine years after his wife's death, for example, Alfred Harvey delivered an account of his loss that began, "She's always been something different from other people to me."[115] Reaching back into their time together, he remembered that between the wars, "She never grumbled, all the times when I was walking and walking, trying to get work." Despite this long history of affection, he mused, "You can't tell how you miss someone until they go." At the time of his wife's death, Alfred's grief was intense: "I don't know how I stood on my feet." Over the intervening years, he thought of his wife often: "There's not a day passes but she's in my mind." He imagined her too. Alfred cried when he listened to couples in dramas on the radio, and sometimes he thought he heard his wife calling from the next room. In his interview with Townsend, Alfred repeatedly returned to his belief that his wife was an "exceptional" person. His story showed that marital bonds could be particularly strong in old age and that widowerhood provided reason to honor them in front of others. The older man's longing did not fit with Townsend's interest in intergenerational support for the elderly, however, and so the sociologist did not describe this aspect of his interview. In this way, social researchers and their readers sometimes missed the depth of people's emotional experiences during later life.

British anthropologist Geoffrey Gorer made little comment on the role of the home in the lives of the bereaved, choosing to focus instead on public rituals.[116] This interest in the public practices of mourning began during Gorer's 1930s education, when reading Sigmund Freud taught him "that the driving forces in humans were sex and death."[117] He became convinced that English culture was emotionally repressed compared to the societies he explored during his tours and anthropological observations in West Africa and Southeast Asia.[118] The *Sunday Times* circulated the questionnaire for Gorer's 1965 survey, *Death, Grief and Mourning*, which elicited 359 responses from recently bereaved people and 212 interview offers.[119] Researchers subsequently interviewed eighty people around Britain.[120] These interviews, Gorer claimed, proved his contention that death had superseded sex as a taboo subject in postwar Britain. He posited that the psychological results of the prohibition were severe, writing that "adults *need* help in living through the phase of intense grief," and questioning "whether they can appeal for help at all" in Britain, "where the majority wish to ignore grief and treat mourning as morbid."[121] Yet there was more to the story of bereavement in Britain.

Interviewees were unconvinced of the importance of public rituals around death and often preferred to mourn in the privacy of their homes. A number of older people volunteered to discuss personal matters, including bereavement, with interviewers for Gorer's project. However, these interviewees maintained a degree of privacy to keep control of their conversations with researchers. Older people described the ways that they were "facing up" to personal tragedies and "getting on" in their aftermath.[122] Stoicism offered comfort and well-worn phrases enabled bereaved people to end exchanges when they became uncomfortable. "Of course you don't like to [discuss grief with others]," one widower explained.[123] This was because he believed that those who were in mourning were divided from most of the people around them: "It's very difficult you see, unless you've been under the same circumstances yourself it's not the same." A widow reinforced the point. You should not "be a bore," she said, by talking about loved ones too much or "butting in" on the domestic lives of married friends.[124] These older Britons were not emotionally repressed; rather, they had realistic expectations of their acquaintances and wished to manage their interactions with others. In doing so, older people frequently prevented researchers from seeing the depth of their feelings. There were silences in the stories told by older people that sociological and anthropological records did not break.

Britons honored the wishes of elderly people, who wanted their roles in family life to continue as they got older and after they died. The bereft decorated their homes with the express purpose of stirring memories.[125] Houses in Preston, Ipswich, and Middlesbrough in the 1960s were kept exactly the same following the death of a spouse.[126] The most treasured items were those that had been worn close to the body of the deceased, such as a watch, suit, hearing aid, or pipe.[127] New domestic memorials were constructed, too. On the birthdays of her husband and son, who were both deceased, a sixty-one-year-old widow placed flowers beside the photographs that she displayed in her home in Birmingham.[128] A seventy-two-year-old widower in West Bromwich had multiple ways of remembering his wife: he "kept all his wife's things, had her buried just round the corner, went three times a week to the cemetery, and had flowers for her birthday and Christmas."[129] These actions had the desired effect of conjuring loved ones in memory. Widows and widowers dreamed of their spouses and saw or heard them, perhaps sitting in a favorite chair or ringing the sick bell for attention.[130] An eighty-five-year-old woman who had been widowed for over three years said that she sometimes saw her husband standing by her: "He says 'Oh Agnes' then I wake up and realize [that it was just a dream]."[131] Reading in her chair, the woman would hear a "rustle" and then "there he was in his dressing gown." The continued presence of her husband in their home was comforting rather than alarming. Agnes explained, "I'm not a bit frightened of anything like that it's rather nice." Just as younger Britons knowingly suspended their disbelief when they enjoyed commercial entertainments like reading the adventures of Sherlock Holmes or attending the cinema, the elderly enjoyed meeting deceased loved ones in what they knew to be visions and dreams.[132]

Aging eventually disrupted close relationships in ways that were permanent and painful. When this happened, storytelling by families and social researchers sometimes failed. Alice Bentley, who had moved out of her house of forty years to make way for a new block of flats, was depressed, felt that her health was poor, and missed the people she had lived among for four decades. She had attempted suicide several times.[133] Sarah Ware began to cry as she recounted her failing physical faculties.[134] James Allford, whose wife had died in 1948, wept when asked if he was ever lonely.[135] In response to these reactions, social researchers retreated from distressing subjects. They tried to introduce a lighter note into the conversation and stopped pursuing particular lines of questioning despite their "great interest."[136] It was such a failure of self-expression that explained the cool reception that Townsend initially encountered at the home of Rose and Charles Ellwood. At the time of the interview, Charles's injured wife had not left their two-room flat for four months. Charles reported, "Sometimes I comes home and there she is sitting in the corner of the room and she doesn't say a word. She just looks at me. She goes on looking at me as I go about getting the tea and I says 'what's the matter? Are you thinking how it was years ago?' and then sometimes she will burst into tears. I don't know how she stands it."[137] Despite talking multiple times with Townsend, Charles could never explain his wife's feelings. And neither could Rose—even to her husband. At times, the chronic pains of old age could disrupt thinking and speech, perhaps to the same degree as traumas of war, which have received greater historical attention.[138] Such moments were rare, however, occurring in only a handful of examples among Townsend's 203 interviewees.

With the implicit support of relatives and researchers, the great majority of older people who spoke to Townsend were articulate about their experiences. Aging interviewees used skilled storytelling, stoicism, and sometimes silence to make sense of their lives. The ability of older people to take control of interviews in these ways challenged the conclusions of contemporary social scientists about isolation and disengagement in more ways than were evident in Townsend's published studies. At the points that aging caused the greatest suffering, however, the social scientific record became almost blank.

CHAPTER THREE

Into the Institution

Residential Care for the Aged

The testimony of older Britons persuaded health and welfare workers like Lilian Chamberlain, who gained a Certificate in Residential Social Work from Middlesex Polytechnic in 1973.[1] Part of a broader apparatus of professional training and accreditation first introduced specifically for care of the elderly in 1950, this course convinced Chamberlain that the attitudes toward caring for the aged she had picked up working first as a clerk and later as matron of the George Moore Lodge care home were wrong.[2] For six years, she had "drifted along on the tide, believing as many others did, that old people needed to be cosseted and 'cared for'" to make up for years of degradation in the "dreaded workhouse."[3] She described how her formal study in a system that ascribed new value to the voices of older people converted her to "a more progressive and less institutional type of care for the elderly" and made her part of a widespread "awakening to the importance of the emotional needs of residents." Chamberlain wrote that afterward, she saw "the future more clearly" and resolved to play her part in realizing change by becoming head of a home. Eight years later, as head of the Oak Tree home on the outskirts of London, Chamberlain put her beliefs in action by shifting the institution's focus from physical care to the "emotional or psychological" needs of residents.[4] She introduced staff meetings, art classes, and reading groups and encouraged residents of the home to become more self-reliant.[5]

Chamberlain identified deep and abiding changes to philosophies of care for the aged, yet the drama of her story resided equally in the contested status of these new ideas. Despite politicians and practitioners boasting of a New Jerusalem, they had not swept away the Poor Law. In Chamberlain's description, George Moore Lodge, with its wide tiled corridors, "impersonal" lounges, and rows of silent residents seated by the walls—women in one room and men in another—felt like a 1960s version of the workhouse.[6] Throughout the 1970s, she feuded with the Oak Tree home's staff, who felt that their primary responsibility was to treat the medical problems of old age, as though their institution were a hospital.[7] By this time, older people had been telling advocacy groups and government ministries of their desire for individuality, independence, and privacy for at least thirty years. Yet it took another eight for Chamberlain to implement these ideas. Historians are familiar with the financial and material factors that limited the planned reforms of residential care. But in addition to this, individuals who were on the front lines of residential care were not wholly convinced of the need to change. This chapter examines the ways that a range of people within old-age institutions— including researchers, workers, and managers—both spread and subverted the testimony of the aged. For inhabitants of residential homes around Britain, face-to-face encounters with these individuals determined much about the experience of old age in the welfare state.

The Last Refuge study was funded by the Nuffield Foundation and carried out by Peter Townsend and his research officer Robert Pinker, with help from Brian Rees, Ruth Townsend, and June Vernon, who all conducted interviews.[8] Rees helped organize the administration and statistical analysis of the survey, and Vernon acted as the project's secretary. In 1958 and 1959, this research team surveyed the 146 local authorities in England and Wales, interviewed 65 chief welfare officers, and visited 173 residential homes selected from lists of all local authority (state-run), private, and voluntary institutions. Evoking the political and intellectual authority of social scientific research, Townsend pointed out that nearly ten years after the Labour government had declared the workhouse doomed, there was still no systematic knowledge of the implementation of new legislation for care of the aged.[9] Older people gave voice to their experiences of institutional life when they participated in the study's questionnaires, interviews, and observations. This chapter uses raw research data from Townsend's study to explore the influence of social scientific ideas on everyday lives within institutions that were both workplaces and homes. It reveals some of the ways that disagreements over ideals of the postwar era—such as the rights of citizenship, the value of universalism, or what it meant to have dignity in old age—shaped the interactions of individual Britons.

Histories of sociology, residential institutions, and old age pay well-deserved attention to Townsend and *The Last Refuge* project.[10] These works celebrate Townsend's pathbreaking contribution to the social sciences, his advocacy for older people, and his critique of the dehumanizing institutional practices that his research revealed. Townsend's recommendations would be influential in British social research and social policy up to the twenty-first century. Shortly after the publication of *The Last Refuge,* for example, local authorities began to close the large institutions that Townsend argued housed older people in the worst conditions.[11] Over subsequent decades, however, governments cited older people's desires for independence and personal choice to introduce cost-saving and privatization measures. Townsend was skeptical of these reforms, and in 1997, he worried that elderly Britons were more vulnerable than ever.[12] As these legacies suggest, the visits of Townsend and his research team had mixed effects on the lives of older Britons in residential homes. *The Last Refuge* research process itself displayed tensions between egalitarianism, hierarchy, and individualism that pulled the attention of researchers away from older people's testimony.

A NEW VISION FOR RESIDENTIAL CARE

The midcentury rethinking of welfare and old age took place in a material and social landscape marked by the long history of the Poor Law and the workhouse, which had offered last-resort lodgings and food at the cost of the separation of families and calculated affronts to the pride and self-sufficiency of inhabitants.[13] Elderly Britons had frequently been forced into the workhouse after being excluded from full-time paid labor, especially if they did not have children who were able to support them.[14] At the beginning of the twentieth century, around twenty-five thousand old people, 2.8 percent of the age group, lived in workhouses.[15] Stephen Hussey has demonstrated that working-class elderly dreaded the workhouse for the hardships it inflicted through labor, a meager diet, the confiscation of personal clothes and possessions, and undignified communal living. He has also shown how the workhouse destroyed valued social roles, such as domestic work and childcare, and symbolized the end of the self-reliance that was essential to working-class respectability.[16] Thanks to these assaults on working-class life, fear of the workhouse was "transported across generations" of working people into the mid-twentieth century.[17]

Toward the end of the nineteenth century, evidence of endemic poverty amid Britain's increased prosperity cast doubt on the laissez-faire ideology that underpinned the Poor Law system.[18] Such questioning became more urgent during the economic turmoil of the interwar period, when many believed that capitalism had failed. Among the responses to critiques of the workhouse, a series of acts introduced from 1925, especially the Local Government Act 1929, formally ended poor relief and introduced more specifically targeted Public Assistance to be provided under legislation such as the Public Health Act and the Education Act.[19] There was, however, little "reforming zeal" in the treatment of older Britons.[20] During the 1930s, there was some marginal improvement to the conditions of older Britons through "a minor share in generally higher living standards," but the decade also brought further difficulties for those living in institutions.[21]

A large amount of care for the elderly has traditionally taken place in medical institutions. Before the National Health Service was established in 1948, access to specialists and medical training was monopolized by voluntary hospitals, which cared for the acute sick, while public hospitals treated most of the aged, chronically ill, and mental health patients in a "neglected backwater" of care.[22] In 1939, at the outbreak of World War II, the discharge from hospitals of 140,000 patients, including many elderly people who were chronically unwell, to make room for wounded civilians drew public attention to the plight of older patients.[23] After the war, the regional hospital boards of the newly formed National Health Service took responsibility for institutions with varied philosophies and practices of care for the aged, including voluntary and municipal hospitals and former Poor Law institutions.[24] The "miserable amenities and staffing standards" of some of these institutions became more apparent when they were compared to others within the same health system.[25] As standards of living rose, the new system supported demands by older people for better, more egalitarian care for the elderly.

The postwar Labour government implemented a new system of residential care and advocated a fresh set of guiding ethics. In 1947, minister of health Aneurin Bevan announced that the workhouse was to go, and he described a utopian vision of residential homes that was characteristic of the New Jerusalem.[26] The workhouse was to be replaced by "sunshine hotels" that would each accommodate twenty-five to thirty older people who were unable to look after themselves.[27] The National Assistance Act 1948 prescribed that local authorities should provide residential housing for old people who needed it due to financial difficulty, ill health, or social isolation. Local authorities could collect means-tested payments for residential care and could also organize for care to be provided by commercial homes that charged fees. Prices per week ranged from three and a half guineas to thirty guineas.[28] The National Assistance Board funded residential care for those who were unable to pay. To begin, 42,000 people were placed in residential homes. In its annual report for 1948 to 1949, the Ministry of Health declared that "local authorities are busy planning and operating small, comfortable Homes, where old people, many of them lonely, can live pleasantly and with dignity."[29] In July 1948, local authorities owned and managed 63 small residential homes. By the end of 1960, they had opened 1,121 more, offering accommodation for 39,000 people.[30] By 1980, the number of older Britons living in residential homes had risen to 126,000, 1.7 percent of the age group.[31]

Yet reimagining residential care was not the same as erasing the workhouse, retraining staff, or shifting the mentalities of people who lived and worked in homes. Shortages of building supplies and limited budgets prevented many large-scale building projects in the postwar period. The optimism of 1948 gradually turned to resignation: few older institutions for the elderly were closed, immediate plans for building conversions were delayed by a shortage of funds, and in the meantime, authorities were reluctant to spend money on existing buildings that were scheduled for eventual abandonment. In 1949, around forty thousand residents of local authority homes lived in such large and outdated buildings; in 1960, these dilapidated institutions housed thirty-five thousand elderly Britons.[32] In 1965, the Ministry of Health estimated that twenty-seven thousand people still lived in two hundred former workhouses, in buildings that exemplified the dehumanizing treatment of older people that was despised by social researchers and policymakers.[33] Oral historian John Adams dated the "last years of the workhouse" to 1965, the date of the closure of Luxborough Lodge, the former St Marylebone Workhouse, which had been a landmark in central London.[34] He pointed out that he could have nominated 1985, the year that the Camberwell Reception Centre, the final incarnation of the Gordon Road Workhouse, closed. As Adams has highlighted, the "sturdy walls" of workhouses ensured they remained both "an essential resource for the new National Health System and a constant reminder of the past that had been renounced" for decades.

In postwar Britain, public, private, and voluntary institutions provided residential care to the elderly. In January 1960, there were 1,573 local authority institutions and 2,071 voluntary and private institutions registered with local authorities.[35] Overall, around two-thirds of beds for the elderly were provided by local authority institutions, which tended to be the largest in size; a quarter were provided by homes run by voluntary and religious associations; and the remaining beds were provided by smaller privately run homes. Welfare officers revealed they had little direct influence over the day-to-day operations of these disparate institutions. The constant pressure created by understaffing and demand for care meant that it was uncommon for councils to refuse or revoke a home's registration and that subsequent formal relations between councils and homes were "often extremely slender."[36] For many homes, local authority inspections were infrequent, "perfunctory," and "amounted to little more than a casual conversation over a cup of tea."[37]

Welfare workers had typically trained and gained their work experience in prewar institutions.[38] Attempting to change this, the National Old People's Welfare Committee, with enthusiastic support from the Ministry of Health, introduced a six-month training course for residential home staff in September 1950.[39] Yet many local authorities and residential home workers opposed the course. The London County Council, for example, wanted to train staff itself and doubted trainees needed the full complement of skills covered in six (later reduced to four) months. By December 1958, only two hundred students had taken the course.[40] A National Council of Social Services study revealed that 80 percent of staff in residential homes still lacked such formal education in 1967.[41] In 1970, the Council for Training in Social Work first awarded the more substantial yearlong Certificate in Residential Social Work in Homes for Adults to twenty-two students.[42] Official qualifications in care for the elderly may have exposed some workers to the new theories of social work—including the implicit stance that welfare work with the elderly was a professional industry that required formal education—but training was patchily attended and did not grant higher pay or status in the workforce.[43] In line with John Bowlby's psychological attachment theories, which popularized a model of fragile but vital psychic development in childhood, social work educators, administrators, and the field's practitioners argued that there was much more at stake in residential care for children than for older people.[44]

Residential home staff mostly learned on the job. After 1948, health departments, which were likely to prioritize medical needs over welfare concerns, administered residential institutions for the elderly. During his research for *The Last Refuge*, Townsend noted that many matrons and staff had been trained as nurses or understood their work according to medical priorities.[45] Under these circumstances, it was unlikely that many staff would follow Townsend in distinguishing between the welfare needs of older people and the medical treatment of hospital patients. Moreover, residential care for the elderly occupied a lowly position in the hierarchy of medicine. When Townsend conducted interviews in geriatric wards in a National Health Service psychiatric hospital, the charge nurses recalled that medical students labeled their department "the punishment ward" and resented being placed in a field that was not considered "real nursing."[46] Townsend speculated that some of the aloofness and reliance on medical ideals he witnessed was a tactic for coping with the gap between the professional ideals of workers and what was possible for them to achieve given the lack of funding, training, and professional pride within their field.[47]

The Last Refuge aligned with the anti-institutional literature of the 1960s and 1970s, which included sociological studies of institutional life and official inquiry reports that followed allegations about the poor living conditions and abuse in long-term hospitals.[48] Townsend asserted that it was neither necessary nor moral to care for older people in institutions, thus undermining the philosophical basis for policies that encouraged improvement of residential care. Older people told the researcher that they entered homes most often for social reasons, such as loneliness and isolation, rather than because of physical debility. Their stories provided Townsend with evidence that institutional life did "not adequately meet the physical, psychological and social needs" of the elderly.[49] Townsend asserted that older people should be cared for in the community with the support of welfare services delivered at home. He advocated the expansion of both voluntary and state services to keep older Britons more active, financially stable, socially integrated, and able to live independently.[50]

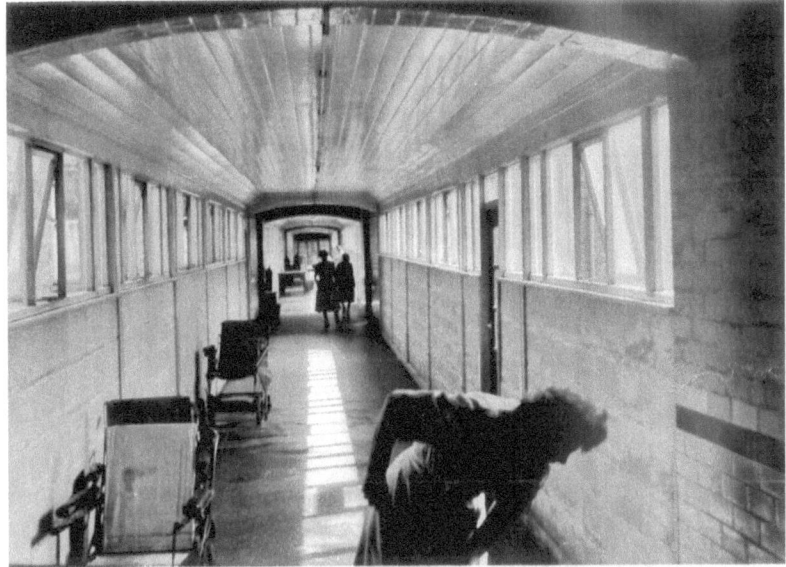

Figure 12. Townsend's unpublished photograph of a corridor in a former workhouse in Wolverhampton. Images, SN 4750 The Last Refuge 1958–1959, Peter Townsend Collection, National Social Policy and Social Change Archive, Albert Sloman Library, University of Essex, Colchester. Copyright Baroness Jean Corston.

Townsend expressed his anti-institutionalism in photographs as well as text (figures 12–15).[51] The researcher was influenced by the photojournalism of the *Picture Post* to capture nearly one hundred photographs of life inside these homes with his Leica camera.[52] In 1962, his publisher, Routledge and Paul, reversed their stance on the images that Townsend had wanted to include in *The Family Life of Old People* and agreed to publish a series of photographs in *The Last Refuge*. The series harnessed the emotional significance of built environments by depicting the long corridors, imposing entrances, and cold stone floors of some institutions and the cozy domestic interiors on offer in others.[53] The passageway of a former workhouse, for example, communicated the discomfort, lack of choices, and isolation of large and traditional institutions. By

Figure 13. A tightly cropped image of a bedroom in a voluntary home in Liverpool. "Voluntary Home, Liverpool 1959," Images, SN 4750 The Last Refuge 1958–1959, Peter Townsend Collection, National Social Policy and Social Change Archive, Albert Sloman Library, University of Essex, Colchester. Copyright Baroness Jean Corston.

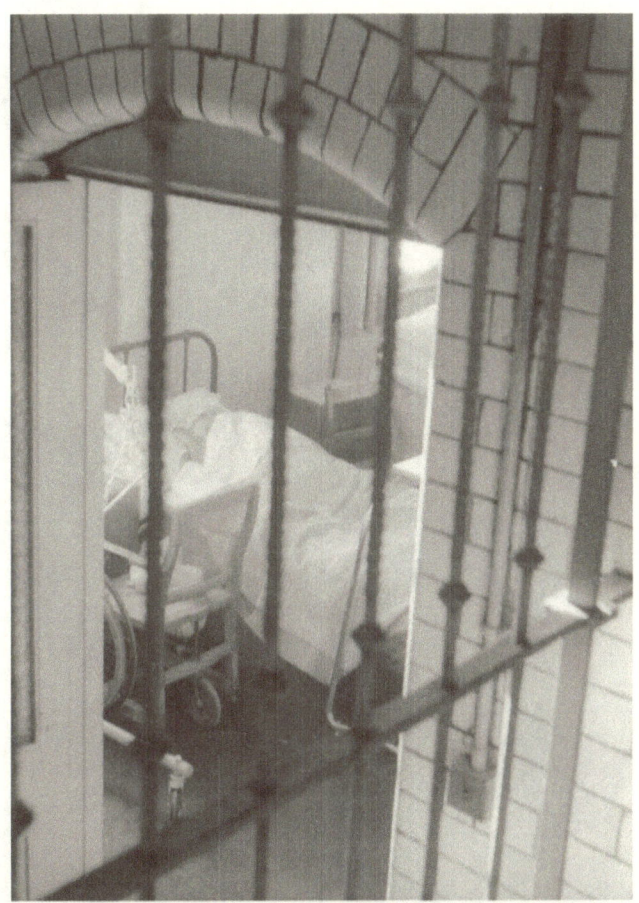

Figure 14. Townsend's portrait of life in a local authority home in London. His images made a visual argument that institutional life was psychologically damaging. Images, SN 4750 The Last Refuge 1958–1959, Peter Townsend Collection, National Social Policy and Social Change Archive, Albert Sloman Library, University of Essex, Colchester. Copyright Baroness Jean Corston.

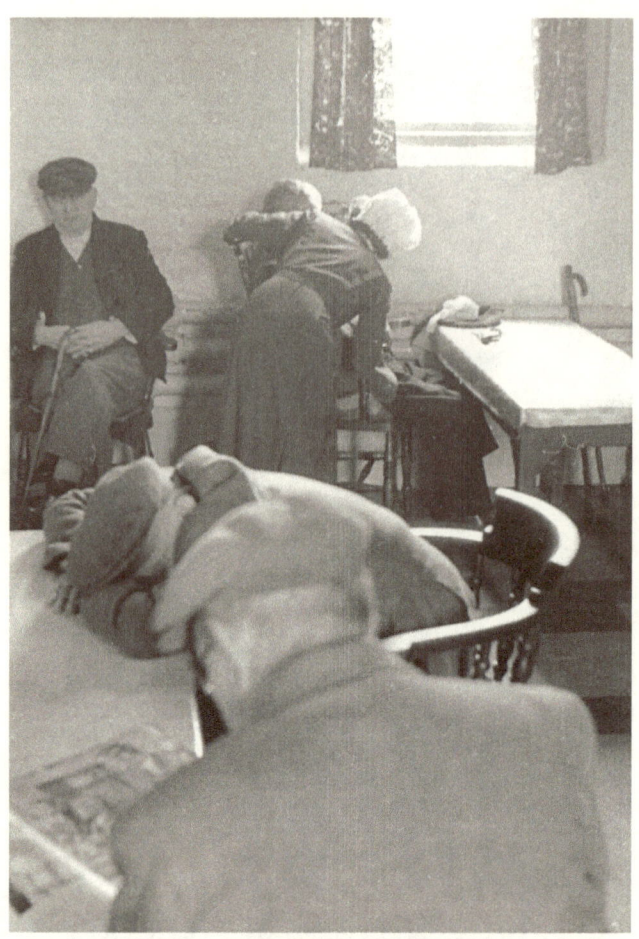

Figure 15. The day room in a local authority institution in Norfolk. Images, SN 4750 The Last Refuge 1958–1959, Peter Townsend Collection, National Social Policy and Social Change Archive, Albert Sloman Library, University of Essex, Colchester. Copyright Baroness Jean Corston.

contrast, the photograph taken of a bedroom in a voluntary home was tightly framed to create a feeling of privacy and to focus on the trappings of domesticity, rest, and relaxation that were widely shared postwar aspirations.[54] Most of Townsend's images, however, remained unpublished. In one of these unpublished photographs, the viewer intrudes on a sleeping resident through a set of bars; in another, the viewer gazes over the shoulder of a resident at the slumped bodies of men dozing in a communal day room. These photographs are visual representations of the misery and apathy that Townsend discerned in the largest institutions. Townsend's positive evaluations of smaller and mostly purpose-built institutions were frequently based on the values of homeliness captured in some of his photographs. However, *The Last Refuge* ultimately argued that a comfortable room in an institution was second best to a room in a home of one's own.

AFFECTIVE LIFE IN RESIDENTIAL HOMES

Townsend's interviews with the residents of residential homes revealed a population of people for whom normal social and familial structures had broken down. Many of the older men and women he spoke to had never had close relationships, or they had lost contact with their loved ones through death, separation, or infirmity.[55] Residents were likely to be aged over eighty and to have been single or childless all their lives. Some had exhibited unusual family behavior, such as deserting their families, living in a common law marriage after the death of a spouse, or living away from relatives for long periods of time.[56] Townsend contrasted the isolation of this minority population with the "marvellously complicated network of family relationships" of those old people he had interviewed in their own homes. He described studying the residents of institutions as "looking at the commonest relationships of society through the wrong end of the telescope, through the eyes of people who had not experienced them."[57] Social welfare systems had also failed many of his subjects. Townsend recorded histories of homelessness and discussed older people's difficulties competing with young families for council flats, calculating that just over a quarter of his interviewees had lost their homes before entering an institution.[58] The long waiting lists to enter residential homes further skewed the populations of these institutions toward the desperate cases of older, poorer, more infirm, and more isolated individuals.

Some older Britons said that their choice to enter residential care served their family life. An eighty-year-old woman who was still living in her home in Eastleigh organized a welfare visit to hold "the threat of going into a Home over the heads of her husband and her daughter."[59] She hoped to win more attention from her offspring. Applications to enter residential homes could be evidence of good familial relations too. One seventy-four-year-old woman, whose doctor had encouraged her to apply for a place in a residential home, remarked, "It's my place to ease my daughter's place."[60] An "extremely active and able" eighty-five-year-old man living in Camberwell reported that his daughter would not "admit that I'm too much for her" but overrode her and requested a bed anyway.[61] In these cases, older Britons were clear in their aims to help relatives. For most, though, entering residential care caused heartbreak and confusion. Townsend observed that welfare officers raced through their visits to older people who had applied or been recommended for residential care, doing little to "calm down the worries of the old person and explain what going into a home meant."[62] The aged received little information or assurance on arrival at their new home. Jovial but insensitive, a receiving ward officer at a home in London boasted, "I can talk them into anything. I just joke them along—they never resent me."[63] Many local authorities used legislation to force older people into homes against their wishes when it was considered dangerous for them to live independently, although most reported exercising this legal power only once or twice each year.[64]

Once inside, residents described how they reacted to hated institutional practices such as public bathing. Some screamed and attempted to escape while others stayed silent out of fright or resignation. A woman living in a home in Southend-on-Sea recounted her response to being bathed and having her hair cut by a rough staff member: "I screamed but where the police are I don't know. It's the only thing I can do."[65] A ninety-two-year-old male living in a home in London reacted to the institutional environment with studied stoicism: "You have to go where you're put. I have to do what I'm told to. I suppose I've no big complaint of this place, and anyway, if I did, they'd tell me to get out."[66] Ruth Townsend interviewed a seventy-eight-year-old woman living in the same home who "appeared to be terrified by authority and [intimidated] by everyone."[67] This woman had believed she was admitted to the home to recover from a fall for a few days, but at the time of her interview she had been there for two weeks and had received no visits from her son or daughter-in-law or information about her future. She did not want to "cause trouble" by commenting on the home in response to the researchers' questions or by asking questions about her situation. The woman felt trapped because she no longer had possession of her own clothes and because she believed that a policeman watched the door. These institutional practices amplified widespread feelings of confusion, helplessness, and panic. Meanwhile, the complaints of the elderly were dismissed in staff interviews as the habitual "grumbling" of the old.[68]

The emotional and psychological needs of residents were assessed by staff members in different ways, depending on the institution. A number of voluntary and religious homes, especially those that had occupied the same building for a long period of time, emphasized charitable relief and moral policing and therefore subverted the midcentury reinterpretation of residential care as a right of citizenship. The legacy of the Poor Law manifested in signs requesting donations and controlled front gates.[69] In fact, one resident of a religious home in London judged that little aside from terminology had changed since his father had died in the St Pancras workhouse: "They don't call it that now, they call it a 'Home'. They put a strip of lino down the middle of the corridor, a few covers on the chairs, and tell us it's different—well, it ain't, it's still the workhouse—I know!"[70] The man punctured claims that postwar legislation had remade old-age institutions. However, he stridently negated the argument made by social researchers, that old-fashioned institutions caused suffering, stating, "I'm real happy here, they couldn't be kinder—you feel you want to help them." The man was grateful to the institution that he had entered after being homeless for a large portion of his life, and he did not expect it to be rid of the vestiges of the workhouse or to treat him very differently from his parents. He demonstrated his loyalty by watching the home's door from 6:15 in the morning until 5:45 each night.

In many of these institutions, the priorities of efficiency and hierarchy shaped the daily lives of residents. In one home, everyone was woken at 5:30 in the morning because staff believed it was vital to get everyone out of bed, washed, and dressed in time for the entire population to breakfast together.[71] The owners of small and privately run homes, which were often operated by families inside their own homes in an effort to balance their household budgets, also frequently astounded researchers with their interpretation of the ethics of care. One matron revealed her lack of interest in the midcentury ideal of independence within residential life when she boasted to Ruth Townsend of her ability to control events in the home by deciding when the women in her care went to bed and got up, when they bathed and changed their clothes, and whether their rooms were sufficiently clean.[72] In contrast, the *Last Refuge* researchers, who had strong feelings about the independence of residents, actually complimented a degree of mess. Research notes from *The Last Refuge* about a Catholic home in Cheshire commented approvingly that the male residents smoked in their beds and said of the lounge, "Lots of rubbish and dust in this room—very pleasant."[73] The researcher also used the term "pleasant" to describe the decorating of the room, the number of personal belongings, and the chat going on between the male residents and the sister superior. In the women's infirmary ward, the researcher admired bunches of tulips and a pet budgie flying around the room, comparing this relative chaos to the repressive order of council institutions: "Imagine this in a Local Authority Home!" The comparison encouraged positive responses to the practice of converting large private homes (often former stately homes) into residential institutions.

The conversion of private homes was a common practice in the postwar period, when local authorities were required to extend their provision of residential care but lacked the funds to begin new building projects.[74] These houses frequently showcased beautiful grounds, unique furniture, and impressive views, which counterbalanced their unsuitability for the technologies of modern health care, such as lifts and adjustable beds. The features of these houses aligned with the researchers' belief in the emotional and psychological satisfactions of individuality, privacy, and material comfort—three central definitions of home. Since the late 1940s, researchers and advocacy groups had recommended that a residential home should "resemble a private home and not an institution."[75] In 1947, for instance, Seebohm Rowntree had insisted that both residential homes and their rooms should be as small, individualized, and private as possible.[76] His report recommended hanging curtains to divide shared rooms, setting up a timetable of occupational and recreational activities in the community, and creating intimate, brightly decorated, and informal areas for socializing.[77] Both the built environment and the routines of eating and sleeping, Rowntree wrote, should "destroy" institutional "symmetry and extreme tidiness."[78] The matron of a home in Liverpool encouraged residents to furnish their own rooms "so they make it a home within a home" and a site of self-expression and personal ease.[79] After Townsend and another researcher visited this home, they wrote, "It was really delightful to walk into a room and imagine that a human being could really live in it," setting out the way their conception of selfhood was wedded to domestic environments. The description of a private home in Surrey cited the possessive phrasing used by a woman who sat proudly surrounded by what she called "my own things" as evidence for these theories.[80] These pleasures were usually on offer in smaller homes. Yet regardless of the size of the institution, a curtain dividing a shared room did not achieve the seclusion of a private house, and attractive decorations did not alter the fact that many residents did not have the freedom to choose their environs, routines, or companions.[81]

Nuns and religious volunteers understood the needs of the elderly through the register of their faith. At a home run by the Methodist Church, the matron believed that the "greatest pleasure" of her residents was their shared religious belief, and so she organized a service every evening, although she kept it to fifteen minutes so residents could also enjoy watching television.[82] Religious homes were the most likely type of institution to offer residents a place until their deaths instead of admitting them to the hospital when their health seriously deteriorated. The sister superior of a Catholic home made the claim that older people came to the home "to prepare for death," a position that was not held outside religious institutions.[83] In this matter, religious homes came closer to the ethos of social researchers than many large institutions, where it was common to hide the dead in bathrooms and arrange for the undertaker to remove the body while residents were sleeping or watching television.[84] Designed to avoid upsetting other aging residents, the practice had the terrifying effect of people disappearing overnight. While researchers typically viewed care for the aged as a right of citizenship that should be provided by the state rather than by charity, they also admired practices of religious homes that mitigated some of the worst aspects of institutionalism.

Administrators and staff judged elderly people and assigned them better or worse care according to hierarchies of social class, health, and mental health. Introducing the National Assistance Act 1948 to the House of Commons, Aneurin Bevan imagined that the populations of residential homes would be self-sufficient: they would be made up of "the type of old person who are still able to look after themselves" but were "unable to do the housework, the laundry, cook meals and things of that sort."[85] As a result of the 1957 Boucher Report, which addressed local authority concerns that their residential homes cared for many people who should have been in hospital, residential homes were charged with care of the infirm and senile.[86] The updated 1965 guidelines expanded the group to include "people so incapacitated that they need help with dressing, toilet and meals," as well as people suffering from some incontinence.[87] During the midcentury period, social scientists and welfare workers had no language that was specific to mental health and frequently intermingled what they saw as "confusion" with other unfavorable characteristics of aging, such as poverty and debility. Midcentury psychiatrists also judged senility to be part of the aging process.[88] These judgments had consequences for the treatment that older people received. The county welfare officer for East Riding, for example, said that large institutions were appropriate housing for what he called the "hard core of low-grade people," a category that included "the mentally defective and dirty people," as well as those with physical limitations.[89] A great number of officials and staff agreed that lower-class elderly would be "quite happy in infirmaries" and that they liked "to be huddled together," a line of argument that denied privacy and self-determination to a large portion of the population they served.[90]

When administrators deemed an older person lower class, physically infirm, or what was consistently termed "confused," they were more likely to send that applicant to a large institution that compromised the freedom and privacy of its residents. Meanwhile, older people who had worked in the professions or exhibited what were called "nice" manners were added to waiting lists for small homes that had been purpose-built during the postwar years.[91] These homes were preferred because of their size, staff-to-resident ratios, and comfortable, homely atmospheres. In Preston, the medical officer of health authored a list of requirements for the admission of older people to smaller homes and made the first criterion "social abilities." The medical officer made it clear that the category was used to rank residents according to social class: "We can't take the sort of person who wants to put his feet up on the fireplace and spit in the fire."[92] Townsend found that a greater proportion of middle-class residents lived in postwar homes, especially in areas where large numbers of elderly lived in former workhouses.[93] The particularly bad conditions of some local institutions appeared to harden the biases of administrators against working-class elderly people and those who were in poor health. Even within institutions, staff gave some residents more attention than others. In a home in Wolverhampton, for example, only the residents living in the "smaller and nicer blocks" were encouraged to celebrate one another's birthdays.[94] Administrators argued that large homes could better care for the infirm and ill adjusted because they could afford more sophisticated equipment and that these residents would feel "out of place" in smaller homes. As a result, working-class and frail elderly lived in the worst conditions.

SOCIAL RESEARCH AND THE ELDERLY

Townsend's research notes record angry encounters between staff and residents and between staff and researchers over such institutional practices. Members of *The Last Refuge* research team recorded particularly strong emotional responses when they were implicated in practices they despised. Researchers felt awkward and ashamed when staff described older people as if they were not in the room.[95] Ruth Townsend enabled a resident to talk back in her observation notes by quoting the woman's bitter remark when a matron displayed her beautiful embroidery and drew attention to her arthritic hands: "I'm the monkey at the Zoo," the resident said.[96] Equally shocking was when residents would stand up as researchers entered a room. Such displays of subservience enacted institutional hierarchies that were reminiscent of the workhouse and disrupted the notion that midcentury Britain was built on democratic citizenship and offered egalitarian social services.[97] On entering a dining room for female residents alongside the home's superintendent and matron and seeing all the women stand up, a *Last Refuge* researcher fled the room, so upset that he was "hardly able to go on with the tour and ask neutral questions."[98] Townsend was similarly aghast when the warden of a home in Lancashire lined up his four interviewees together on a bench to wait, instead of calling them one by one.[99] He insisted, "There was nothing I could do about it." Yet *The Last*

Refuge project operated within the same power structures it critiqued, and, distressingly, the study was frequently used to justify further inconvenience and disempowerment for its subjects.

The Last Refuge project's influence over institutional behavior was revealed when residential homeowners and workers performed the psychologically aware and egalitarian actions that social researchers favored. A married couple who owned a privately run home in St Leonards put on a show for the visiting research team when they sat down to the same "very unappetizing" midday meal as their residents. This was meant to demonstrate the couple's egalitarian practices, as residents were treated to the same standards of comfort—and the same dish of mashed potato and macaroni and cheese—as the couple's own family.[100] However, their five-year-old daughter revealed that the family was only enacting what they felt to be correct practice when she indignantly inquired, "Auntie is having lamb chops. Why aren't we having that?" The researcher concluded that the couple usually served themselves different and more luxurious fare than what the residents were offered. Food had long been accorded social and emotional importance in social research. Debates over the minimum nutrition an adult required, for example, had also considered the social status of consuming meat, especially for working men.[101]

While some attempts to impress were particularly clumsy, even a flawless performance of professional practice was not sufficient to impress Townsend and his team. True to their interest in internal lives, the *Last Refuge* researchers judged the feelings and intentions of residential home staff as well as their behavior. Knocking at a resident's door and pausing for permission to enter was usually a sign of a sensitive and humane worker, but the "hearty, overbearing" clergyman at a private home in Midhurst was reported to have done so only to ensure "that the niceties of tact had been observed."[102] A researcher cynically noted that the warden leading a tour of a home in London "made a lot" of the fact that he called residents by their Christian names and "kept making a point" of doing so, thus inserting a gap between the warden's words and intentions.[103] The researchers suggested that the language and practices they advocated could be employed tactically in competition for professional status. Residential homeowners, administrators, and staff wanted to show that they were up to date with the latest professional standards, even if they did not normally observe them. Of course, at least in their project notes and publications, social researchers always had the last say.

Mirroring the power structures that operated in residential institutions, research interviews were molded by public spaces and the intrusions of administrators and staff who listened in. At a private home in Skegness, interviews could not be conducted in the rooms of residents due to their "extreme cold" and had to take place in a downstairs parlor with doors on either side, one of which did not close properly, so that interviewees "were constantly looking nervously at the door" for spies.[104] Elsewhere, interviewers believed they were being watched or "harried" by staff on the pretense of serving tea or making beds.[105] The sensitivity of social researchers to the presence of onlookers was partly the result of their new insistence on authentic first-person reflections and partly due to the acknowledgment of the sometimes conflicting interests of administrators, staff, and residents.[106] The technical difficulties that researchers encountered when they attempted to record first-person interviews with elderly residents revealed the tenuousness of privacy within institutional life.

Townsend's commitment to measuring emotional and psychological need and gathering first-person evidence meant that the *Last Refuge* researchers viewed their 489 interviews with older people as "the most important single task of the research."[107] The interviewers aimed to speak with every resident who had recently moved into each home they visited. Each questionnaire took just over half an hour to complete, and the researchers would spend four hours in small homes and up to two or three days in larger ones. Aiming for accuracy, researchers cross-checked their answers with matrons and local authority case files. They wrote out the questions for deaf subjects. Townsend reported that "quiet conversation" with disabled people produced "patchy responses" when none had been expected. In pursuit of deeper knowledge, Townsend lived for several days in a postwar home in Leicester. While there, he interviewed all but one of the thirty-seven residents using a special questionnaire that asked residents whether they felt happy or experienced loneliness. Their answers, he wrote, were "complex."[108]

Residents claimed emotional needs that included material comforts, freedom, companionship, and privacy. A man living in a private home in Brighton complained of the home's lack of heating and its "shocking" menu of burnt food. He said that there was a single lavatory for fourteen men: "The cistern won't work properly and you have to wait 20 minutes for the flush to fill."[109] There was "no comfort" in the home, he said: "A prison wouldn't be worse." A woman living in a religious home in Boscombe described a very different reality. She pronounced the head sister "a dear" and the home "very comfortable," with "excellent" food, but lonely.[110] Expressing similar reservations, one female resident of a local authority home in Bury described the home's bedrooms as "beautiful, with plenty of blankets and sheets," but felt bored and as if she were under surveillance.[111] She wept when she was asked whether she would like to stay, concluding, "Sometimes I feel I could go out and not come back."[112] Interviewees typically expressed fulfillment in some areas and want in others, making it difficult to label their feelings about residential care.

The emotional experience of living in a home was not contained within its walls but rather connected with the outside world and noninstitutional dimensions of the aging process.[113] A widower of eighty-three, who had been admitted to a hospital in London, started to "sob his heart out" during a welfare visit, and "every time he would try to speak he would begin sobbing again."[114] These notes record that the man was depressed by the hospital's "regimented routine" but he was also saddened because his property had recently been sold. He cheered up when describing the recent arrival of a great-grandchild. A man living in a home in Salisbury was close to tears as he described thinking of his village and feeling its "draw." He put out an arm and made "a tense pulling movement to illustrate this feeling" of longing.[115] Another resident sat at the local traffic circle to watch coaches until he saw one coming from his home in the West Country, but "by the time he has read the name of the proprietor it has gone and he hasn't had time to search for a familiar face." These scenes of men holding back tears, physically reaching toward their home, or sitting on the street for hours suggested bittersweet emotional lives that operated outside of institutional culture through memory and imaginative connections to familiar landscapes and people.

When they got the chance, a number of older Britons rejected *The Last Refuge*'s key questions and research methods. Early in an exchange with Townsend about the residential home she lived in, an elderly woman named Emma confidently said, "I have noted your suggestion as to the kind of report you need.... Unfortunately, the routine outline mentioned by you, would not give a picture of the life as lived in this Home by us."[116] She may have been emboldened by her prior experience as a researcher at the Merrill-Palmer Institute of Human Development and Family Life in Michigan. Emma and her husband had been living in a private home for the aged in Surrey for around seventeen months when, in May 1960, she read an article Townsend penned for the *Times* and volunteered to keep a diary for the project.[117] Emma was keenly aware of the driving purpose of social research to understand the lives of individuals. However, instead of answering the researcher's request for a timeline of her day, with activities such as getting up, reading the newspaper, and dining, Emma wrote a detailed account of her life over the month of June 1960 and provided narratives of the couple's "outstanding experiences" since they moved into the home.[118] Emma's diary entries and essays turned on the emotional significance of social hierarchy and power struggles within the home, especially the couple's resistance to a matron who was able to use her professional status to control the home's meal plan and access to medical supplies. By contrast, a second diarist, Arthur, aligned his authorial identity with the routines of his residential home, where he voluntarily rose at 5:30 each morning to help set tables in the dining room before breakfast.[119]

Despite his different take on institutional life, Arthur was no less resistant to the prescriptions of the *Last Refuge* researchers. He wrote general comments throughout the model diary entry that research officer Pinker intended to be reproduced on a daily basis, and he penned unsolicited essays on his life that asserted his persona as a cheerful, hardworking, and humorous older man.[120]

In the published version of *The Last Refuge,* the voices of people who advocated and cared for older people often drowned out the voices of the aged themselves. The section of the book titled "Life in an Institution," for example, included over two hundred quotations from "those in charge" of institutions, as well as comments from lower-ranked staff members.[121] In contrast, there were only thirty-eight direct quotations from elderly residents. An excerpt taken from the diary that Townsend kept while he worked as an attendant in a home ran to forty-five lines, while most quotations from residents recorded a single line or just a turn of phrase.[122] In subsequent chapters, the researcher made greater use of the voices of the elderly. A chapter about the effects of living in residential care, for example, included seventy-five quotations from residents.[123] These numbers identify the limits to Townsend's interest in individual experiences. In his opinion, individuals were "unique" mostly because of "the structural situation" of their lives, which was revealed by the words of those who were "in charge."[124] It was "utterly wrong," he later reflected, to have an "individualistic preoccupation" during research. The *Last Refuge* researchers may have sent a different message to elderly residents when they took the time to talk to these individuals about their lives. However, it is likely that interviewees were aware of the contradictions of a research process that both complimented and inconvenienced its subjects. After all, many of the same tensions were apparent in mid-twentieth-century reforms of the institutions in which the elderly lived.

• • •

By the postwar years, residential care in Britain had become symbolic of continuous state support from the cradle to the grave. The daily interactions that made up life in residential homes, however, display the ragged edges of midcentury claims to egalitarianism and respect for the feelings of the old. In practice, the system was disparate, and it divided the old by their social and physical characteristics. In his publications, Peter Townsend uncovered the ways that residential care was a source of great suffering. Yet the influence of his research began earlier, during the interview process. When Townsend invited the residents of old-age homes to tell him their stories, he voiced the argument that the inner lives of the old should be of public concern and also put this philosophy into action, frequently creating a dramatic break in the working culture of residential homes. As this chapter has explored, however, social research sometimes reproduced the conditions it critiqued and sometimes created the ideals that researchers wanted to see. In this way, long before the publication of their studies, social researchers drove as well as documented social change in twentieth-century Britain.

CHAPTER FOUR

"Making the Best of My Appearance"

Grooming in Old Age

For writers in midcentury Britain and for historians looking back at that period, the vision of old women clad in Victorian black symbolized the hardship of the lives of these women through the visual symbolism of mourning. Historians have suggested that dark hues were considered the most "suitable" and "becoming" shades for older women in 1920s and 1930s Britain, partly because widows were likely to wear black.[1] When Mass Observation researchers walked the streets of London's East End to study working-class clothing in 1940 and 1941, they made this symbolism central to their questionnaires and analysis. Women over forty-five were described as "down-at-heel," scruffy, and dressed in clothes that were, "almost exclusively, brown, navy and black."[2] In contrast, they observed that women younger than thirty-five took "great interest" in their appearances and wore high-heeled shoes, unwrinkled stockings, and silk frocks dotted with flowers. However, the impression the researchers had of drab older women and colorful youth was not supported by their interviews. In fact, women of all ages named black as their favorite color by an "overwhelming" majority, and navy blue was the second most popular shade.[3] Similarly, when the organization studied the colors worn by women in the streets in 1941, researchers found that young women did not favor bright colors more often than older women and that brown, navy, black, and grey were equally appreciated by each age group.[4] The color divide was more evident in people's minds and in conventional imagery than it was in the everyday grooming of British women.

The shopping and grooming habits of elderly women and men at midcentury pointed to the unequal resources of older Britons in the 1950s. While some older people were admitted to charitable institutions, those with good health, enough cash, free time, and the inclination could choose to enjoy commercial pastimes, such as shopping. British *Vogue* invited older women with means to participate in the sensuous world of fashion. Mrs. Exeter, the magazine's sixty-year-old fictional character who dispensed advice to older readers in her column, described having "very strong feelings" about color and often chose luxurious tones such as "a rich red, or deep sapphire, or steel grey" for evening wear.[5] In the January 1950 issue of the magazine, she was attired in "midnight blue velvet" and discussed the pleasure of discovering colors that were flattering when worn with grey hair. Older men generally selected tones that were more discreet, and they took care to groom their faces and bodies. Depictions of both older women and older men in women's magazines reveal that these individuals had a prominent place in midcentury visual and commercial culture, especially during the 1950s. Public discussion of aging included fashion and beauty and was therefore broader than historians have previously thought. While black clothing had practical and symbolic value during this period, we have been wrong to cloak our understanding of old age in its folds. The bright colors of midcentury beauty and fashion culture highlight some of the pleasures that older people experienced as they made their bodies beautiful and admired the look of their garb.[6] The way that older Britons wrote about shopping and grooming reveals a set of personal responses to physiological aging and its strong connections to selfhood.

The counternarrative to this chapter—that is, the idea that older women and men in the past felt disconnected from and confused by their bodies rather than able to find pleasure in them—makes sense to us, as this is a common message in contemporary media and academic publications. We expect aging bodies to be placed out of sight or experienced as shocking in modern culture.[7] We are told they are hard to look at and heartbreaking for older people, especially women, to consider in the mirror. Midcentury social scientists focused on struggling older bodies: those of people who were in pain, in need, and trapped in their houses. These figures were not readily included in the visual culture of modern Britain. Sociologists working in the later part of the twentieth century theorized that women "disappear" as they age.[8] Scholars published the testimony of women who felt eyes slipping over them in the street and who argued that they were ascribed no personal attributes other than their age. Other social scientists have described how wrinkled faces, stooped backs, and shuffling walks define old age for those outside the category but are rejected by those who display those characteristics, who say, "[This body] isn't me."[9] The horror of old age in the past is enhanced by the knowledge that people endured harsher material realities—such as greater poverty and shorter lives—and by the self-congratulatory notion that images of aging have become more positive since the 1960s.[10] A few sociologists have questioned whether ageism has had this hegemonic influence. Peter Öberg surveyed men and women of a range of ages about their feelings toward their bodies and received 1,250 replies that revealed a complicated relationship between age and body confidence.[11] The number of men who reported feeling satisfied with their bodies declined somewhat with age, but women's responses demonstrated the opposite pattern. As they grew older, women became more likely to feel happy, with the exception of a dip among thirty-five to forty-five year olds.[12] Despite these findings, the idea that aging bodies are a source of emotional suffering has proved to be a long-lasting motif in academic and popular culture. Older men and women were in fact celebrated in the fashion and beauty culture of the mid-twentieth century in ways that have not been recognized or understood, in part because twenty-first-century historians are the inheritors of the particular age-conscious gaze that developed during the 1960s.

FASHION AND WOMEN'S MAGAZINES

Dress has been an important symbol of generational conflict in histories and autobiographies that discuss the mid-twentieth century. Fashions connote sexual and social repression in descriptions of the 1950s and newfound freedom in memories of life in the 1960s. Callum Brown has noted the pleasure midcentury British women felt as they donned their Sunday best and attended church feeling attractive and looking forward to meeting young men.[13] Yet autobiographies by women who came of sexual age in the 1960s discount the value of 1950s style and use it to denounce the period's class-based standards of behavior. As author Angela Carter recounted, "I grew up in the late fifties—that is, I was twenty in 1960, and by God I *deserved* what happened later on. It was tough, in the fifties, girls wore white gloves."[14] In these personal narratives and in many historical accounts, young women in white gloves are treated as evidence of a repressed younger generation and society. The unrealistic expectation that young women's gloves should remain unsullied symbolizes the way they were denied useful work and meaningful social roles and were forced to conform to stultifying social and sexual norms. By contrast, the 1960s are now described as a time when young people found their voice and their own beliefs as they fought for the liberation of private life and their right to personal happiness, political influence, and the pleasures of a vibrant pop culture.

Historians have begun the work of complicating this narrative of sexual and sartorial revolution. Becky Conekin has located the roots of 1960s style in the professional practices of fashion models and photographers working in London in the 1950s, who "set the scene" for the apparently sudden shifts of the subsequent decade.[15] This chapter tells another side of the story by reclaiming the expressive value of midcentury style for an older generation. Older women viewed the signatures of midcentury ladylike style, gloves included, as tools of beauty and self-worth as well as symbols of propriety. The fastidiousness of this older generation's standards is part of what gave youthful fashion rebellion its potency. If good grooming had not been so closely tied to respectability and self-respect, looser standards and long-haired men would not have made older people feel so disturbed. Amid the stories of the liberation some felt as they wore their skirts shorter and their eyelashes thick, we might also consider what was lost in the transition, including a world of fashion and beauty that welcomed older consumers.

Older women fit in different ways with the commercial appeal of women's publications that defined reading audiences by their homemaking roles, social class, or age. First published in Britain in 1922, *Good Housekeeping* continued an established nineteenth-century tradition of domestic magazines aimed at middle-class women.[16] During the early 1930s, for example, over half of the magazine's features addressed the subjects of home and family.[17] Older women featured in *Good Housekeeping* in poetry and serial fiction, advertising for household goods, and editorial features that described the achievements of notable women, such as Eleanor Rathbone and Beatrice Webb, in the fields of politics, intellect, and philanthropy.[18] Established in 1911, *Women's Weekly* was most popular in the early 1930s, when its mostly working-class readership numbered 1.1 million.[19] Near the height of its popularity, in June 1930, *Women's Weekly* argued, "Never has the older woman had such a chance to beautify herself as now, when skirts are of a becoming length and necklines so soft."[20] By 1935, Ruth M. Ayers was writing a regular column under the headline "Middle Age Is Not a Thing to Dread." Ayers suggested that "the woman of forty-five, or even much older," was "amongst the most sought after and attractive" because she knew "how to dress, and how to be interesting."[21] Perhaps historians have overemphasized the beguiling imagery of the lithe flapper of the 1920s and wrongly implied a twentieth-century obsession with youth.[22] In fact, the first half of the twentieth century also offered mature fashions, from the "statuesque, heavy-chested grandeur" of Edwardian fashions to the "huge swirling skirts" and "formal demeanour" of the "New Look" championed by Christian Dior in his debut collection of 1947.[23]

The women's magazine industry transformed in the 1930s, when publishers introduced periodicals aimed at young, working-class women with rising incomes.[24] Magazines such as *Woman's Own* and *Woman* (launched in 1932 and 1937, respectively) kept the most successful elements of working-class periodicals, such as informal editorials and serial fiction, but adopted a new, classless tone to reach the widest audience.[25] By 1939, *Woman* was selling one million copies per week.[26] These magazines printed fewer romantic stories and knitting patterns, introduced features on beauty and fashion alongside those on domestic life, and increased the amount of advertising between their pages so that they could publish attractive issues at cheap prices.[27] Nearly half of the articles that appeared in *Woman's Own* in the 1930s were about women's appearances. The focus on youth was obvious, especially in beauty advertising and the magazine's choice of active, cheerful, and glamorous models as cover girls.[28] Older women appeared in the pages of these periodicals as grandmothers who recommended particular household products and as supporting characters in serialized stories that described the romances and adventures of young people. By 1951, *Women's Weekly* had been displaced by *Woman* and *Woman's Own*. Nearly a quarter of all women read at least one of the newly popular titles, while *Women's Weekly* had less than half as many readers.[29]

Published from 1916, the British edition of *Vogue* became both profitable and influential during the 1920s and 1930s.[30] Its publisher, Condé Nast, had purchased American *Vogue* in 1909 and recast it as a "class magazine" that was designed to attract wealthy readers, and it relied on the revenue from advertising for luxury goods to subsidize the high-quality printing.[31] Nast employed the same approach in the British market. In the 1930s, British *Vogue* fashion spreads featured clothes that knew "no age limit" but were appropriate for what the magazine called "the age of discretion."[32] For middle- and upper-class women who studied *Vogue*'s fashion advice, aging was no barrier to good style. "A few added years," the editors opined, "hold no terrors for women who choose clothes like these."[33] In the July 1937 feature "After Fifty, What?" readers could choose between six illustrated "answers," including "pleats to promote length," "elbow sleeves to cover too-plump arms," and an "elongating panel of printed crêpe-de-chine down a plain navy-blue satin backed crêpe dress."[34] *Vogue* models appeared womanly and wore dresses of "tailored, architectural severity" or "studied, yet easy formality" that were marketed as "distinctively English."[35] *Vogue* suggested that readers who followed the magazine's careful fashion advice could look "smart for your age" or "fifty years young" (figure 16).[36] Accompanying such articles, angular line drawings denoted high fashion, slimness, and age. In the 1930s, these fashion sketches seemed to be an expression of modern life and its panache.[37] Line drawings appeared in Vogue until the mid-1960s, although Condé Nast introduced an increasing number of photographs after he surveyed newsstand sales in 1936 and concluded that photographic covers sold better than illustrated ones. By the early 1950s, *Vogue* had the sixth largest readership among women's periodicals thanks to its significant middle-class circulation.[38]

Wartime fashions were primarily designed for economical use of fabrics, featuring short, military-style dresses and utility skirts.[39] Women of all ages used "elaborate make-up, inventive hairstyles, and coupon-free accessories" to brighten the look. After Dior introduced his New Look in the late 1940s, British women adopted the style despite restrictions and in the face of public outrage over its perceived waste.[40] Women appreciated the look's sturdy foundations, flowing skirts, and discreet shoulder padding. They donned voluminous Dior-inspired skirts "supported by crinolines or layers of petticoats, nipped-in waist, boned torso and cantilevered bust, sweeping necklines for evening wear and tightly-sleeved jackets for day."[41] The Board of Trade forbade *Vogue* editor Alison Settle from mentioning Dior in the magazine because the government feared that it would spur an increased demand for fabric.[42] The corsets that were required to achieve the tiny waists and wide hips of the New Look were banned under rationing. Many women created a version of the style with home sewing machines, sometimes by inserting a broad band of fabric near the hem of shorter

Figure 16. The line drawings and photographs that appeared in *Vogue* emphasized the glamour and dignity of older women. *Vogue* (UK), February 2, 1938, p. 52. *Vogue* © Condé Nast Publications.

skirts that they already owned. The contrasting stripe was a fashion item in its own right.[43] Whether women wore Dior or a homemade version of the designer's clothes, they aimed to express fashionable qualities of poise and perfect grooming. These were virtues of experience rather than the gifts of youth.

In 1949, *Vogue* created a character who embodied the magazine's ideals for older women: Mrs. Exeter, a woman who was "approaching sixty" and did not look "a day younger."[44] Writers for the magazine played up the character's age. In March 1949, Mrs. Exeter was accused of mumbling. In June, she daydreamed about the past.[45] In September, she knitted for her granddaughter.[46] Mrs. Exeter was "prehistoric" in the eyes of her grandchildren.[47] The style icon mused about challenges that had been delivered by recent years, including her "33-inch" waist, "yellowing" complexion, and rheumatism. Mrs. Exeter's sense of style, however, was undimmed by the passage of time. "My new suit?" she wrote, "Ah, now that *is* up-to-date." In November 1950, Mrs. Exeter appeared on the cover of the magazine in a vision of her ladylike style (figure 17). The fact that she was definitively not "young-looking," her creators wrote, did not preclude her from being "*good*-looking."[48] In 1952, *Vogue* ran a competition to find their "real-life Mrs Exeter."[49] Mrs. Eastley, who was a justice of the peace in Devonshire, won the title.[50] However, model Margot Smyly—who was only thirty-nine when she appeared on the *Vogue* cover in 1950—became Mrs. Exeter's most recognizable face (figures 18–20).[51]

Mrs. Exeter's high status was reflected by supporting characters who depended on her social nous. In the summer of 1953 alone, the older woman escorted her niece through the season, accompanied her grandchildren to the coronation, and hosted friends from abroad.[52] As an older woman of financial means, she had much to offer her family and community in committee work and at garden parties, dinners, theater outings, and weddings.[53] The older woman's ever-stylish and suitable clothes, *Vogue* was quick to remind readers, were signs of her success: she was "businesslike and charming" at meetings and radiated a "restrained and formal beauty" during dinners. The character usually wore sharply

Figure 17. Mrs. Exeter graced the cover of British *Vogue* in November 1950. Photograph by Horst P. Horst. *Vogue* © Condé Nast Publications.

Figure 18. This spread shows a typical example of the well-groomed style that Mrs. Exeter wore until the 1960s, when she reconsidered the hard edges of her look. Photograph by Eugene Vernier. Illustration by Eric Stemp. *Vogue* (UK), October 1957, p. 154. *Vogue* © Condé Nast Publications.

tailored suits and pearls, but she also embodied the glamour and desirability of a black velvet evening dress. Few older women could hope to stand at a table surrounded by glittering crystal and fine works of art, but they could be inspired by the poise that was on display in photographs of Mrs. Exeter. By aspiring to even a touch of this sophistication, older

Figure 19. Mrs. Exeter photographed stepping out into the limelight at a dinner, framed by an attentive and appreciative audience. The soft fabric and loose fit of her outfit in this spread shows that she kept up with the increasingly relaxed styling of the late 1950s. *Vogue* (UK), February 1959, 68. Don Honeyman / *Vogue* © Condé Nast Publications.

"Making the Best of My Appearance" / 115

Figure 20. In this photograph, Mrs. Exeter's averted eyes allow the reader uninterrupted access to her body, especially to her décolletage, which is emphasized by a plunging neckline and draped stole. Her waist is highlighted by a giant rose gleaming white against the black velvet of her dress. *Vogue* (UK), October 1953, p. 163. Photograph © Norman Parkinson. Courtesy of the Norman Parkinson Archive.

women could claim a portion of the "assertive and powerful" identity that was on offer in these images.[54]

Mrs. Exeter achieved a perfect fit with the fashion culture that *Vogue* marketed to women of all ages. During the 1950s, the character typically appeared in well-cut, flattering suits with a fashionable twist in color or

Figure 21. Photographs of Barbara Goalen showcased her striking facial features and the ease with which she wore formal and luxurious clothing. *Vogue* (UK), August 1956, p. 34. Photograph © Norman Parkinson. Courtesy of the Norman Parkinson Archive.

tailoring that marked her out as attractive and up to date. Advertisers and feature writers agreed with Mrs. Exeter about the vital importance of "quality" and "clothes of distinction."[55] The same styling made Barbara Goalen, who has been called Britain's first supermodel, a queen of British fashion pages between 1947 and 1954 (figure 21).[56] Goalen enjoyed the limelight from her midtwenties to her early thirties, yet she embodied a mature femininity that could be emulated by women of a range of ages.[57] One photographer described the angularity of her face as "sharp and memorable, every plane jutted and recessed like some Cubist sculpture, a photographer's dream. She was drawn with a knife," reminiscent of the line drawings of Mrs. Exeter in *Vogue*.[58] As a commentator later observed, Goalen modeled expensive clothes that were "designed for women, not girls."[59] Against this background, *Vogue* judged their missives to older women a success. In an autobiography published the year she turned ninety-one, literary editor and author Diana Athill agreed that Mrs. Exeter persuaded elderly women to wear stylish clothes.[60]

Vogue gradually changed the way that it treated age during the 1950s. In 1953, for example, *Vogue* launched "Young Idea," a section designed to appeal to the "booming" youth market.[61] Norman Parkinson provided the key photograph for the new section. He celebrated the informality of young people by photographing models in energetic poses and enjoying the outdoors rather than in the studio. During its first decade, this section and similar features were points of intersection between *Vogue*'s increasing interest in young women and its celebration of ageless style. Fashion features, advertisements, and *Vogue* patterns that were all titled "Clothes with No Age Tag" insisted that the same looks were appropriate for women of any age (figure 22). This message was challenged elsewhere in the magazine, though, when *Vogue*'s visual cues emphasized the differences between younger and older women's bodies and pastimes in ways that earlier images had not. A 1956 feature, for example, pictured the actresses Elizabeth Seal (aged twenty-two) and Adrianne Allen (aged forty-eight) wearing matching twinsets.[62] The magazine did not mention the ages of the women, yet the developing aesthetics of youth culture highlighted the differences between the two through the juxtaposition of jeans with a tweed skirt, the clean white space of a studio with a drawing room, and a pixie cut with a perm. By 1959, younger and older women who appeared in the "Clothes with No Age Tag" feature wore different outfits.[63] The magazine made an increasingly clear distinction between the visual signifiers of youth and age. By 1964, most

Figure 22. Older and younger women were pictured wearing exactly the same clothes in numerous fashion spreads, dressmaking patterns, and advertisements during the 1950s. *Vogue* (UK), October 1957, p. 169. Helmut Newton / *Vogue* © Condé Nast Publications.

of *Vogue*'s style suggestions—including patent leather knee-high boots, miniskirts, and false eyelashes—were no longer marketed to older women. At the same time, Mrs. Exeter's column became an advertorial, with only a few tangential references to the character's identity as an older woman. High fashion ceased to be an appropriate location for the celebration of older bodies during the mid-1960s. Yet we should not ignore what came before, when fashion illustrations and photography championed mature, statuesque women and Mrs. Exeter was a symbol of glamour for those approaching and on the other side of sixty.

MEN'S FASHION

Men trod riskier ground than women when they fretted about the style of their shoes or the cut of their clothes. The relatively conservative and slow-changing male fashion market in late nineteenth-century and early twentieth-century London turned men's attention to "minor changes" in their choices of hat, gloves, shirt, or tie.[64] However, a lack of ostentation did not mean that men were unconcerned with style. On the contrary, achieving a "plain" appearance required considerable thought and effort. In 1870s tailoring journalism, for example, plainness meant "an attention to neatness in finish and the provision of an uncompromised setting against which accessories and detail could be more clearly displayed."[65] Men needed to be alert to the details of their dress. Yet those who knew too much about beauty and fashion culture might appear effeminate, a charge that carried harsh legal and social penalties. Appropriately masculine behavior was sometimes policed by monitoring men's possession and use of beauty accessories such as the powder puff.[66] In the early decades of the twentieth century, physical culture and its celebration of muscular and barely clothed bodybuilders, like Eugene Sandow, further encouraged male disdain for consumer culture.[67]

Despite the uncertainty of the territory, magazine writers and shop owners wooed men as consumers of style from the 1930s. Between 1935 and 1939, for example, one-fifth of the articles in the lifestyle magazine *Men Only* and one-third of its advertising dealt with men's bodies and clothes. However, the magazine's editorial staff was careful to point out that men shopped for practical reasons, not out of vanity.[68] British men also saw products for purchase in the windows and catalogs of tailors' shops, such as the Leeds-based tailoring company House of Burton.[69]

Figure 23. A dashing older man accompanies Mrs. Exeter as she models a suit and blouse made from a Vogue pattern. *Vogue* (UK), January 1954, p. 77. The photograph, shot by Clifford Coffin, was originally published in American *Vogue*, October 1953, p. 173. Clifford Coffin/*Vogue* © Condé Nast Publications.

Burton's aimed to sell suits to lower-middle and respectable working-class men by suggesting that they should look like gentlemen. Burton's ideal gentleman was represented as "indeterminate in age, but secure in position," and always "correctly dressed."[70] In doing so, Burton's took into account the era's contradictory expectations about masculine consumption. In its stores, a gentleman shopper "acquired status by being absolutely normal."[71] This balancing act was pursued by men of all ages. One seventy-three-year-old who wrote for Mass Observation, for example, hoped to look "neat and tidy but not conspicuous."[72] Encouraged by consumer culture, this older man groomed himself to appear at the midpoint between the undesirable poles of overdressing and carelessness.

In the pages of *Vogue,* advancing age did not undermine the attractiveness of men. Well-groomed male models with graying hair and wrinkled skin played supporting roles to women of a range of ages, accompanying them to the races, the theater, and cocktail parties (figure 23). In 1954, an older male model embodied the aristocratic ambitions of the brand Aristoc in a printed advertisement for the company.[73] The image anticipated romance, showing the man grooming himself, applying cologne, and putting on cufflinks and a bowtie. In the bottom portion of the page, his refined female companion revealed only her hands and her Aristoc hosiery. Their connection was emphasized by pairing the photograph of the man with a promise printed beneath: "*She* of course will be wearing ... Aristoc." A 1955 image that advertised a brand of French jersey depicted a similarly amorous scene between an older man and a younger woman.[74] The couple leaned their bodies inward in a way that, combined with their downward gazes, suggested erotic interest. Whether they were depicted looking into a mirror or enjoying a private moment with a female companion, older men maintained their aesthetic appeal in the pages of magazines.

STYLE AND SELF-WORTH IN LATER LIFE

Historians have depicted the sartorial lives of older people as staid and conventional. Some have imagined that older women and men clung stubbornly to their outdated stiff collars, hats, and gloves and ignored comfort, convenience, and exciting new fashions.[75] Yet the pursuit of respectability meant more than achieving class conformity and keeping up appearances. For many, careful grooming displayed inner character and affirmed one's place in the community. Looking respectable was not just mindlessly adhering to tradition; it was about keeping one's job, pleasing one's family and friends, and affirming one's sense of self. Older Britons typically approached new fashions with flexibility. While older women did not usually wish to be absolutely up-to-the-minute in their dress, they were interested in wearing colorful and stylish clothes and in being noticed for their attractive faces, hands, hair, and accessories.

Older men were usually more cautious about inviting attention because they operated in an environment of simultaneous encouragement of, and anxiety over, men's interest in fashion, but they still wanted to look good.[76] Some older people had difficulty meeting the sartorial standards of the day, and this had as much to do with limited resources or interest in fashion as with physical signs of aging.

Mid-twentieth-century Britons were acutely aware of being observed. As in America, "new urban sites of consumption and display, a flourishing fashion economy, the spread of image-making technologies, and a nascent culture of celebrity" in Britain meant that "seeing and being seen" took on greater cultural importance starting in the late nineteenth century.[77] In the 1920s, consumer culture around the British world linked feminine identity to "techniques of appearing" so that "it was as visual images, spectacles, that women could appear modern to themselves and others."[78] Twentieth-century beauty culture required "knowledge of the self" that was achieved through "a calculated regime of care" and performed for the mirror and the public.[79] Established traditions of the "reciprocal relation of the inner and outer body" survived the scientific ideas about beauty and hygiene that were popular in the twentieth century.[80] Just as nineteenth-century physiognomy and phrenology taught that personality could be revealed through face and skull, 1930s beauty advertising used the "therapeutic language" of psychology and psychiatry to sell the possibility of simultaneous "transformation of external appearance and inner well-being."[81]

Older Britons participated in the visual culture of the twentieth century. In 1950, for example, a sixty-three-year-old music teacher told Mass Observation, "One ought to try as far as possible to make a pleasing 'picture' for others to look at."[82] Much was at stake in her efforts. As a sixty-one-year-old man put it in his own writing for the organization, "A person's appearance is an index of his character." According to him, the cut of a man's hair, for example, displayed personality traits such as "self-esteem, conscientiousness, energy, carefulness and balance (between vanity and slovenliness)."[83] While many older people writing for Mass Observation described their grooming rituals with pride, their exacting requirements of dress and appearance could be oppressive as well as pleasurable. A Durham housewife of sixty-three years, for example, listed multiple criteria that she set for the appearance of acquaintances, many of whom failed to impress her: "I examine the appearances of all I meet. I might be saying to myself 'You're really a nice face & figure if only you (1) bought the right hats, (2) clothes, (3) did your hair differently and (4) carried yourself well.' Or I might be thinking 'Your smartness makes you for you've a very poor face.'"[84] This woman held herself to high standards that sometimes disrupted her daily life. She declined to visit the shops and would "leave the milk in the hands of the milkman" rather than let anyone see her looking "any old sight." Her writing displayed her own skillful choices of garb, accessories, grooming, and posture. It also revealed the shame that she perceived to be the consequence a poorly groomed, rather than a poorly aged, body.

Many older Britons with means had a clear vision of how they wished to appear that was related to—but not identical to—the fashions they observed in advertising and shop windows. In May 1939, a sixty-four-year-old retired office worker detailed the way that she chose an item of clothing, a process that spanned a period of months. The woman was inspired by fashions she saw displayed in printed advertising and along the shopping streets and markets of London.[85] Yet everyday concerns were central, too, especially her budget and the critical eye of friends and family. A sixty-one-year-old man was critical of the idea that he might follow fads.[86] Nevertheless, he asserted a specific vision of the way his suits should be designed: they should be indigo blue with pockets on the inside, the trousers should be short in the body, and the waistcoat should be long. He was not willing to accept less than his ideal and found it "surprising how difficult it is to make a tailor understand that I know what I want and mean to have it." Both these elderly Britons presented themselves as competent, and perhaps unusually clever, in their navigation of the world of marketing and outfitting. Both the woman and the man judged that appearing correctly, according to their own exacting standards, was vital.

Older women were often proud of their appearances, particularly of their skin and hair, and did not feel that age was an insurmountable barrier to attractiveness. For example, a sixty-two-year-old writer reported that she had used cosmetics for just a few years, "having been blessed with a fair smooth skin and a good complexion," and continued to be happy with only a small amount of powder. Even then, her friends assured her, "Of course you don't need it."[87] Beauty was a topic of conversation and cause for compliment among older women. Three women—aged sixty-three, sixty-five, and eighty-six—reported that they found it unnecessary to hide or boost their "naturally good," clear, and tanned complexions.[88] Women of all ages could have beautiful hair. A Dorset housewife wrote that her short white hair was "often admired," and another woman maintained that grey hair "seems to add to youthfulness."[89] The pleasures of well-groomed and luxuriant locks, good skin, and beautifully shaped hands were both attainable and socially significant for many women over sixty. In their own words, older women got "confidence," "comfort," and the "uplift of feeling of equality with others" from these attributes.[90] Older women felt the internal satisfaction of attractive appearances and stylish dress because these provided visual affirmation that women were important and valued members of social circles, families, and community life.

Putting together their outfits, older women typically positioned themselves on a scale of style consciousness. At sixty-three, a Suffolk housewife and secretary considered herself "too old to wear clothes simply because they are in fashion" but liked "to wear things sufficiently still in fashion to look Right."[91] She capitalized the final term to emphasize its significance. The woman's language was similar to the text used in fashion advertising in the middle decades of the twentieth century that addressed "those who want to look Right," perhaps by dressing in well-styled suits.[92] Similarly, an eighty-six-year-old wrote to Mass Observation that did not wish to look "'smart' whatever that may be, nor dull nor dowdy, just right for my size, age & type & dressed for the occasion."[93] This woman understood smartness to connote a degree of attention to trends that would be unbecoming at her age, but she was not discouraged from looking "just right." In July 1950, another woman, who was sixty years old, mused that she could not say truthfully that she was "very clothes conscious as regards up to the minute fashion," but she stressed that her clothes needed to "fit perfectly" and "be immaculately clean."[94] While she did not feel attuned to the latest fashions, style was important to her: "wide flamboyant checks" or "ugly" slingback shoes made her "positively cringe," and she would "go to any trouble to try & make exactly" what she wanted to wear. She reflected, "It's not always been easy to keep my 'finicky' standards but I know if I gave them up—when illness has made me have to for instance, something inside me suffers." The woman's writing demonstrated both her careful adjustments to physical aging and the high emotional stakes of getting her appearance right.

Men generally wrote shorter and less enthusiastic descriptions of their clothes. A number of older men pronounced themselves "indifferent" to their appearance. Yet, like older women, these men usually listened carefully to the advice about their appearances that was offered by family and friends. They, too, felt that their appearances expressed their character and found pleasures in good grooming. One retiree, for example, wrote, "[I'm] quite critical of the get-up of my friends."[95] Another man, who was still working in a Glasgow pressroom at seventy, described how he would "get on to" any "unsightly" colleagues and insist that they shaved.[96] These men were active in community policing of standards of appearance, which, in turn, affected their own habits. A retired clergyman recorded that "remarks from the lady members of the family" caused him to take greater care with his appearances.[97] A sixty-three-year-old man reported that he shaved his beard after a fellow train passenger addressed him as "dad," a title he felt his years did not yet deserve.[98] Some elderly men made superior efforts. One said that dressing "so that one's appearance should not offend canons of propriety and good taste" was only the first, or "lowest," rung on the ladder of style and good looks.[99] A pensioner of sixty-eight aimed to "please [himself] and others" by looking "spruce."[100] This man equated cleanliness with happiness, celebrated that he looked younger than his age, and explained that being "fresh in appearance" conferred "ease and confidence." Wives, daughters, workmates, and passersby often agreed with these older men about the importance of masculine grooming.

Many elderly Britons worked hard to achieve the right look and avoid the indignity of poor grooming. When a sixty-year-old housewife and voluntary social worker wrote a description of her wardrobe for Mass Observation in June 1950, she recorded that she chose her clothes "with very great care."[101] She purchased clothes of "the best cut and material" that she could afford, in styles that would provide "something suitable for every occasion" she could foresee. The woman treasured the items she selected. She changed out of her better clothes and into house gowns as soon as she could and never threw pieces of clothing on the bed; instead, she hung them on "shoulder" hangers and made sure to "air them well." The woman removed "small spots" on sight and washed or dry-cleaned items "as soon as they lose freshness." She stored her shoes carefully and washed her stockings daily. She pressed "lightweight garments before wearing it all crumpled, & put things carefully away in tissue paper." And that was just for outfits. Her hair required biweekly trips to the hairdresser, a "thorough" brushing daily, and pinning up at night under a net to protect the set from steam in the bath. She spent ten minutes on makeup in the morning, changed the cosmetics if she changed her clothes during the day, and took "plenty of time" to prepare her face for an evening out. In search of "cleanliness & freshness, good grooming & suitability of turn out," she devoted "a great deal of time, trouble and as much expense" as possible to "making the best" of her appearance. This especially fastidious woman listed four "conscious reasons for taking great pains" with herself: vanity, aesthetics, self-discipline, and a love of clothes. Along with many older Britons, the woman believed that fashion and beauty revealed more than what was skin deep, and she described the numerous satisfactions awaiting those who had the time and money to look good.

OLDER WOMEN AND COSMETICS

Most older women who wore makeup were not cowed by the perpetually youthful faces displayed in cosmetics advertising. One woman wrote that she had started to use rouge in her early fifties after being told that she looked unwell.[102] She sounded self-effacing but lighthearted as she responded to her husband's compliments with the explanation that she had "put a touch of rouge in the right place." A woman from Lancashire had a similar experience. She recorded a steady escalation of cosmetics use: she powdered her face as a "girl," added rouge after an illness robbed her cheeks of color, and applied lipstick at sixty to "disguise" lips that seemed "leaden."[103] Her story revealed her experience of physical aging and her search for some continuity with the visage of her youth. The older woman wanted to be herself—only better. The woman's tale also tracked societal shifts in the kinds of cosmetics that were judged respectable. Reflecting its widespread use from the 1920s, powder was seen as benign by a number of older women in the 1950s. Even the writer who labeled lipstick atavistic and "revolting" conceded that powder was "quite tolerable" as an "anti-shine treatment."[104] Many older women were comfortable with the use of rouge or lipstick, although they often used only one or the other and in moderation. However, for many of them, eye shadow and mascara remained beyond the pale, belonging "on the stage," and red nail polish seemed repulsive.[105] By 1950, older women's make up habits were related to but slightly altered from those of the middle-class readers of *Good Housekeeping* in 1930, 20 percent of whom used lipstick and 7 percent, rouge.[106] Among the older women who wrote to Mass Observation in July 1950, for example, just over 20 percent used lipstick, while almost 30 percent used rouge, which they considered more effective against the paleness they understood as a sign of aging.[107] In part, this reflects a generational attitude to cosmetics, because a far greater percentage of young women were wearing lipstick by 1950.[108] It also suggests that the sexualized meanings of makeup changed with the age of the women who wore it. While a young girl who applied lipstick and rouge risked being regarded as "fast," older women wearing lipstick were more likely to be praised for maintaining a dignified portion of sexual appeal.

Kin and community influenced the beauty practices of older women. While a number of women named the brand of powder they used or wrote about "skin food" or "tonic lotion," in the language of advertising, their purchases of specific products were often motivated by the comments and habits of people they knew.[109] In 1939, a sixty-three-year-old widow living in Kent sounded grateful for the advice of her daughter and sister-in-law: "[They] took me in hand about ten years ago & insisted on my using an eyebrow pencil as I was going so grey."[110] Many older women made judgments about cosmetics based on their observations of members of their local communities. A retired governess supported her contention that most people looked better without makeup by describing a "pretty girl" she had seen at a wedding, whose ill-advised application of rouge was apparent when "she became excited and flushed, & the natural color did not blend with the artificial, which looked like a patch on her cheekbones."[111] The woman was inspired by the beauty practices of others. She used Drene shampoo on the recommendation of a young woman whose hair seemed particularly "glossy and shiny and attractive." The common pattern of these decisions was not the expression of generational difference. Rather, the writers paid attention to women across generational lines and made confident assessments about which beauty regimes were worth following.

The pleasures of beauty culture came from both everyday life and commercial desires. The success in America of door-to-door cosmetics sales and in-store demonstrators showed that cosmetics businesses had to do more than present women with "fantasy images of glamour and romance."[112] To sell makeup to women, businesses needed to provide them with knowledge, services, and fun. Women's choices took in "the sensuous creams and tiny compacts, the riot of colours, the mastery of makeup skills, the touch of hands, the sharing of knowledge and advice."[113] Consumers were not duped by advertising. American market studies in the 1920s and 1930s revealed that the opinions of friends and neighbors were more influential than commercial promotions.[114] Women's use of cosmetics typically originated in their social circles, initiated by gift giving, advice, and gossip. A sixty-year-old Lancashire housewife, for example, linked the pleasure she felt when her sons admired her appearance to her request that they replenish her supply of "good powder, cream, [and] lipstick refills" for Christmas.[115] Women who purchased cosmetics in Britain knew "precisely what they were buying" and that their acquisitions delivered them both entertainment and affection.[116]

Women of all ages embedded the fantastical aspects of cosmetics in the reality of their less-than-perfect lives. Beauty practices that were developed over a lifetime enabled older women to enjoy the promise of makeup without measuring themselves by the brand of youthful beauty that was featured in cosmetics advertising. A sixty-three-year-old music teacher's description of her beauty practices illustrated the layered meanings of applying cosmetics. This woman made cutting remarks about the look of old age and dismissed makeup's potential to make a difference. She applied cosmetics "in the forlorn hope that it may help in some magical way to rejuvenate the depressing spectacle that confronts me whenever I look in a mirror."[117] However, seeing other older women wearing makeup made her realize that this was "a complete illusion." Yet this fantasy gave her a "temporary feeling of confidence" that showed on the outside. She wrote that after applying lipstick, "one's face *feels* younger; even if it doesn't look it for long, and the moral support this induces gives one a pleasanter, more refreshed expression." Thus, she explained that in the face of "the stress of daily life," women chose to "do up" their faces to "feel better, and at once look it." Her description shifted from the internal dimensions of this "magical" experience (the greater confidence and "moral support" makeup gave her) to its outward expression (a "pleasanter, more refreshed" appearance). The passage recorded both the emotional impact of physical aging and the writer's belief in her underlying beauty, which could be rediscovered through the application of makeup.

• • •

Historians routinely focus on trends, especially the ones that we know caught on and changed the ways people thought and behaved.[118] We tend to see change as meaningful while conservative impulses are treated as relics of times past. However, if we listen to some of the things older men and women had to say about beauty and fashion around the middle of the twentieth century, we can see them engaging in a delicate balancing act as they groomed themselves with the right amount of concern for fashion and comfort, glamour and neatness, and standing out and blending in. Older people's choices about dress, conservative or otherwise, signaled their participation in family and community life and expressed their values and self-worth. The appearance they aimed for was class-specific, and the voices in this chapter are disproportionately from the middle and upper classes, but it was also shaped by age and by personal style.[119] In fact, there were multiple reasons that older people strived to make the best of their appearances, and they felt a corresponding array of pleasures when they achieved their goals. When older Britons tried on mid-twentieth-century fashion and beauty culture for size, they frequently found that it fit.

Writing about this sartorial pleasure opens a window into realms of emotional experience in later life that have barely been touched on by historians. The grooming practices of many older Britons reached beyond respectability to access the satisfactions of sensuous enjoyment and sexual appeal. A sixty-five-year-old nursery superintendent's aim in 1950 to be "nice & neat" could be interpreted as showing a stuffy lack of interest in fashion and beauty.[120] However, she was keen to match or contrast colors and sought out expensive shoes and hats. She admired "elegance," which was closely aligned with sexuality and charm. Considering these topics allows us to understand the experiences of inhabiting aging bodies that delivered pleasures as well as pains. In the pages of twentieth-century fashion magazines, youth and beauty were often equated. Before the mid-1960s, though, upmarket publications paid equal admiration to stylish, mature women whose ages were ambiguous. The enticing imagery of high-end fashion magazines—realized in sketches, fashion photography, advertising, the successful career of model Barbara Goalen, and the aspirational character of Mrs. Exeter in British *Vogue*—was the most lavish expression of a midcentury beauty culture that welcomed the participation and the purchasing power of older women.

Both men and women who wrote to Mass Observation recorded their habits of self-observation and studious grooming, but they did so within gendered boundaries and therefore with different things at stake. Men were more likely to enthuse over their skills in thriftiness than their delight in beautiful colors and flattering cuts. But they put just as much thought into how they appeared to others and could take equal pride in the aesthetic effects of their choices. In addition, older men and women agreed on the kinds of things that their outward appearances revealed about character. A person's knowledge of dress-styles and the time and money they could devote to grooming aligned with occupation and social class. Yet this behavior was widely believed to reveal deeper truths. By cultivating appearances, older men and women hoped to demonstrate their value to friends, family, and the community and to display inner characteristics such as intelligence, self-esteem, and subtlety.

Growing older brought new challenges and required people to constantly adjust their relationship to ideals of fashion and beauty, but this was a process that people had been engaged in over the life course. As Graham Dawson has shown, cultural representations are always "aspired to rather than actually being achieved," and all "imagined identities are shot through with wish fulfilling fantasies."[121] These practices did not encourage a continuous yearning to replicate the flawless images of youthful health and beauty that Britons encountered in advertising and popular culture. Instead, as a man from Penzance who reported feeling "less ugly at 73 than twenty" noted, they held himself to different standards as they aged.[122] Being soignée at seventy-three, discovering new combinations of silvery tones, and keeping one's hair barbered all signified a life successfully lived. In the mid-twentieth century, the joys of youth did not completely eclipse the satisfactions of maturity. There is time enough in the lifecycle to feel both these sensations, and there is space on the pages of our histories to record them.

CHAPTER FIVE

Games with Time

Autobiography and Aging

The writer Storm Jameson played games with time.[1] Or perhaps time played games with her. In Jameson's autobiography, which was published in 1969, when she was seventy-eight, the past constantly intruded on the present, and the present reshaped memories of the past. Childhood was never really gone, Storm wrote: "We only live in one house" all our lives.[2] Jameson's "one house" was in Whitby, the fishing village she had grown up in. Throughout her life, she heard echoes of the chime of the bell-buoys and the calls of children as ships cast off from the dock, even when she lived in Leeds and, later, South London.[3] In her old age, Storm still heard the "thunder" of the North Sea breaking on the pier beneath the sound of London traffic.[4] These soundscapes instilled in her a hatred of domesticity and a longing for freedom and independence, attributes that she said directed her decision making over her lifetime.

Late in Jameson's life, memories appeared to her suddenly and vividly—or not at all. The past was an "underworld" through which she was "trying to move backwards against the current."[5] Remembering was a taxing, nearly impossible task. On her autobiographical journey, she found "centres of total blackness" surrounding some moments, while other experiences remained clear and full. Jameson wrote of her happiness with her baby son in 1917: "[It] rings in my head with the sound given out by a flawless glass."[6] Visions of her mother also appeared unbidden: "A scene, a colour, a sound, split open as I brushed past it, and for an instant she was there."[7] For Storm, the process of writing an autobiography was not a matter of sitting down to remember and recreate but rather an engagement with aspects of her past that continuously intruded on her experience of the present.

Autobiographers such as Jameson (1891–1986) wrote versions of their lives that they planned to publish, making their stories permanent in the public record. Like her fellow author Catherine Cookson (1906–98), who also published her autobiography, *Our Kate*, in 1969, Jameson drafted multiple versions of her story before its publication. Michael Roper has described writing as a "psychological activity" that allows individuals to deal with difficult feelings in the face of social expectations.[8] Engaging in this process, Jameson wrote every page of her text four or five times. Cookson produced eight versions of her autobiography over twelve years before it was published when she was in her sixties.[9] As Deborah Cohen has written, the 1930s were "the first modern age of confession," but the 1970s marked the "high tide of psychoanalytical influence" in Britain, and it was a time of such rapid change that "sentiments that seemed daring to express in 1967" soon became "entirely commonplace."[10] Using the language of psychoanalysis, Storm attempted to "collect the fragments" of the self, and Catherine found that each rehearsal of her story was "more therapeutic as I deleted the bitterness from it."[11] Both authors said that writing about memories had changed the content of those memories. Jameson regretted the way her passion for reshaping the world into phrases had distanced her from it, as the "very act of writing, of turning pain, grief, joy, into words," created echoes of those feelings that could blur or replace them.[12] Cookson celebrated her transcendence of the past. Writing, she said, could "alleviate" the "torment" of her unhappy childhood and the shame she felt over her illegitimate birth.[13] Publication of the book, Catherine said, would complete her autobiographical "cure."

Jameson and Cookson told stories that were intensely personal. They did not often employ generational or chronological labels, such as old age, to explain their lives. Yet autobiography was a response to collective circumstances that included literary traditions, new technologies, and shifts in popular culture. Both established literary figures, Jameson and Cookson were also the inheritors of genre traditions that were established in the first half of the century by autobiographical writing that described the professional and creative lives of men. The autobiographies of the two women fit with the grassroots production and popularity of working-class autobiographies in Britain between the 1960s and the 1980s. Catherine, for example, was born in the deprived area of South Tyneside, North East England, and had worked as a domestic servant after leaving school at fourteen. New interest in working-class lives coincided with changing technologies in publishing that made printing cheaper. This enabled the establishment of community presses with keen interest in the autobiographies of working people. Older Britons who embraced these developments took up the difficult task of parsing social changes that had taken place over half a century or more. By the 1960s, an expanded group of British autobiographers published their life stories to wide interest. Jameson and Cookson released their autobiographies during a period when confessional writing about the experiences and private lives of women had new purchase in public life.[14] This chapter examines developments in publishing and popular culture that widened the pool of elderly authors in twentieth-century Britain. These diverse autobiographers revealed the emotional qualities of aging when they described the joys and frustrations of reminiscence and evoked a constant comparison of the present and the past.

AGING AND AUTOBIOGRAPHY

The romantic tradition helped define the aging process and determine its meaning for older generations in the twentieth century. In his 1807 poem "The Rainbow," William Wordsworth described the adult significance of the habits and behavior of childhood by reversing lineage in the line, "The child is the father of the man." Wordsworth's poem was included in the 1919 edition of *The Oxford Book of English Verse*, which was widely used in schools and carried by soldiers during World War II.[15] The lifelong significance of childhood was further emphasized in several strands of midcentury scientific and psychological thought. The most famous examples were Sigmund Freud's theories and their multiple iterations in British popular culture, which emphasized the enduring influence of childhood experiences on the adult subconscious.[16] Later, especially with the full articulation of cell theory during the middle of the century, medical textbooks and child-care manuals revealed the way that each human cell's decline and death was preprogrammed from its beginning. The theory illustrated that "we are ever dying—ever mutating—ever changing," setting out a biological model of the life course that "more closely elided the beginning with the end, the child with death."[17] The connection between aging and childhood was a feature of the midcentury literary scene as well as the mental life of many older individuals. While autobiographers struggled to explain the precise meaning of their fascination with scenes of youth, their engagement with the changing meaning of childhood experiences shows that old age was far from simply a "second childhood," an idea that has been too often invoked in both mid-twentieth-century and twenty-first-century commentary.[18] Scenes of youth provided the readers of autobiographies with access to the far-off past. Conveniently, it was exactly these early memories that appeared most vividly in the minds of the aged. Through discussion of their early lives, older Britons attempted to comprehend both the aging process and the nature of rapid social change in twentieth-century Britain.

Many aging autobiographers gave their memories organic and unpredictable qualities. They compared their visions of the past to wild landscapes and shifting light, evoking the work of romantics who had also celebrated inspiration, subjectivity, and the individual. The artist Augustus John (1878–1961) described his past as a "landscape" and the workings of his memory as the sun. When the light of memory broke through the clouds, it revealed full vignettes of his past, complete with sounds of laughter, tears, and hymns sung in Welsh.[19] Herbert Read (1893–1968) also imagined a "shimmering" picture of the past when he held a stem from an honesty plant in his hand and found that it evoked an entire scene from his childhood in a "widening circle" of memory.[20] Evelyn Waugh (1903–66) recounted "uncertain flashes" of childhood memory, around which his mind was "dark," or more precisely, "an even glow of pure happiness."[21] Conjuring a more dangerous scene, Richard Church (1893–1972) pictured himself navigating the "obstructions" of "preconceived ideas and prejudices" looming in his imagination "like rocks out of the sea."[22] Memory supplied him a "defective compass" for his mental journey into the past. For all of these autobiographers, memory was irregular and embedded in unique sensory and emotional experiences, particularly those of early life.

Like many others, the writer and critic Victor Pritchett (1900–1997) found his childhood relatively easy to retell because its plot and central character were obvious: "One's life has a natural defining frame. One knows who one is."[23] After the age of twenty, however, this frame became "uncertain," and life's turning points were "hard to pin down."[24] Church agreed. The first of his three autobiographical volumes described his close-knit family life and the dawning of his creative consciousness in childhood. Repeating the bright imagery used by others, he recorded that his early life seemed a "unique story" of "fabulous adventures in a dew-glittering world."[25] He wondered, though, how the story of childhood could be continued: "Who wants to hear of the gradual slowing-down and subsistence of early raptures" as the story's hero "falls into step with the rest of the breadwinners, worthy but indistinct, for the long remainder of his life"?[26] All of the writers featured in this chapter found it difficult to shape middle and old age into the narratives of growth and progress that most of them associated with the autobiographical genre. By setting their texts in childhood, though, autobiographers communicated important points about their experience of adulthood. These included the major decisions and ethical commitments that had shaped their lives and the awe and confusion they felt looking back to the early years of the century.

For many, old age stood a little outside the narrative frame. It was, however, a time when reflective and valuable storytelling became possible. A number of autobiographers claimed that a long life was a basis for interesting stories because it meant that one had a connection to the distant past. They believed that the past would likely interest their readers since it had equipped older writers with wide-ranging experience and an even-handed perspective.[27] Augustus John had the first volume of his autobiography published in 1952, when he was seventy-four years old. In it, he defined the "consolations" of his old age as his existence "a little apart from the general turmoil," where he felt better placed to contemplate and accurately judge his life.[28] A few years later, in 1955, the author and biographer Winifred Peck (1882–1962) claimed that the young were incapable of looking back with clarity or understanding and classed the "great advantage in being old" as the ability to remember experiences in a "kinder" mode and "recapture happiness."[29] For Richard Church, late life was a time of precarious balance and greater ability to cope with hardship. The death of his brother had delivered him a "knockout blow" during middle age. In old age, he said, "I have at least risen to my knees."[30] None of the authors claimed that age made them more willing to rescind their existing prejudices. Rather, they prioritized clarity of feeling about a personalized, subjective past.

WRITING AND PUBLISHING IN BRITAIN

Historians have traced the emergence of the modern autobiography to shifts in identity formation after the eighteenth century.[31] The genre's conventions include the use of first-person narrative, allegiance to truth telling, and attention to individual achievements. Philippe Lejeune has written influentially of the "autobiographical pact," which requires the author's commitment "not to some impossible historical exactitude but rather to the sincere effort to come to terms with and to understand his or her own life."[32] This pact has been a defining feature of modern autobiography. By the end of the nineteenth century, an increasing proportion of British autobiographies were authored by middle-class, professional men pursuing just this aim.[33] In the twentieth century, male authors described wide-scale social changes that had influenced their accomplishments, such as the expansion of the education system in Britain. However, these autobiographers highlighted personal achievements above generational experiences by detailing the challenges they had encountered and overcome during their lives, and thus attributing their successes to individual effort. The individualistic model, however, did not fit with the way women described their lives as entwined with the needs and accomplishments of others.[34]

The presentation of the self via the life story was reformulated in the early decades of the twentieth century by the success of human-interest journalism and the competition for readers among British newspapers. Interwar newspaper editors commercialized the popular "crook life story," for example, because it was salable.[35] After World War I, the increasing flexibility of both social mores and hierarchies of class caused public concern. At the same time, individuals were increasingly able to purchase a new social identity when they shopped for ready-made clothing or engaged in new commercial entertainments. Autobiographies, too, were tools of self-fashioning—and sometimes reinvention—rather than only self-expression.[36] Historians of subjectivity have identified the discovery by the 1920s of "the self *within*—a quite richly detailed self," which became the primary subject of autobiographies.[37] In the early decades of the twentieth century, a deepening interest in self-reflection coexisted with new opportunities for self-representation.

Especially before the 1960s, the cost of publishing and marketing books meant that most published autobiographies were written by upper-class and literary authors. Examples include the autobiographies that Marie Belloc Lowndes and Horace Horsnell published during the 1940s, when she was in her seventies and he in his early sixties. Lowndes was a successful and prolific writer, most well known for romances and crime novels, especially *The Chink in the Armour* (1912) and *The Lodger* (1913). Her four autobiographies were published between 1941 and 1948, to critical acclaim. Macmillan's print run of the first volume sold out before its publication date. The *Times Literary Supplement* praised Lowndes for achieving objectivity about her younger self.[38] Moving in the same literary world, Horsnell had acted as secretary to H. G. Wells, written the successful play *Advertising for April*, conducted a "varied and notable career" as a dramatic critic for the *Observer* and *Punch*, and published several novels.[39] The autobiographies of these two notable individuals were celebrated for their famous characters, literary merit, and upper-class concerns. The reading public was assured that the texts were "full of the past" by virtue of the advanced ages of the authors.[40] Yet, to repeat the advertising copy, it was a particular kind of "cultured, elegant, leisured past" that was on offer.

Postwar social change sparked interest in working-class lives as they had been lived in the first half of the twentieth century. The wide-scale clearance of terraced housing and the construction of council estates on the edges of cities, for example, transformed urban environments around Britain. Wages rose, especially for manual workers and lower-grade clerical staff.[41] Full employment did the most to alleviate poverty. The extension of credit to working-class people financed widespread ownership of the consumer goods that would become symbols of economic plenty, especially televisions.[42] For some, these developments seemed to wipe out the culture and practices of so-called traditional working-class communities, such as close living quarters and reliance on mutual aid. At the same time, working-class culture became fashionable in Britain, including in autobiography.[43] The apparent affluence of working people became a source of anxiety for some, who worried about the social consequences of this changing world. Yet the transformation had been overstated. As Selina Todd has shown, groups such as the elderly had been denied access to greater wealth, which always depended on employment, and working-class families remained vulnerable to poverty throughout the period.[44] Living costs rose alongside wages, the income gap between the rich and the poor increased during the 1950s, and unskilled workers were never provided with the same financial stability as other Britons.

A wider group of Britons were encouraged to study and write, which was a significant development in the history of British culture and selfhood. As Christopher Hilliard has established, advice manuals, writers' circles, and working-class authors contributed to the democratization of British culture that started in the interwar period.[45] Reading novels and writing letters gave women the opportunity to understand their lives in new ways, even if this exploration of fiction and selfhood was sometimes used against them to disastrous effect, as it was in the trial of Edith Thompson, who was charged with murder and executed on the basis of letters she wrote to her lover.[46] The postwar welfare state and the national education system encouraged autobiographical and expressive writing among working-class children through, for example, the introduction of creative writing to school curricula in the 1950s.[47] This midcentury celebration of self-reflection contrasted with the "enforced narratives" that were performed by earlier generations of the poor to access charitable aid.[48] The new forms of politics, popular culture, and citizenship that reshaped midcentury Britain encouraged a different style of autobiography that critiqued social class and discussed formerly taboo aspects of private life, including depression, illegitimacy, and poverty.[49] Victor Pritchett's autobiography, for example, which discussed his family's poverty, was entitled *A Cab at the Door* in reference to early memories of his parents calling taxis to move between rented flats in and around London.[50]

A crucial difference between the working-class autobiographical writing that "flowered" in the late 1960s and the narratives of workers who had long "struggled to tell their stories" were the conditions of their production.[51] New publications were made possible by a series of technological innovations. Lithography (the use of photography to generate text) and offset printing were first introduced in Britain in the late

1950s.⁵² These techniques lowered the cost of printing, including color printing, and meant that presses could operate at high speeds. The availability of electronic typewriters in the early 1960s meant that authors could submit "camera-ready copy," thus avoiding the significant costs of typesetting and proofing.⁵³ As a result, hundreds of working-class autobiographies were published during this period, mostly in the 1970s and 1980s.⁵⁴ The work was coordinated by community groups such as Centerprise, a community center and bookshop in Hackney, and the People's History classes that were run by the Workers' Education Association.⁵⁵ Such community organizing culminated in 1976 with the founding of the Federation of Worker Writers and Community Publishers.⁵⁶ The publications of these organizations circulated widely in local communities. Centerprise, for example, published 3,500 to 13,000 copies of each of its early titles.⁵⁷

Reflections on the working-class past had significant popular and personal appeal among the British public, due in part to the joys of reminiscence they offered to the old. When Walter Greenwood (1903–74) published *There was a Time* (1967), a memoir of growing up in Salford, Manchester, he garnered dozens of letters from his readers. Most of these letter writers were elderly themselves and had spent their early life in the Manchester area, and many noted that they felt compelled to write after finding themselves "so moved" by his account of the past.⁵⁸ One writer thanked Walter for "reminding [him] so forcibly and entertainingly about [his] own life," and many others quibbled with his recollections of the geography and inhabitants of Salford and recited their own stories of life in the first half of the twentieth century.⁵⁹ Greenwood was most famous for his socially influential novel *Love on the Dole* (1932). He invited older Britons to send him their autobiographical information in his midcentury radio broadcasts and newspaper articles and in the final chapter of his popular history of Lancashire, and he received over one hundred letters in response to the latter.⁶⁰ This enthusiastic and detailed correspondence suggested a widespread enjoyment of reminiscence among older Britons, many of whom were reminded of their memories of youth as they listened to the radio or read newspaper articles, even if they did not publish their accounts.

Nearing the end of the life cycle made resolving questions about the meaning and value of life especially urgent.[61] Many older Britons saw producing an autobiography as a strategy to achieve status and what Alistair Thomson has called the "composure" or the "personal coherence" of a life history.[62] But writing an autobiography is no simple task. As literary scholars and oral historians have argued, there are actually "two pasts" in life stories, and these describe both the time of the event and the time when the story is told.[63] This makes creating an autobiography a difficult undertaking because the author must "negotiate" with "former selves" to produce a text that belongs to both the past and the present.[64] Such theories about the malleability of memories were circulating in the midcentury period. In 1932, experimental psychologist Frederic Bartlett showed that memories "are not eidetically exact but partially reconstructed, reshaped by the mind at every stage: in initial perception, in encoding, during storage, and in retrieval."[65] Older autobiographers were particularly likely to share Bartlett's views. Rather than presenting their lives chronologically, writers described their memories as a feedback loop in which past and present experiences were a "mutually constructing pair."[66] The same process of comparison governed people's recognition of aging and their attitudes toward growing older.

Working-class memories took on new significance from the mid-1970s, when the postwar economic boom ended and working-class people experienced deindustrialization and high levels of unemployment. The makeup of the working classes changed as skilled manual labor disappeared and greater numbers of families relied on state welfare.[67] Historian Chris Waters has identified that in this context, working-class autobiographies of the era were "organized around a positive evaluation of the past—even to the point of mythologizing that past."[68] The texts "romanticized" life in traditional working-class communities and "lamented the loss" of neighborhood customs. However, historian Ben Jones has shown that working-class autobiographers took a more critical stance than this by commenting on both contemporary denigrations of the working classes that were made by Conservative governments and the poverty and intermittent violence of slum neighborhoods in the first half of the century.[69] Questions about the engagement of autobiographers with the present are at the heart of the debate over whether the boom in working-class autobiographies between the 1960s and the 1980s was a narrow exercise in nostalgia. Did working-class authors view the setting of the past as a "container of memories" about the "minutiae of a vanished way of life" that did not require serious engagement with the present?[70] Or did they work to "register their experiences of living with inequality" at least in part to comment on contemporary politics and social life?[71]

These questions about the nature and purpose of working-class autobiographies invite consideration of experiences of aging and the ways they were connected to public and private storytelling. Working-class autobiographers certainly reveled in childhood memories and in describing the rituals of early twentieth-century working-class communities. Virtually all of them concluded their tales in young adulthood, at the moment when the world of their childhood was transformed by the outbreak of World War II, marriage, or by moving away from the neighborhoods of their youth.[72] Thus, working-class autobiographers did not often retell the scenes of their life that were set in old age. Yet these attributes of the texts should not be interpreted as proof of limited engagement with history or politics on the part of their working-class authors, who were keen to record and comment on social change.[73] Nor should the fact that the stories ended at the brink of adulthood preclude historians from analyzing experiences of later life. In fact, the aging of an author informed his or her entire narrative. Older Britons acted as translators for the young of the experience of living through the twentieth century.

WITNESSES TO THE TWENTIETH CENTURY

Older autobiographers writing in the twentieth century expressed their astonishment at the changes to British society, culture, and landscape that had taken place during their lifetimes. Elizabeth Sanderson Haldane, an author, nursing administrator, and welfare worker, wrote in 1937 that life had changed "almost incredibly" during the fifty years that her autobiography described.[74] In particular, she described how the Education Act 1870, which made elementary school education mandatory for children between the ages of five and thirteen, had provided new opportunities. The technological developments of the late nineteenth century, such as the telephone and new forms of transport, and the democratic social transformations that followed World War I were so great that they seemed "inconceivable" in hindsight.[75] Former suffragette and magistrate Hannah Mitchell (1871–1956) argued that anyone over the age of sixty had an interesting life story to tell and that this was "especially true" of the members of her generation, who had "witnessed the merging of one century into another" and the "far-reaching changes of the period," including women's right to vote.[76] Influential book curator and trader Thomas Joy was defensive of some aspects of early twentieth-century life and morality. He chose to call his 1971 autobiography *Mostly Joy*. Yet the older man wrote that on balance, "things have improved almost beyond belief," especially due to the alleviation of poverty.[77]

Autobiographers marked the boundaries of their lifetimes and of the twentieth century with descriptions of iconic public occasions. These events evoked the priorities and customs of the past and provided an opportunity to discuss habits of family and social life that could be dated precisely. Walter Greenwood opened his autobiography with the scene of his father visiting the eight public houses in his Salford street on two celebratory occasions: the end of the Siege of Mafeking in South Africa in 1900 and Walter's birth in 1903.[78] The death of Queen Victoria in 1901 was the starting point of many life stories, even when it predated the birth of the author. English teacher and writer Robert Roberts, for example, was born in 1905, but he recorded his family's memories of the event in the tradition of every "decent Edwardian biography."[79] Elizabeth Sanderson Haldane compared King George V's 1935 jubilee to the nineteenth-century celebrations that marked the length of Queen

Victoria's reign to illustrate changes in the conditions of life and behavior that had occurred in the intervening years. She favorably compared the comfort and order that she observed on the streets in 1935 to public behavior during earlier events, which she claimed were occasions of drunkenness, fighting, and pickpocketing.[80] Events that honored British royalty were milestones in the lives of British people, whether they celebrated them by visiting the pub or lauding the apparent passing of public intoxication. The world wars, too, were recalled as solemn and dramatic ruptures in the private lives of autobiographers that also altered the mood of entire generations.[81] These scenes—which readers could verify—were presented as evidence of the immense variety of social life that older autobiographers had witnessed by the middle decades of the twentieth century.

Autobiographies discussed policies and social customs that had widespread significance and were linked to developments in the personal lives of their authors. Harry Burton introduced his 1958 autobiography as an assessment of the effects of the Education Act 1902, which began a rapid expansion of secondary schooling.[82] Burton's scholarship to a grammar school made it possible for him to study at Cambridge and later find work as an educational assessor in local government. Reflecting the literary tastes and talents of many midcentury autobiographers, he wrote that his "changes of heart and mind," especially his engagement with art, literature, and music, were more important than his new income and profession.[83] In terms of social class, Harry understood himself to be, while not upper class, "distinctive," mostly due to his intellectual and emotional engagement with high culture.[84] By writing about his personal experiences and their implications for his relationship with his working-class family, Burton responded to midcentury interest in both selfhood and social hierarchy. Like other members of the reading public, he expected memoirs to offer "inimitable personal details, subjective internal processes, and self-reflexive accounts of the development of perception and expression," in the style that had been developed in modernist memoirs of the 1930s.[85]

The writing of French-born Madeleine Henrey (née Gal) focused on family, femininity, and familiar households. Henrey, who was born in 1906 and moved to London as a child, published over thirty books between 1941 and 1979 to commercial success and public acclaim in Britain. Writing under the name of her journalist husband, Robert Henrey, she told the story of her childhood in Clichy, on the industrial northern edge of Paris, her migration with her mother to Soho, and her experiences of World War II in Normandy and London. In her books, Henrey made sense of growing older generationally. She wrote with particular emotion about the death of her mother, Matilda, in 1962 and the visits of her young granddaughter in the 1970s.[86] In the volume of her autobiography that told the story of Matilda's worsening health in old age and eventual death, Henrey expressed conflicted feelings about caring for her mother and waiting for her death.[87] Her mother resented her arthritis-riddled body, and Madeleine shared this resentment, often comparing the state of Matilda's aged body with its beauty and grace in the past.[88] Henrey became acutely aware of her own aging and was determined to enjoy herself.[89] Soon after Matilda's death, Henrey wrote, "She and I had spent fifty-five years together. I would never know such a space of time again."[90] She tried to stave off age by exercising, and she worried when she noticed her own mind wandering.[91] Madeleine expressed sadness about the consequences of growing older for her body and dress and nostalgia about the passage of time, which she measured by the changing landscape around the farmhouse that she owned in Normandy. Visits by her young granddaughter were the only events that lessened the "revolt" she "felt upon reaching the age of seventy."[92]

Henrey used shared narratives of British courage and pride to connect the domestic scenes of her later life to her earlier experiences. While Henrey was selling her family's furniture in the mid-1960s, for instance, an armchair reminded her of the battle for London. She described how she had sat down on the chair to sew during the worst of the bombing and how her husband had fallen asleep on it after nights out fire watching.⁹³ In her new role as a grandmother during the 1970s, Madeleine remembered of one of her son's teddy bears, "This one had lived right through the Battle of Britain, had been squeezed by nervous baby fingers when heavy explosives and incendiaries rained down upon our apartment in Shepherd Market, blasting the smooth road of Piccadilly, starting fires all along Curzon Street, sending the glass out from our window panes piercing the opposite walls like cruel daggers."⁹⁴ Henrey marked out her aging against momentous and public events, such as the occupation of France, the Blitz, and the end of the war.⁹⁵ Her melancholy feeling about growing older was a generational and gendered response to the experience. While "for a woman, youth and happiness are synonymous," she opined that "the man, like a good wine, matures with age."⁹⁶ Henrey acted in common with many autobiographers when she meshed national, generational, and personal experiences to understand the meaning of growing old. Hers was a feminine version of the mid-twentieth century that was not described in the same way by male writers.

Transformations in the twentieth-century workplace and economy were so great that the gap between past and present seemed impossibly vast, even to working-class men, like Walter Greenwood, who had lived through the changes. Greenwood reported great changes that he witnessed in the place of his birth, Hanky Park, in Pendleton, Salford. As he wrote his 1967 autobiography, Walter watched the Hanky Park slum clearance take place, predicting that it "soon will have obliterated all trace of yesterday." He described the building of new tower blocks: "Steel skeletons of the multi-storied flats are rising gaunt above the skyline, the world of tomorrow springing from the ruins of yesterday."⁹⁷ In his mind's eye, he saw the old Hanky Park as it had been early in the century. Standing on Brindleheath Road, Walter inhabited "one of the old ways home from the pits, mills, factories and railway sheds" with a "shallow channel scuffed out over the years by the weary homeward plod of forgotten generations." He venerated this memory as much as the more distant Roman past: "For me, the channel is as eloquent of bygone days as are the groves of chariot wheels along the Appian way."[98] Greenwood believed that the new tenants of the area would have a different "modern," "mobile outlook." As a result of their access to consumer goods, travel, and higher education, they would not wear paths down familiar roads. He wrote, "Yesterday the Depression and lo! By a hop, skip and jump the Space Age and a Welfare State. A five-day, forty-hour week, holidays with pay, superannuation pension schemes, lunch vouchers and workers' canteens; an inrush of immigrants to fill the rising tide of jobs gone begging; and organized Labour in conference with employers on equal terms."[99] As he looked back, it seemed that time had sped by, and the pace of change was incredible.

Aging autobiographers described feeling confounded by and ambivalent about the changes in society and urban and rural landscapes that they described. Their vacillation was expressed in the title of Albert Paul's autobiography, *Poverty—Hardship but Happiness: Those Were the Days, 1903–1917* (1974), the first book published by community press QueenSpark Books. Older autobiographers like Paul described an earlier time of abject poverty, which they deplored. Yet the same period featured the pleasures of childhood play, familial love, adventure, and learning. Authors were concerned with impressing on their reading audience both the injustice of the past and the contributions of privation to personal qualities of which they felt proud. As Paul concluded, the "poverty days" of the early 1900s were a period that he and his family had "endured" but also "enjoyed."[100]

Over time, Britons attained living standards and expectations that gave them a new viewpoint on earlier experiences of poverty. Midcentury expectations about a satisfied and comfortable life were at odds with the childhood memories of many autobiographers. Harry Burton, for example, wrote that he had enjoyed a happy childhood, even though he had been aware of the hardships of his father's unemployment, his mother's struggle to keep house, and the couple's quarrels.[101] He wrote that the family's lack of money kept their "horizons small," without exposure to the artistic and cultural life that he loved later in his life or the popular entertainments of cinema or radio.[102] Yet, he repeated, "If all this seems grey and depressing, ... we were far from depressed ourselves." In fact, Harry missed the "close-knit domestic unity" of his childhood after the family's fortunes improved with his father's earnings and the contributions of his grown siblings. Puzzling over these memories, he simultaneously celebrated and denigrated a family "spirit" that was "narrow, prejudiced and unintelligent" but "had a fuzzy kind of warm cheerfulness which was endearing."[103] His memories of family life seemed appealing, at least at a distance of fifty years.

The front and back cover of Grace Foakes's (1901–79) autobiography seemed to replicate the nostalgic replaying of the past that has been attributed to working-class autobiography. The front cover featured a sketch of a sweet-looking child surrounded by elegant handwriting (figure 24). This imagery suggested the intimacy of a diary but hid the financial hardships and lack of privacy that had characterized Grace's childhood. The blurb on the back cover further depoliticized Foakes's autobiographical writing by suggesting that the book offered a "child's uncluttered observation" of the past. It went on to celebrate Grace's memories for their "little details—Saturday shopping in Watney Street market, men waiting for work at the dock gates, the inside of the tenement flat which for her was home, the sights and sounds and smells of East London." Alongside this text were two portraits of Foakes (figure 25). One, a portrait of her as a girl, evoked a far-off world because of its sepia tone, faded appearance, and Grace's formal three-quarter pose and hairstyle. Next to it was a contemporary black-and-white photograph of Foakes as an old woman. The contrast of the two images visually emphasized the passage of time.

Taken together, these elements suggested that a reader of Foakes's book would experience "a breakage with the past, a world frozen in time that can now be recaptured only through writing."[104] In fact, the

> When I was a little girl I lived with my parents, my three brothers and my sister in one of the tenement flats in Royal Jubilee Buildings. It consisted of two bedrooms and a kitchen. My parents occupied one bedroom, and we five children shared the other. Mother divided the room with a large clothes' horse covered with a sheet, to separate boys from girls. All the available space was taken up by three beds and my Father's large toolchest. The walls were distempered in a dull brown colour. What a dark and cheerless room it was!

Figure 24. The front cover illustration for Grace Foakes's autobiography. The images on the front and back cover emphasize intimacy, authenticity, and the passage of time, although the author took a critical perspective on the past in the text of the book. Grace Foakes, *Between High Walls: A London Childhood*, 2nd ed. (Oxford: Athena Books, 1972).

dramatic tension and nostalgic appeal of Foakes's account of growing up in Wapping, East London, were created by the transformation of the area during the twentieth century, which she skillfully described:

> Now I see a great change on the river. Gone are the great docks, gone is the hustle and bustle of fussy little ships. The great clanking cranes are rusting and silent. The small isolated communities who lived and worked on the river are gone. I revisited my part of the river some time ago, and could scarcely recognise it. It was a dead and derelict place. The people were gone, and the place seemed to be filled with the sound of the tramp of men

Figure 25. The back cover illustrations for Grace Foakes's autobiography. Grace Foakes, *Between High Walls: A London Childhood*, 2nd ed. (Oxford: Athena Books, 1972).

searching for work, of the laughter of the children who once played here, all I suspect now cooped up in high rise flats; for not far off I saw them shutting out the skyline, just as did the high dock walls so many years ago.[105]

This account of changes to the landscape referenced the decline of shipping and industry in London and alterations to working-class culture and neighborhoods. Grace celebrated the people who had previously lived in the area and their experiences of hardships, like unemployment, as well as the joy of laughing children. Her account of the present was a similarly mixed one. She wrote that children were "cooped up" in high-rise buildings that blocked the horizon but acknowledged that dock walls had done the same in years past.[106] The motif of youth allowed the free interplay of past and present in Foakes's writing. Childhood scenes, for example, provided an explanation for Grace's adult decision to leave Wapping and its "high brick walls" for a London County Council housing estate at Dagenham in Essex.[107] Her stories about her own childhood were often about the restrictions of urban life and especially her unfulfilled longing to play on grass and see plants and flowers. In one scene, she stood on Green Bank Street and imagined a natural glade instead of the noise and dirt of the city.[108] Despite some fond memories of London, Foakes wanted to raise her daughter, Kathleen, outside of the city.

Grace's memories of the past, so powerfully encoded in street scenes of Wapping, were sufficiently different from the present that she confessed, "I sometimes wonder if I have dreamt these things."[109] She wrote her autobiography to explain this "bewilderment" to younger generations and also to close the gap created by time by describing "a world of people who were just as you are but without opportunities or knowledge."[110] The lives of Foakes's grandchildren and their generation threw into relief the significance of the details of her Victorian and Edwardian childhood. Occasionally, she addressed them directly. "You," she lectured the young readers whom she wrote for, could not imagine the "thick and yellow" London fogs, the ache of fingers after washing a family's laundry, the noise of the street, or the poverty of the homeless population in years gone by.[111] In her autobiography, we glimpse Grace's attempt to integrate conflicted feelings about the lost world of the past, where her family had happily gathered around the fire at Christmas but also where her mother had died in poverty and her father had beaten his son "black and blue."[112] Her idealized descriptions of family celebrations stand alongside her memories of violence and squalor, complicating the psychological and social messages of her nostalgia. Together with other autobiographers, Foakes made a plea to simultaneously value individual memories of the past and the communal and political projects that had raised standards of living in the present.

· · ·

Storm Jameson reveled in the experiences of recollection that she directly associated with aging and death. She described old age as "time to settle the account. To arrange to make a friend of the knowledge that wherever you go in the short time left you will find yourself in the same street, the same place, landing in the same harbor."[113] She welcomed the pull of the past. Anticipating death, she hoped that "the very last moment" of her life would be "a pure act of memory," an immersion in the oldest "images I carry in my skull."[114] Both Jameson and Catherine Cookson adjusted their expectations of life as they aged and judged themselves to have become gentler in their treatment of themselves and others. Cookson wrote that the interwoven processes of aging and autobiographical writing had brought her to the happiest point of her life. When she began writing, her mind had been "bent on retaliation" and without "one happy memory."[115] In the foreword to the 1990 edition of *Our Kate,* she wrote that she had achieved a partial "peace of mind" that would "soothe the residue of those sad feelings which still linger, and get me through each day as it comes."[116] Jameson lamented the passing of her youthful strength but dismissed the character traits that had accompanied it when she had been "an ignorant clumsy provincial fool."[117] She considered herself to be more informed and worldly in later life.

Older autobiographers like Jameson and Cookson took comparative and reflective perspectives on their experiences over time. The close relationship of the past to the present in autobiographical writing, in which each one made sense of the other, meant that aging was understood to be relative. In these ways, autobiography allows us to think about old age in a different way from the identification of the life chances of a particular generation. As aging Britons remembered their past and attempted to understand their present, they continued to view childhood with wonder but felt that, with age, they had gained a clearer perspective on the events of the past. They explained the personal impact of widespread social changes and confessed to contradictions between joyful memories of youth and their firsthand knowledge of deprivation and violence. These writers gave full descriptions of memory and the ways that it continually reshaped their daily lives. The writing of autobiography, restricted at various times by class, profession, and skill, was an extension of quotidian habits of remembering that were enjoyed by many. The detail and the literary qualities of autobiographical sources illuminate the personal dimensions of growing older in the twentieth century and beautifully open up the history of old age.

Epilogue

What is means to be old is among the most pressing questions of our time. Global news publications regularly report on the rapidly aging populations of developed nations. The issue made the cover story of every region's edition of the *Economist* in April 2014.[1] Only days later, Ari Seth Cohen presented the European premiere of his documentary, *Advanced Style*. Born of Cohen's popular New York–based fashion blog, the film promised to introduce its audience to the personal style of "the silver-haired set" and to depict "a much more joyous way of ageing" along the way.[2] In the face of changing demographics, we are fascinated by the ethical and emotional dimensions of aging and by new fashions and technologies that might ameliorate its effects. Knowledge of recent history is vital to understanding these issues in our own time, whether we are discussing beauty or government budgets. This book has examined both by seeking out the voices of the aged and identifying the extent of their agency in the history of old age in the twentieth century. It argues that viewing older Britons as whole people—as individuals with varied experiences and wide-ranging interests—will give us a fuller picture of old age as it was lived in the British past.

By the mid-twentieth century, the British state had established collective markers of old age, such as retirement and residential care, but individuals experienced aging before, after, and independently of these apparent parameters of late life. A paradox of aging in the twentieth century was the mismatch between personal experiences of growing older and the state's administration of old age. Publicity for welfare services for the aged, for example, strengthened the notion that elderly people were frail and dependent on the state. Such narrow views of what it was to be old have dominated public discussions of aging in recent years and contributed to widespread anxiety over the effects of population aging. Yet in reality, Britons have contributed more to the state and to their communities during their lives than they have taken. At midcentury, the public image of older people was expansive enough that some elderly individuals were treated as icons of beauty, fashion, and good grooming.

BRITAIN'S "AGING POPULATION"

Currently, the United Nations describes population aging as one of the most significant social transformations of this century and warns that it will have potentially dire effects, including poverty, inequality, and environmental degradation.[3] The World Economic Forum considers the aging of the population to be "the financial equivalent of climate change," which is understood as a threat to the world and the future of the human race.[4] The extent and consequences of population aging vary by region. The World Bank reports that East Asian and Pacific countries are home to more than a third of people aged sixty-five and above and that their populations are aging faster than those of any region in history.[5] In economically developed countries, aging populations are commonly viewed as a financial problem. In Britain, for example, government researchers emphasize that around 55 percent of welfare spending is paid to pensioners.[6] They also point to high government spending on long-term health conditions, estimated at 70 percent of health and welfare costs in Britain, and to the decline in the tax-paying working population relative to the number of retired people. In this presentation, older people are ruinously expensive and their growing numbers mean that the activities of the state must be reduced.

In the twentieth century, new technologies and forms of knowledge affected the way that demographic change was measured and judged.[7] The aging population came to public attention in the early 1930s, when Britain's birth rate reached a low point, sparking fears of national economic decline and international war.[8] New methods in statistics propagated the notion of population aging and specifically the idea that there had been a sudden expansion in numbers of elderly Britons. Statisticians drew public attention by using the concepts of net and gross reproduction rates to make specific predictions about the age composition of the British population in the future.[9] Commentators described historic and current demographic changes and, more sensationally, projected the proportion of older people that would inhabit Britain ten, twenty, or fifty years in the future. Statistician Grace Leybourne, for example, predicted that the low birth rates of the 1930s would persist and therefore the population of Britain would both shrink and become older. In 1939, when 14 percent of the population of England and Wales was aged over sixty, Leybourne and others predicted that the proportion would rise to 29 percent by 2000 and 35 percent by 2019.[10] Social biologist Enid Charles also assumed that birth rates would remain at their historically low rate.[11] Much of the debate that took place during the 1930s also made the assumption that an older population was inferior. Prominent social scientist Richard Titmuss argued that an older Britain would be less intelligent, more conservative, more hierarchical, and militarily weak.[12] Economists feared that British workplaces could not adjust to the aging population. Demographic statistics helped deflect public attention away from the improved health of old people over time and their contributions to social, political, cultural, and economic life.[13]

However, these forecasts about the rapid and dramatic aging of the population were made irrelevant by high birth rates and immigration after World War II.[14] Britain had multiple baby booms, the first peaking in 1947 and the second in 1964.[15] During the same period, greater numbers of women and migrants entered the workforce and provided increased financial support for pensions and healthcare. Postwar labor shortages encouraged social scientists to more carefully consider the potential contributions of older workers. But even in the 1950s and 1960s, people remained concerned that the higher birth rates would be short-lived.[16] Commentators relied on shaky logic when they assumed that trends they observed would continue indefinitely.[17] In fact, the proportion of the British population that was aged over sixty-five was lower than predicted in 2006, at 15.9 percent, and in 2016, at 18 percent.[18] However, even rebuttal by influential figures such as David Glass and John Maynard Keynes did not prevent dire predictions from becoming common sense or from informing reform movements and social policy.[19]

Starting in the 1970s, demographers once again predicted the dire consequences of population aging. This time, commentators worried about the escalating costs of welfare rather than the projected decline in the quality of the population that was feared in the 1930s. Economists and politicians anticipated that increasing numbers of older people would bankrupt welfare states due to the high demands the elderly made on national health systems and public pensions.[20] Some took a generational perspective on the issue by claiming that aging societies placed undue burden on younger generations, which would have to support the needs of the old, and arguing for "intergenerational equity."[21] In recent decades, discussion of population aging has been dominated by the particular demographic measurement of the dependency ratio. This statistical tool aims to express the number of "dependent" people who rely on each financially independent member of a society. Its proponents produce the ratio by dividing the population into two groups: those aged sixty-five and above, and everyone aged twenty to sixty-four.[22] This is a rough measurement that calls wealthy older people "dependents" and assumes that all adults under sixty-five are employed. In reality, changes such as people's later entry into employment and earlier exit from it have been balanced by the greater participation of women in the workforce so that the proportion of the population in employment in 2013 (48 percent) was similar to what is was in 1953 (46 percent).[23] The dependent population is not predicted to reach the level that Britain supported for much of the twentieth century until 2050.[24] Critics of the dependency ratio point to other causes for the financial problems of modern welfare states, such as reductions in tax payments of various types since the 1970s and monetary policies of the 1980s and 1990s that pursued low inflation.[25] On this reading, demographic aging has become a scapegoat for difficulties of financing government spending and slow economic growth.[26]

Some economists argue that the apparent "fact" of population aging has served as a convenient justification for the reduction of state activity and the unwinding of mid-twentieth-century policy changes.[27] Alternative measurements that account for the improved health and longer life expectancy of Britons paint a different picture of demographic change. Recent research has found that people's behaviors and attitudes are more closely related to remaining life expectancy than to the number of years they have lived.[28] When the category of dependence is altered to include Britons with fifteen years or fewer left to live, researchers conclude that dependency in Britain has fallen by one third since the 1980s.[29] Some even argue that the British population has been getting younger because more people have a greater number of years left to live.

PERSONAL EXPERIENCES OF AGING

Twentieth-century Britons described aging differently from statisticians and policymakers. When visited in their own homes, most aging East Londoners asserted continuities of later life that they viewed as more significant than the social and medical changes age had brought them. These elderly women and men spoke, for example, about their ongoing roles as workers, parents, and spouses. If retirement or death had intervened, then it was reminiscence and its domestic rituals that kept the past alive. In these contexts, aging Britons told stories that demonstrated the stability of self-identity in late life and that celebrated persistent character traits that ranged from resilience to industriousness to humor. The grooming routines of older Britons who devoted time and resources to making the best of their appearances also expressed both continuity and change. Most of the aging Britons who cataloged their grooming routines described calibrating the use of cosmetics or the purchase of new fashions in response to physical aging. This process, however, was an extension of existing desires to look good and to adopt styles that were "just right" for each stage of life.

The chances that older Britons had to speak about their lives were determined by their wealth, health, and family situation. At midcentury, older Britons with the least access to material and social resources were the most likely to live in old-age institutions that restricted their opportunities to discuss their experiences. By this time, researchers and policymakers alike professed their interest in the subjectivity of the old. The stated values of experts, however, frequently came into conflict with one another. It was difficult to balance egalitarianism with respect for the dignity of individuals. Social researchers pursued both ideals by interviewing aging individuals to inform state policies, but they ended up compromising on each of their hopes.

In 1997, Peter Townsend looked back on his research in Bethnal Green and reflected on the experiences of older Britons who had become absorbed in storytelling and felt bewildered by the feelings their distant memories evoked. "Most people got lost in their narrative," Townsend remembered, "rather like I am now."[30] Despite such disquieting emotions, most older people did not treat talking about the past as an occasion to register losses. Instead, elderly Britons used a range of plot lines to interweave the past and the present and thus manage their feelings about growing older. In the twentieth century, older people also told stories to influence public life, including as participants in social scientific projects that interpreted their testimonies as an emblem of intellectual authority. However, as these doorstep interviews were turned into social scientific studies, most of the contributions of older people slipped out of view. The voices of the aged were lost to the narratives of social science as often as interviewees became absorbed in their own stories. Perhaps both of these processes diminished older Britons' chances to influence the public face of aging. As a consequence, while the drive to discover individual stories of the elderly has persisted long past the midcentury, the political consequences of their storytelling are ambiguous.[31]

CARE FOR THE AGED, 1970–2000

The outrage that Townsend expressed over the conditions of residential care was shared by policymakers, and it was decisive in determining the future of the dated public institutions that he visited near the end of the 1950s. Their demise came quickly. A wave of closures began not long after the publication of *The Last Refuge* and peaked in the late 1960s and early 1970s.[32] By 2010, nearly two-thirds of the thirty-nine large institutions that Townsend observed had been demolished. Researchers found only four old-age homes still located at their former addresses, and in each of these cases, new buildings had been constructed on the sites during the 1960s and 1970s. Researchers in 2010 declared, "The era of the workhouse has ended," something that Townsend had wanted to precipitate.[33] Most of the public homes that were in converted Georgian and Victorian houses, a number of which Townsend had admired, closed their doors about a decade after the larger institutions.[34] Many of the voluntary homes that Townsend judged the most humane examples of residential care shut down, too.[35] The most common way that such homes stayed open was by being sold to large nonprofit trusts and private companies.[36] In 1997, Townsend was worried anew about the "even more vulnerable" condition of elderly Britons.[37] He felt troubled that "profit-oriented" residential care was not well regulated. Meanwhile, care for the aged in the community, which Townsend had long espoused, had received "lip-service" from politicians without the "good planning" or resources necessary to make it effective.[38] *The Last Refuge* had left a mixed legacy for the aged.

By the 1970s, older people seemed to have secured the right to community care. The Health Services and Public Health Act 1968 had made the provision of domestic help a duty of local authorities, and some had stopped charging for the service.[39] In one London borough, 90 percent of the 2,057 people who received help at home in 1972 and 1973 received it for free, and the borough abolished all charges shortly afterward.[40] Other services that made up care in the community, such as meal deliveries and social clubs, had largely been provided by volunteers since the 1940s.[41] Many volunteers were themselves older people, so that some clubs were "run virtually on a self-help basis."[42] In the 1970s and 1980s, it was mostly the Women's Royal Voluntary Service that delivered meals to the elderly, except in large cities, where the number of willing volunteers was small and local authorities took responsibility instead.

Care for the elderly was changed by the oil and sterling crises of the mid-1970s, when governments began to cut spending. The National Health Service closed its long-stay hospitals, including large psychiatric hospitals where many residents had been older people with dementia.[43] Community care was seen as a cost-saving measure because its services were designed to keep older people healthy and living in their own homes.[44] Accordingly, local authorities attempted to close residential homes, which caused public protests over where elderly residents would live. It proved easier to cut welfare services. One solution that local authorities came up with was to offer community care only in "crisis situations."[45] This was opposite to the preemptive intentions of its designers. As the elderly became older and more in need, care began to include increasingly personal acts, such as dressing, washing, and feeding.[46] The same happened in residential homes because the definition of older people who were "in need of care and attention" and therefore had the right to residential care was progressively narrowed to people of greater frailty and dependence.[47] As welfare services and residential homes served older Britons with increasingly serious and complex needs, they required upgraded medical facilities and staff training that needed to be funded by local authorities with tight budgets.

From 1979, Conservative governments discouraged the provision of care for the aged by local authorities. Conservatives saw state care as expensive and unresponsive to the needs of elderly people, whom they described as consumers of these services. In 1970, the majority of people who lived in residential and nursing homes lived in public institutions. However, the number of beds available in private homes grew from 49,000 in 1982 to 161,200 in 1991.[48] The fastest growth came after 1983, when regulations enabled residents of private and voluntary homes to claim board and lodging allowances from the social security system on the basis of financial, not health or welfare, need.[49] The privatization of residential care caused concern about care for the aged that was motivated by profits and that drew from public funds without civic accountability.[50] The government responded by establishing standards of care in 1984.[51] This caused problems for local authorities because the required upgrades were expensive, and this led many to close a proportion of their homes to improve the remainder.[52] Later Conservative governments made local authorities the "arrangers and purchasers" of care for the aged and, by 1993, required 85 percent of social security payments to fund services in the private sector.[53] Between 1991 and 2001, local authority homes decreased by over 50 percent in England but by only 30 percent in Wales, where there was greater commitment to the public provision of care.[54] Of the five public homes that Townsend visited in Wales, three were still run by local authorities in 2010.[55] Still, by 2007, three in four residents of old-age homes lived in private institutions.[56]

At the close of the twentieth century, care for the aged was provided on the basis of midcentury policy, including the National Assistance Act 1948 and legislation for community care that was enacted in the late 1960s and early 1970s.[57] While the laws were the same, much else had changed.[58] Late twentieth-century governments repeated Townsend's language when they advocated "personalization, early intervention and prevention" as the guiding principles of care.[59] Policymakers repeated his arguments that care for the aged should be provided in the homes of older people and by the community. Up to today, however, successive governments have not solved the bind of inadequate funding and the rising needs of the oldest generation. As researchers have pointed out, while independent living for all has been a popular policy objective, it denies the reality of the lives of that proportion of older people whose needs are already greater than community care can meet and are growing with time.[60]

After steadily growing for a century, the rate of increase of life expectancy in the United Kingdom has halved since 2010.[61] Michael Marmot, director of the Institute of Health Equity at University College London, points to inequality as a probable cause. In 2015, the highest life expectancy in the United Kingdom was in its richest borough, Kensington and Chelsea, where life expectancy was eighty-three for men and eighty-six for women. Life expectancy was fourteen years shorter among the borough's most disadvantaged residents. The lowest life expectancy in Britain was in the north of the country: men in Blackpool lived to an average age of seventy-four, and women in Manchester lived to an average age of seventy-nine.[62] There was a nine-year difference in life expectancy between men who lived in Blackpool compared to those in Kensington and Chelsea, and a seven-year difference among women who were from Manchester and from Kensington and Chelsea; the disparity was strongly linked to social class. The slowdown of the rate of increase of life expectancy began at the time of the election of a Conservative coalition that introduced a new period of austerity politics in Britain. Commentators have drawn attention to "miserly" spending on social care and health in recent years and its negative effects on the quality of life of the elderly.[63] The incomes of older people have been protected by the government's triple guarantee of the value of state pensions.[64] But the elderly have become more vulnerable to cuts to health and social welfare services.[65] Marmot has concluded that now "it is urgent to determine whether austerity also shortens lives."[66]

· · ·

Social scientists have continued to research the experiences of older people in residential care. In 2005 and 2006, researchers revisited the homes where Townsend studied institutional life in the late 1950s. They gathered information about the older people and staff who lived and worked in the twenty homes that remained open and conducted interviews with seventy-five residents and twenty home managers.[67] In line with national trends, the people living in these homes were older and needed greater care than the population that Townsend had researched fifty years before.[68] Townsend made few references to ethnicity in his study, saying only that some of the residents of large institutions were "elderly Jamaicans, Hungarians, Poles or German Jews."[69] The 2010 follow-up study found that 95 percent of residents in the surveyed homes were white British and that almost half of the residents of other ethnic backgrounds lived in a single home in London, which had a separate unit for Polish people.[70] A majority of home workers, 86 percent, were white British or Irish, but staff also included Britons of African and Caribbean descent and others who identified as Indian and Chinese.[71] In 2005 and 2006, homes were governed by requirements for staff ratios, training, and qualifications.[72] The conditions of employment, however, were poor. The work, said the manager of a religious home, was low paid, low status, and demanding enough that staff were often sick because of stress, and there was little opportunity for promotion as a reward for hard labor.[73]

These twenty-first-century researchers replicated a number of Townsend's methods, including asking residents to keep diaries for the project. Comparison of the diaries from the late 1950s and those from the first decade of the twenty-first century showed that the lives of the elderly were different in the two time periods but not always better. Diarists had led busier lives in 1958 and 1959. Many residents had worked in the homes in which they lived, for example, and their daily activities included entertainment and errands outside of the institutions. Townsend had watched residents washing dishes, setting tables, dusting and sweeping, gardening, sewing, and helping with the laundry, and he took photographs of them arranging flowers, making beds, feeding chickens, and gardening.[74] Although not all of them would have enjoyed this labor, residents were precluded from such work in the early twenty-first century by regulations.[75] Instead, residents enjoyed greater privacy than before, as they lived in single rooms where they ate, watched television, listened to the radio, spent time with visitors, and talked on the telephone.[76] Although secluded, their bedrooms were not always attractive, and many of them looked like hospital rooms that were arranged for the convenience of staff.[77] There were more organized recreational activities in the twenty-first-century homes, but not everyone participated. Some viewed the activities on offer as infantilizing, and others preferred to keep their own company.[78] Still, residents found moments of peace and enjoyment in both periods, for example, by spending time in the gardens of homes and by gazing out of windows with a view.[79]

Researchers returning in the 1990s to the East London location of Peter Townsend's study *The Family Life of Old People* encountered a new social landscape. Bethnal Green had a larger share of older people: the proportion of people who were aged over eighty-five had increased from 2.5 percent in 1951 to 7.5 percent in 1991.[80] Both the social life and the physical geography of the borough had been transformed: two-storied houses had been replaced by blocks of flats, opportunities for local employment had dropped after the 1970s, and the population had fallen by half between 1951 and 1981.[81] By the end of the twentieth century, 40 percent of the local population was drawn from minority ethnic groups. From the 1960s, a significant number of Bangladeshis had moved to London from elsewhere in Britain to seek employment in the garment trade and in restaurants during times of recession.[82] The number of Bangladeshi families living in Bethnal Green by the close of the twentieth century meant that the proportion of multigenerational families there was greater than the national average, although the 26 percent of households in the borough that housed multiple generations was less than the 41 percent that Townsend's study had reported.[83] Changes to the ethnic makeup of East London contributed to some continuity in domestic arrangements within the borough.

Since the 1950s, a majority of elderly East Londoners had experienced the geographic dispersal of their families but had no access to the greater material and welfare resources that have compensated elderly people in wealthier areas.[84] This local population suffered the effects of inner-city deprivation and marginalization during the closing decades of the twentieth century. People in Wolverhampton, where Joseph Sheldon studied old age in 1945, experienced deindustrialization. Suburbanization drove social change in Woodford, where Peter Willmott and Michael Young had done research for *Family and Class in a London Suburb*. Despite these developments, researchers found that at the century's close, family was "still doing what it did forty or fifty years ago" in all of these places.[85] In the 1990s, the period between when children left home and when their aging parents required care was longer than it had ever been, and this meant that adult children were often raising their own offspring while also caring for their elderly parents.[86] Family life had to be "worked at" and managed in new ways, often with the help of a different set of tools, such as the telephone and family cars.[87] Yet the ties of kinship remained strong.[88]

In 1950, men in Britain retired, on average, soon after they turned sixty-seven. The decline of manufacturing jobs in the early 1980s caused considerable numbers of older men to leave the workforce.[89] A decade later, in the early 1990s, there was an increased level of redundancies and early retirement from white-collar positions. Senior employees who benefitted from generous retirement packages helped create an image of prosperous retirees. The age at which men retired fell to 64.6 in 1980 and to 63.1 in 1990. These patterns reversed in the mid-1990s, when economic recovery supported some older men re-entering the workforce. At the same time, fewer companies were able to provide luxurious pension packages, so white-collar workers worked until they were older. The Conservative coalition that was elected in 2010 accelerated planned increases to the pension age. By 2020, the state pension age will be sixty-seven for both men and women.[90]

During this time, older Britons have continued their efforts to narrate their own lives. The aged contributed to the twenty-first-century version of Townsend's study of residential homes, for example, by serving as voluntary researchers who conducted oral histories and scoured the records of local archives. Of the hundred volunteers who researched the fate of the institutions that Townsend visited in the 1950s, just over three-quarters were aged between sixty and seventy-nine, and 10 percent were aged eighty and over.[91] Most of these elderly people felt that academic research was an extension of their contributions to the University of the Third Age, history societies, and older people's forums. A common reason elderly individuals gave for volunteering was that they possessed "skills, knowledge and experience" that added to the project.[92] Some had worked in the social services, and a few remembered the effects of the original research. One volunteer said, "Peter Townsend was something of a 'guru' in my social work training," and another recalled reading *The Last Refuge* in a course in 1966. In the twenty-first century, a widening circle of older people have spoken to social scientists about their lives and detailed experiences as diverse as ballet dancing, elite running, and the effects of living with HIV.[93] Others have contributed to the public discussion of old age through artistic projects. As photographer Jo Spence (1934–92) aged, for example, she began to doubt her right "to act on behalf of those [she] photographed," and turned instead to representing her own life.[94] Spence documented her responses to breast cancer in the photographic exhibitions *Cancer Shock* (1982) and *The Picture of Health* (1982–86), and to leukemia in *The Final Project* (1991–92).

Today, older people around Britain are likely to contribute to their families and communities as well as to social research projects. A large-scale survey of babies born in 2001 and 2002 found that grandparents cared for children in 42 percent of families, and in 71 percent of families in which the mother worked or studied.[95] Data collected in 2006 to 2007 for the European Social Survey has shown that older people are likely to stop working to care for their grandchildren. Just over 50 percent of grandmothers in the study retired before reaching the age of sixty, compared to 37 percent of women without grandchildren.[96] By 2011, 49 percent of Britons aged sixty-five and over looked after young children.[97] Older people have increasingly made financial contributions to their families, too. Many have saved to help grandchildren buy homes, and since the global recession, older Britons have been more likely to lend financial support to their adult children.[98] It is only later in life, when Britons reach the age of seventy-five, that they are more likely to receive than to give this financial and practical help.

The history and contemporary politics of care for the aged are connected to struggles that are experienced by parents, migrants, women in the workforce, unwell and disabled people, and international workers who are all part of lengthening "global care chains."[99] The contradictions of capital and care, as Nancy Fraser has put it, unite social movements that are fighting for "housing, healthcare, food security and an unconditional basic income" with groups working to secure public services such as day care, elder care, shorter working hours, and paid parental leave.[100] Since the 1980s, responsibility for care has been assigned to families and communities while states have simultaneously stripped away the social protections that had allowed some families to provide it. Viewed from the standpoint of the twenty-first century—a new age of austerity in Britain—public faith in social welfare and social science is particular to the middle decades of the twentieth century, and it has left a mixed legacy.

• • •

This project was motivated by my frustration as I sought out the stories of older people in the twentieth century and found that they were often missing from histories of old age. Seeking to find out more about the everyday and internal lives of the elderly, I discovered that older people raised their voices in diverse fields of twentieth-century life and that they spoke with particular authority at midcentury. What they had to say about aging poses a number of challenges for historians like myself. The testimonies of the aged have a variety and depth that demand an expanded role for older people in the history of modern Britain. Aging narrators make clear, for example, that consideration of their experiences is vital to the histories of creative pursuits, family life, work, the body, and the state in the twentieth century. Some among them have been better equipped than others to craft and live the lives that they have wanted, and this distinction provides an alternative measurement of the inequalities of twentieth-century life. Most challenging of all for the practice of historians, older Britons have testified to the significance of the frequently disconcerting experience of living through time. This means that the history of old age is nested in stories of national politics and culture, family life, personal biography, and selfhood. Aging Britons have asked to be understood by the course of their own lives as well as according to the social context, generation, and historical period in which we find them. Their personal experiences of aging are a vital piece of British history and the history of old age.

NOTES

INTRODUCTION

1. Mike Savage, *Identities and Social Change in Britain since 1940: The Politics of Method* (Oxford: Oxford University Press, 2010); Claire Langhamer, "'Who the Hell Are Ordinary People?': Ordinariness as a Category of Historical Analysis" (paper presented at the Royal Historical Society Lecture, University College London, February 10, 2017).

2. James Hinton, *The Mass Observers: A History, 1937–1949* (Oxford: Oxford University Press, 2013), 371.

3. Ibid., 373, 75.

4. Jordanna Bailkin, *The Afterlife of Empire* (Berkeley: University of California Press, 2012), 8.

5. Peter Townsend, *The Last Refuge: A Survey of Residential Institutions and Homes for the Aged in England and Wales* (London: Routledge and Paul, 1962).

6. Peter Townsend, *The Family Life of Old People: An Inquiry in East London* (London: Routledge and Kegan Paul, 1957).

7. Jeremy Tunstall, *Old and Alone: A Sociological Study of Old People* (London: Routledge and Kegan Paul, 1966), 24–27.

8. Interview with Annie Waller (aged seventy-eight), 15 November 1954, SN 4723 Family Life of Old People, 1865–1955, Peter Townsend Collection, National Social Policy and Social Change Archive, Albert Sloman Library, University of Essex, Colchester (hereafter cited as Townsend Collection), available digitally from United Kingdom Data Archives, University of Essex (hereafter cited as UKDA), http://dx.doi.org/10.5255/UKDA-SN-4723-1.

9. Interviews with Elizabeth Thompson (aged seventy-three), 24 June 1954; Rose Smith (aged seventy-two), 14 June 1955; John Knight (aged seventy), 9 August 1955; and Elizabeth Petken (aged seventy-nine), 23 November 1954, Family Life of Old People, Townsend Collection, UKDA.

10. Interviews with Mrs. C. (aged eighty-five), pilot study; and George Thornley (aged seventy), 20 December 1954, Family Life of Old People, Townsend Collection, UKDA.

11. Interview notes from interview 36 (aged seventy-three), in Gateshead, interview transcripts, 1H, Survey Material, Death, Grief, and Mourning in Contemporary Britain, Geoffrey Gorer Archive, University of Sussex (hereafter cited as Death, Grief and Mourning, Gorer Archive).

12. Interview with residents of a welfare home in Southend-on-Sea, 18 March 1959; interview with the warden of a voluntary home in Cheltenham, 6 March 1959; interview with the secretary of the Cornwall County Association for the Blind and the matron of a home for the blind in Truro, Cornwall, 20 July 1959, SN 4750 The Last Refuge, 1958–59, Peter Townsend Collection, available digitally from UKDA, http://doi.org/10.5255/UKDA-SN-4750-1.

13. Julia Johnson, Sheena Rolph, and Randall Smith, *Residential Care Transformed: Revisiting "The Last Refuge"* (Basingstoke: Palgrave Macmillan, 2010).

14. Mass Observation directive (author 914, aged eighty-six), reply to July 1950 directive, Mass Observation Archive, University of Sussex (hereafter cited as MOA).

15. Mass Observation directive, author 3981, reply to June 1950 directive, MOA.

16. For an example of a description of professional life, in this case as an academic, see John H. Muirhead and John W. Harvey, *Reflections by a Journeyman in Philosophy on the Movements of Thought and Practice in His Time* (London: George Allen and Unwin, 1942). For an example of an investigation of a mystery in the life of a family, see J.R. Ackerley, *My Father and Myself* (Harmondsworth: Penguin, 1971). For an example of writing aimed, at least initially, to exact revenge, see Catherine Cookson, *Our Kate* (London: Macdonald, 1969).

17. Hannah Maria Webster Mitchell, *The Hard Way Up: The Autobiography of Hannah Mitchell, Suffragette and Rebel* (London: Faber, 1968), 37.

18. Ibid.

19. This point was first made in the 1940s. See Claire Hilton, "The Origins of Old Age Psychiatry in Britain in the 1940s," *History of Psychiatry* 16, no. 3 (2005): 271.

20. Pat Thane, *Old Age in English History: Past Experiences, Present Issues* (Oxford: Oxford University Press, 2000), 453.

21. Townsend, *The Last Refuge,* 152–53, 61.

22. Peter Laslett, *A Fresh Map of Life: The Emergence of the Third Age,* 2nd. ed. (Basingstoke: Macmillan, 1996), 4–5; I. M. Richardson, *Age and Need: A Study of Older People in North-East Scotland* (Edinburgh: E. and S. Livingstone, 1964), 4. The first and second ages are childhood and adulthood, respectively.

23. Thane, *Old Age in English History,* 479.

24. Ibid., 333.

25. Spijker Jeroen and MacInnes John, "Population Ageing: The Time-bomb That Isn't?," *BMJ,* no. 347 (2013): 1.

26. Ibid.

27. Pat Thane, "'My Age Is a Lusty Winter': The Age of Old Age," in *The Long History of Old Age,* ed. Pat Thane (London: Thames and Hudson, 2005), 9.

28. Pat Thane, *The Long History of Old Age* (London: Thames and Hudson, 2005), 113, 75, 220.

29. Shulamith Shahar, "'All Want to Reach Old Age but Nobody Wants to Be Old': The Middle Ages and Renaissance," in Thane, *Long History of Old Age,* 75.

30. Lynn A. Botelho, "'An Idle Youth Makes a Needy Old Age': The 17th Century," in Thane, *Long History of Old Age,* 157–67.

31. David G. Troyansky, "'Long Live the Republic Where Old Men Preside': The 18th Century," in Thane, *Long History of Old Age,* 183, 90.

32. Ibid., 183.

33. Thomas R. Cole and Claudia Edwards, "'Don't Complain About Old Age': The 19th Century," in Thane, *Long History of Old Age,* 233.

34. Kay Heath, *Aging by the Book: The Emergence of Midlife in Victorian Britain* (Albany: SUNY Press, 2009), 12.

35. Ibid.

36. Thane, *Old Age in English History,* 225.

37. Ibid., 228–29.

38. Sarah Harper and Pat Thane, "The Consolidation of 'Old Age' as a Phase of Life, 1945–1965," in *Growing Old in the Twentieth Century,* ed. Margot Jefferys (London: Routledge, 1989), 43.

39. Thane, *Old Age in English History,* 21.

40. Ibid., 441, 88.

41. Ibid., 329.

42. Ibid., 441.

43. Ibid., 397.

44. Ibid., 284.

45. Ibid., 331; Pat Thane, "Old Women in Twentieth-Century Britain," in *Women and Ageing in British Society since 1500*, ed. L. A. Botelho and Pat Thane (Harlow: Longman, 2001), 210–11.

46. Pat Thane, "Older People and Equality," in *Unequal Britain: Equalities in Britain since 1945*, ed. Pat Thane (London: Continuum UK, 2010), 8–9.

47. Hilary Land and Hilary Rose, "Peter Townsend, a Man ahead of His Time: Re-Reading *The Family Life of Old People* and *the Last Refuge*," in *Fighting Poverty, Inequality and Injustice: A Manifesto Inspired by Peter Townsend*, ed. Alan Walker, Adrian Sinfield, and Carol Walker (Bristol: Policy, 2011), 69.

48. Robin Means and Randall Smith, *From Poor Law to Community Care: The Development of Welfare Services for Elderly People 1939–1971*, 2nd ed. (Bristol: Policy, 1998), 81, 92–103, 11, 36, 206–7.

49. Christopher Conrad, "Old Age and the Health Care System in the Nineteenth and Twentieth Centuries," in *Old Age from Antiquity to Post-Modernity*, ed. Paul Johnson and Pat Thane (London: Routledge, 1998), 136.

50. Interviews with Lillian Niner (aged seventy-four), 2 December 1945; June 1955; 3 November 1955, Family Life of Old People, Townsend Collection, UKDA.

51. Townsend, *The Last Refuge*, 228.

52. See, for example, Jon Lawrence, "Paternalism, Class, and the British Path to Modernity," in *The Peculiarities of Liberal Modernity in Imperial Britain*, ed. Simon Gunn and James Vernon (Berkeley: University of California Press, 2011), 147–64; and Susan Pedersen, *Family, Dependence, and the Origins of the Welfare State: Britain and France, 1914–1945* (Cambridge: Cambridge University Press, 1993); Bailkin, *Afterlife of Empire*.

53. Nancy Fraser, "Contradictions of Capital and Care," *New Left Review* 100 (2016): 108–12.

54. Thane, "Older People and Equality," 7–28.

55. Paul Johnson, "Parallel Histories of Retirement in Modern Britain," in *Old Age from Antiquity to Post-Modernity*, ed. Paul Johnson and Pat Thane (London: Routledge, 1998), 211–12.

56. John Benson, *Prime Time: A History of Middle Age in Twentieth-Century Britain* (London: Longman, 1997), 1; Peter Laslett, "Necessary Knowledge: Age and Aging in the Societies of the Past," in *Aging in the Past: Demography, Society, and Old Age*, ed. David I. Kertzer and Peter Laslett (Berkeley: University of California Press, 1995), 4; Peter Öberg, "Images versus Experience of the Aging Body," in *Aging Bodies: Images and Everyday Experience*, ed. Christopher A. Faircloth (Walnut Creek, CA: AltaMira, 2003), 106.

57. Thane, *Old Age in English History*, 333.

58. Ibid., 436–37, 44–49; Dale A. Matthews, "Dr. Marjory Warren and the Origin of British Geriatrics," *Journal of the American Geriatrics Society* 32, no. 4 (1984): 253–58.

59. Hilton, "Origins of Old Age Psychiatry in Britain," 267–89; Claire Hilton, "The Clinical Psychiatry of Late Life in Britain from 1950 to 1970: An Overview," *International Journal of Geriatric Psychiatry* 20, no. 5 (2005): 423–28.

60. See Thane, *Old Age in English History*; John Macnicol, *The Politics of Retirement in Britain, 1878–1948* (Cambridge: Cambridge University Press, 1998); Tony Salter, *100 Years of State Pension: Learning from the Past* (London: Faculty of Actuaries and Institute of Actuaries, 2009); Conrad, "Old Age and the Health Care System," 132–45; P. Johnson, "Parallel Histories."

61. Thane, *Old Age in English History*, 367–78.

62. Thane, "Older People and Equality," 7–28.

63. P. Johnson, "Parallel Histories."

64. Thane, *Old Age in English History*, 399.

65. Ibid., 400–401.

66. Ibid., 403.

67. Javier Moscoso, *Pain: A Cultural History* (Basingstoke: Palgrave Macmillan, 2012), 1.

68. Monique Scheer, "Are Emotions a Kind of Practice (and Is That What Makes Them Have a History)? A Bourdieuian Approach to Understanding Emotion," *History and Theory* 51, no. 2 (2012): 193–220.

69. In the past, historians aiming to establish public norms of feeling have followed the method of "emotionology," which was developed in the work of Peter Stearns and Carol Stearns.

70. See the concept of "emotives" in William M. Reddy, *The Navigation of Feeling: A Framework for the History of Emotions* (Cambridge: Cambridge University Press, 2001).

71. Deborah Cohen, *Family Secrets: Living with Shame from the Victorians to the Present Day* (London: Viking, 2013), xv.

72. Carolyn Steedman, *Landscape for a Good Woman* (London: Virago, 1986), 122; Frank Mort, "Social and Symbolic Fathers and Sons in Postwar Britain," *Journal of British Studies* 38, no. 3 (1999): 353–84; Abigail Wills, "Delinquency, Masculinity and Citizenship in England 1950–1970," *Past and Present* 187, no. 1 (2005): 157–85.

73. W. Andrew Achenbaum, "Toward a Pschohistory of Late-Life Emotionality," in *An Emotional History of the United States*, ed. Peter N. Stearns and Jan Lewis (New York: New York University Press, 1998), 417–30.

74. Thane, *Old Age in English History*, 259–70.

75. Johnson, "Historical Readings of Old Age and Ageing," 16–17.

76. Selina Todd, *Young Women, Work, and Family in England, 1918–1950* (Oxford: Oxford University Press, 2005); Claire Langhamer, *Women's Leisure in England, 1920–60* (Manchester: Manchester University Press, 2000).

77. Michael Roper, *The Secret Battle: Emotional Survival in the Great War* (Manchester: Manchester University Press, 2009).

78. Claire Langhamer, *The English in Love: The Intimate Story of an Emotional Revolution* (Oxford: Oxford University Press, 2013); Simon Szreter and Kate Fisher, *Sex before the Sexual Revolution: Intimate Life in England 1918–1963* (Cambridge: Cambridge University Press, 2010).

79. Mass Observation's material was donated to the University of Sussex in 1970. It has recently been digitized and made searchable at Mass Observation Online, www.massobservation.amdigital.co.uk.

80. See Louise Corti and Paul Thompson, "Secondary Analysis of Archive Data," in *Qualitative Research Practice,* ed. Clive Seale, Giampietro Gobo, Jaber F. Gubrium, and David Silverman (London: Sage Publications, 2004), 327–43; Louise Corti, "Recent Developments in Archiving Social Research," *International Journal of Social Research Methodology* 15, no. 4 (2012): 281–90; Nigel Fielding, "Getting the Most from Archived Qualitative Data: Epistemological, Practical and Professional Obstacles," *International Journal of Social Research Methodology* 7, no. 1 (2004): 97–104; and Val Gillies and Rosalind Edwards, "Working with Archived Classic Family and Community Studies: Illuminating Past and Present Conventions around Acceptable Research Practice," *International Journal of Social Research Methodology* 15, no. 4 (2012): 321–30.

81. Mike Savage, "Working-Class Identities in the 1960s: Revisiting the Affluent Worker Study," *Sociology* 39, no. 5 (2005): 937.

82. Selina Todd, "Affluence, Class and Crown Street: Reinvestigating the Post-War Working Class," *Contemporary British History* 22, no. 4 (2008): 502.

83. Jon Lawrence, "Social-Science Encounters and the Negotiation of Difference in Early 1960s England," *History Workshop Journal* 77, no. 1 (2014): 215–39.

84. Tim Parkin, "'Old Age Has Always Been Revered': The Ancient Greek and Roman Worlds," in Thane, *Long History of Old Age,* 31–70; Shulamith Shahar, *Growing Old in the Middle Ages: "Winter Clothes Us in Shadow and Pain"* (London: Routledge, 1997); Helen Small, *The Long Life* (Oxford: Oxford University Press, 2007); Karen Chase, *The Victorians and Old Age* (Oxford: Oxford University Press, 2009); and Heath, *Aging by the Book.*

85. This essay was written in reply to Mass Observation's inquiry "How do you FEEL about 1946?" Mass Observation directive, author 1095, reply to December 1945–January 1946 directive, MOA.

1. EXPERTS AND THE ELDERLY

1. Henry Mayhew and William Tuckniss, *London Labour and the London Poor: A Cyclopædia of the Condition and Earnings of Those That Will Work, Those That Cannot Work, and Those That Will Not Work*, 4 vols. (London: Griffin, Bohn, and Company, 1861), 144.

2. Townsend, *Family Life of Old People*, 17.

3. Ibid., 18.

4. Jordanna Bailkin, *The Afterlife of Empire* (Berkeley: University of California Press, 2012), 8.

5. Thane, *Old Age in English History*, 392–93, 98–404, 11–13.

6. Carl Chinn, *Poverty amidst Prosperity: The Urban Poor in England, 1834–1914* (Lancaster: Carnegie, 2006), 17–18.

7. Martin Bulmer, Kevin Bales, and Kathryn Kish Sklar, introduction to *The Social Survey in Historical Perspective, 1880–1940*, ed. Martin Bulmer, Kevin Bales, and Kathryn Kish Sklar (Cambridge: Cambridge University Press, 1991), 23–24.

8. Judith R. Walkowitz, *City of Dreadful Delight: Narratives of Sexual Danger in Late-Victorian London* (London: Virago, 1992), 27.

9. Ibid., 28; Bulmer, Bales, and Sklar, introduction to *The Social Survey in Historical Perspective*, 12.

10. Walkowitz, *City of Dreadful Delight*, 29.

11. Charles Booth, Richard M. Elman, and Albert Fried, *Charles Booth's London: A Portrait of the Poor at the Turn of the Century, Drawn from "Life and Labour of the People in London"* (London: Hutchinson, 1969), xxviii.

12. Belinda Norman-Butler, *Victorian Aspirations: The Life and Labour of Charles and Mary Booth* (London: Allen and Unwin, 1972), 71.

13. David Englander and Rosemary O'Day, *Retrieved Riches: Social Investigation in Britain 1840–1914* (Aldershot: Scolar, 1995), 18.

14. Walkowitz, *City of Dreadful Delight*, 30.

15. Norman-Butler, *Victorian Aspirations*, 72.

16. Ben Gidley, *The Proletarian Other: Charles Booth and the Politics of Representation* (London: Goldsmiths University of London, 2000), 1.

17. Kevin Bales, "Charles Booth's Survey of Life and Labour of the People in London 1889–1903," in *The Social Survey in Historical Perspective, 1880–1940*, ed.

Martin Bulmer, Kevin Bales, and Kathryn Kish Sklar (Cambridge: Cambridge University Press, 1991), 89; Notebooks, Charles Booth Archive, London School of Economics Library, London School of Economics.

18. Booth, *Life and Labour of the People in London: 1st Series*, 2:25–31.

19. Norman-Butler, *Victorian Aspirations*, 72; Englander and O'Day, *Retrieved Riches*, 36.

20. Charles Booth, *Pauperism, a Picture; And Endowment of Old Age, an Argument* (London: Macmillan, 1892), 148.

21. Norman-Butler, *Victorian Aspirations*, 118.

22. John Macnicol, *The Politics of Retirement in Britain, 1878–1948* (Cambridge: Cambridge University Press, 1998), 76.

23. B. Seebohm Rowntree, *Poverty: A Study of Town Life* (London: Macmillan, 1901).

24. A. L. Bowley and Alexander Robert Burnett-Hurst, *Livelihood and Poverty: A Study in the Economic Conditions of Working-Class Households in Northampton, Warrington, Stanley and Reading* (London: G. Bell and Sons, 1915), 47.

25. Englander and O'Day, *Retrieved Riches*, 8.

26. Charles Booth, *Life and Labour of the People in London: 2nd Series; Industry*, 5 vols. (London: Macmillan, 1903).

27. Charles Booth, *Life and Labour of the People in London: 3rd Series; Religious Influences*, 8 vols. (London: Macmillan, 1902).

28. Seth Koven, "The Dangers of Castle Building: Surveying the Social Survey," in *The Social Survey in Historical Perspective, 1880–1940*, ed. Martin Bulmer, Kevin Bales, and Kathryn Kish Sklar (Cambridge: Cambridge University Press, 1991), 371.

29. See, for example, the story describing the life of Mrs. Bennett, a seventy-three-year-old woman who was blind and widowed in Booth, *Pauperism*, 39–40.

30. Alison Light, *Common People: The History of an English Family* (London: Fig Tree, 2014), 233.

31. Peter Mandler, *The Uses of Charity: The Poor on Relief in the Nineteenth-Century Metropolis* (Philadelphia: University of Pennsylvania Press, 1990), 2.

32. Stephen Hussey, "'An Inheritance of Fear': Older Women in the Twentieth-Century Countryside," in *Women and Ageing in British Society since 1500*, ed. Lynn Botelho and Pat Thane (Harlow: Longman, 2001), 186–206.

33. Mandler, *Uses of Charity*, 2.

34. Booth, *Pauperism*, v, 90, 135.

35. Ibid., 87.

36. Rowntree, *Poverty*, 87.

37. Thane, *Old Age in English History*, 328.

38. Hubert Llewellyn Smith, *The New Survey of London Life and Labour*, vol. 3 (London: P. S. King and Son, 1930), 76–77.

39. The "line of poverty" was 18–21 shillings for a family. Charles Booth, *Old Age Pensions and the Aged Poor: A Proposal* (London: Macmillan, 1899), 44–45.

40. Macnicol, *Politics of Retirement*, 31.

41. Thane, *Old Age in English History*, 198–99.

42. Ibid., 200.

43. Ibid., 228–29.

44. Ibid., 255.

45. On the popular appeal of psychology, see Mathew Thomson, *Psychological Subjects: Identity, Culture, and Health in Twentieth-Century Britain* (Oxford: Oxford University Press, 2006).

46. G. Stanley Hall, *Senescence, the Last Half of Life* (New York: D. Appleton, 1922), 172–73.

47. Ibid., 411.

48. Ibid., 321.

49. Leonard Llewelyn Bulkeley Williams, *Middle Age and Old Age* (London: Oxford University Press, 1925), vi.

50. Ibid., 5.

51. Ibid., 265.

52. Ibid., 4.

53. Tom Jeffery, *Mass-Observation: A Short History*, 2nd ed. (Brighton: Mass-Observation Archive, 1999), 4.

54. Jennie Taylor, "Mass Observation as Cultural Critic: The Problem of Leisure in the Worktown Study, 1937–1940" (PhD diss., University of Sydney, 2012), 2.

55. James Hinton, *The Mass Observers: A History, 1937–1949* (Oxford: Oxford University Press, 2013), 368–69.

56. Ibid., 370.

57. James Hinton, "'The "Class" Complex': Mass-Observation and Cultural Distinction in Pre-War Britain," *Past and Present* 199, no. 1 (2008): 207–36.

58. Hinton, *The Mass Observers*, 375.

59. Ibid., 371.

60. Robin Means and Randall Smith, *From Poor Law to Community Care: The Development of Welfare Services for Elderly People 1939–1971*, 2nd ed. (Bristol: Policy, 1998), 21.

61. Ibid., 25, 3, 13.

62. The organization changed its name to the National Old People's Welfare Council in 1955. Henry J. Pratt, *Gray Agendas: Interest Groups and Public Pensions in Canada, Britain, and the United States* (Ann Arbor: University of Michigan Press, 1993), 128.

63. Means and Smith, *From Poor Law to Community Care,* 98–100; Pratt, *Gray Agendas,* 129.

64. James Vernon, *Hunger: A Modern History* (Cambridge, MA: Belknap Press of Harvard University Press, 2007), 146.

65. Brian Abel-Smith, "The Beveridge Report: Its Origins and Outcomes," in *Beveridge and Social Security: An International Retrospective,* ed. John Hills, John Ditch, and Howard Glennerster (Oxford: Clarendon Press, 1994), 13.

66. Ibid., 15.

67. Thane, *Old Age in English History,* 367.

68. Abel-Smith, "Beveridge Report," 18.

69. Thane, *Old Age in English History,* 368–69.

70. Ibid., 367.

71. Ibid., 371–72.

72. Ibid., 374–76.

73. Ibid., 369.

74. Ibid., 371.

75. National Old People's Welfare Committee, *Report of the Conference on "The Care of Old People"* (London: National Council of Social Service, 1947), 19–20.

76. A. T. Welford, *Skill and Age: An Experimental Approach* (London: Published for the Trustees of the Nuffield Foundation by the Oxford University Press, 1951), 3.

77. William Warrender Mackenzie Amulree, *Adding Life to Years* (London: National Council of Social Service, 1951), 1; Trevor Henry Howell, *Our Advancing Years: An Essay on Modern Problems of Old Age* (London: Phoenix House, 1953), 56.

78. M. Thomson, *Psychological Subjects,* 45.

79. National Old People's Welfare Committee, *Working Together for Old People's Welfare* (London: National Council of Social Service, 1948), 6.

80. Ministry of Health (UK), *Welfare of Old People,* Circular 11/50 (London: Ministry of Health, 1950).

81. National Old People's Welfare Committee, *Old People's Welfare: A Guide to Practical Work for the Welfare of Old People* (London: National Council of Social Service, 1945), 13–14; Howell, *Our Advancing Years,* 81–82.

82. As imagined, for example, in National Old People's Welfare Committee, *Old People's Welfare,* 11–12.

83. Ibid., 6–7, 15; Nesta Roberts, *Our Future Selves* (London: Allen and Unwin, 1970), 115, 23–25.

84. Robin Means, Hazel Morbey, and Randall Smith, *From Community Care to Market Care? The Development of Welfare Services for Older People* (Bristol: Policy, 2002), 29.

85. Ibid., 28–29.

86. Hilary Land and Hilary Rose, "Peter Townsend, a Man ahead of His Time: Re-Reading *The Family Life of Old People* and *The Last Refuge*," in *Fighting Poverty, Inequality and Injustice: A Manifesto Inspired by Peter Townsend*, ed. Alan Walker, Adrian Sinfield, and Carol Walker (Bristol: Policy, 2011), 70–71.

87. Means, Morbey, and Smith, *From Community Care to Market Care?*, 29.

88. Ibid., 30–31.

89. Becky Conekin, Frank Mort, and Chris Waters, introduction to *Moments of Modernity: Reconstructing Britain 1945–1964*, ed. Becky Conekin, Frank Mort, and Chris Waters (London: Rivers Oram, 1999), 14; Guy Ortolano, *The Two Cultures Controversy: Science, Literature and Cultural Politics in Postwar Britain* (New York: Cambridge University Press, 2009), 17.

90. Mike Savage, *Identities and Social Change in Britain since 1940: The Politics of Method* (Oxford: Oxford University Press, 2010), 128.

91. Eileen Louise Younghusband, *The Newest Profession: A Short History of Social Work* (Sutton: Community Care, 1981), 29–30.

92. Pat Barr and National Old People's Welfare Council, *The Elderly: Handbook on Care and Services* (London: National Council of Social Service, 1968), 79.

93. A. H. Halsey, *A History of Sociology in Britain: Science, Literature, and Society* (Oxford: Oxford University Press, 2004), 13.

94. Savage, *Identities and Social Change*, 51.

95. See the publications of the National Old People's Welfare Committee, established in 1940, and the National Corporation for the Care of Old People, established in 1947.

96. G. F. Adams, Eric Arthur Cheeseman, and Northern Ireland Hospitals Authority, *Old People in Northern Ireland: A Report to the Northern Ireland Hospitals Authority on the Medical Social Problems of Old Age* (Belfast: Northern Ireland Hospitals Authority, 1951); Will Hobson and John Pemberton, *The Health of the Elderly at Home: A Medical, Social and Dietary Study of Elderly People Living at Home in Sheffield* (London: Butterworth, 1955); P. L. Parsons, "Mental Health of Swansea's Old Folk," *British Journal of Preventive and Social Medicine* 19, no. 1 (1965): 43–47; I. M. Richardson, *Age and Need: A Study of Older People in North-East Scotland* (Edinburgh: E. and S. Livingstone, 1964); Fraser Brockington and Susanne

M. Lempert, *The Social Needs of the Over-80's: The Stockport Survey* (Manchester: Manchester University Press, 1966).

97. B. Seebohm Rowntree and G.R. Lavers, *Poverty and the Welfare State: A Third Social Survey of York Dealing Only with Economic Questions* (London: Longmans Green, 1951); Welford, *Skill and Age*.

98. See E.W. Burgess, *Aging in Western Societies* (Chicago: University of Chicago Press, 1960); Elaine Cumming and William Earl Henry, *Growing Old: The Process of Disengagement* (New York: Basic Books, 1961); Jeremy Tunstall, *Old and Alone: A Sociological Study of Old People* (London: Routledge and Kegan Paul, 1966).

99. Kathleen M. Slack, *Councils, Committees, and Concern for the Old: A Study of the Provision, Extent, and Co-ordination of Certain Services for the Old People in the County of London* (Welwyn: Codicote Press, 1960); Amelia I. Harris et al., *Social Welfare for the Elderly: A Study in Thirteen Local Authority Areas in England, Wales and Scotland* (London: Her Majesty's Stationery Office, 1968); R.B. Bamlett and H.C. Milligan, "Health and Welfare Services and the Over 75s: A Geriatric Survey at West Hartlepool," *Medical Officer* 109 (1963): 379–85; J.R. Edge and I.D.M. Nelson, "Survey of Arrangements for the Elderly in Barrow-in-Furness," *Medical Care* 1, no. 4 (1963): 202–18.

100. Tunstall, *Old and Alone*; Douglas R. Snellgrove, *Elderly Housebound: A Report on Elderly People Who Are Incapacitated* (Luton: White Crescent, 1963); Townsend, *The Last Refuge*.

101. Peter Townsend et al., *The Aged in the Welfare State: The Interim Report of a Survey of Persons Aged 65 and over in Britain, 1962 and 1963* (London: G. Bell, 1965); Dorothy Wedderburn, "Old People in Britain," *American Behavioral Scientist* 14, no. 1 (1970): 97–110.

102. Herbert Crossley Miller, *The Ageing Countryman: A Socio-Medical Report on Old Age in a Country Practice* (London: National Corporation for the Care of Old People, 1963). See also National Old People's Welfare Committee, *Welfare Problems of Old People* (London: National Council of Social Service, 1950), 41; and National Old People's Welfare Committee, *The Welfare of Old People in Rural Areas* (London: National Council of Social Service, 1951).

103. "Book Notes," *Public Administration* 41, no. 4 (1963): 432.

104. National Old People's Welfare Committee, *Welfare Problems of Old People*, 34–35.

105. N. Roberts, *Our Future Selves*, 102.

106. Tunstall, *Old and Alone*, 8–9.

107. Ibid., 10.

108. Ibid., 24.
109. Savage, *Identities and Social Change*, 165.
110. Ibid., 94.
111. Ibid., 165.
112. Ibid., 167.
113. Paul Thompson, "The Making of a Pioneer Researcher: Reflections from Peter Townsend's Life Story," in *Fighting Poverty, Inequality and Injustice: A Manifesto Inspired by Peter Townsend*, ed. Alan Walker, Adrian Sinfield, and Carol Walker (Bristol: Policy, 2011), 30.
114. Ibid., 29.
115. Ibid., 32.
116. Ibid., 34.
117. Peter Townsend interviewed by Paul Thompson, part 7, 14 September 1998, SN 6226—Pioneers of Social Research, 1996–2012, available digitally through UKDA, http://doi.org/10.5255/UKDA-SN-6226-4.
118. Bailkin, *Afterlife of Empire*, 8.
119. Ibid.
120. Peter Townsend interviewed by Paul Thompson, part 7, 14 September 1998, Pioneers of Social Research, UKDA.
121. Ibid.
122. Ibid.
123. Alan Walker, "Professor Peter Townsend: Campaigner for Social Justice Who Co-founded the Child Poverty Action Group," *Independent*, June 13, 2009; Robert Holman, *Champions for Children: The Lives of Modern Child Care Pioneers* (Bristol: Policy, 2001), 134–42, 49.
124. Peter Townsend, "Reflections on Becoming a Researcher," *International Journal of Social Research Methodology* 7, no. 1 (2004): 91.
125. Walker, "Professor Peter Townsend."
126. Peter Townsend interviewed by Paul Thompson, part 1, 30 June 1997, Pioneers of Social Research, UKDA.
127. Peter Townsend interviewed by Paul Thompson, part 1, 30 June 1997, Pioneers of Social Research, UKDA.
128. Thompson, "The Making of a Pioneer Researcher," 35.
129. Peter Townsend, interview by Paul Thompson, part 1, 30 June 1997, Pioneers of Social Research, UKDA.
130. Ibid.; Thompson, "The Making of a Pioneer Researcher," 41.
131. Peter Townsend interviewed by Paul Thompson, part 1, 30 June 1997, Pioneers of Social Research, UKDA.

132. Peter Townsend interviewed by Paul Thompson, part 3, 24 November 1997, Pioneers of Social Research, UKDA.

133. Townsend, *The Last Refuge*, 10.

134. Ibid., 11.

135. Peter Townsend interviewed by Paul Thompson, part 4, 24 January 1998, Pioneers of Social Research, UKDA.

136. Peter Townsend interviewed by Paul Thompson, part 3, 24 November 1997, Pioneers of Social Research, UKDA.

137. Peter Townsend interviewed by Paul Thompson, part 4, 24 January 1998, Pioneers of Social Research, UKDA.

138. Thompson, "The Making of a Pioneer Researcher," 49.

139. Peter Townsend interviewed by Paul Thompson, part 8, 1 February 1999, Pioneers of Social Research, UKDA.

140. Peter Townsend interviewed by Paul Thompson, part 2, 13 October 1997, Pioneers of Social Research, UKDA.

141. N. Roberts, *Our Future Selves*, 114–15.

142. Ibid., 115.

143. Ibid.

144. See Macnicol, *Politics of Retirement*; Tony Salter, *100 Years of State Pension: Learning from the Past* (London: Faculty of Actuaries and Institute of Actuaries, 2009); Thane, *Old Age in English History*; and Christopher Conrad, "Old Age and the Health Care System in the Nineteenth and Twentieth Centuries," in *Old Age from Antiquity to Post-Modernity*, ed. Paul Johnson and Pat Thane (London: Routledge, 1998).

2. TALKING WITH PETER TOWNSEND

1. Interview with Charles Ellwood (aged seventy-one), 15 June 1954, Family Life of Old People, Townsend Collection, UKDA, http://dx.doi.org/10.5255/UKDA-SN-4723-1.

2. Peter Townsend interviewed by Paul Thompson, part 1, 30 June 1997, Pioneers of Social Research, UKDA.

3. Cohen, *Family Secrets*, 182–83.

4. Townsend, *Family Life of Old People*, 11.

5. Ibid., 11–12.

6. Ibid., 14–15.

7. Ibid., 166–78.

8. Ibid., 27.

9. Ibid., 31.
10. Ibid., 39.
11. Ibid., 36.
12. Peter Townsend was aged twenty-six and twenty-seven during this fieldwork.
13. Nikolas S. Rose, *Inventing Our Selves: Psychology, Power and Personhood* (Cambridge: Cambridge University Press, 1996), 73–74.
14. Bowley and Burnett-Hurst, *Livelihood and Poverty*, 188–89.
15. Ibid., 46.
16. B. Seebohm Rowntree, *Poverty: A Study of Town Life* (London: Macmillan, 1901), 152–54, 77.
17. Political and Economic Planning, *The Exit from Industry* (London: Political and Economic Planning, 1935), 15.
18. Means and Smith, *From Poor Law to Community Care*, 206–07.
19. Thane, *Old Age in English History*, 304–6.
20. Talcott Parsons, "The Kinship System of Contemporary United States," *American Anthropologist* 45 (1943): 22–38.
21. Townsend, *Family Life of Old People*, 5.
22. Howell, *Our Advancing Years*, 18–19.
23. Kenneth Hazell, *Social and Medical Problems of the Elderly* (London: Hutchinson Medical Publications, 1960), 179–80.
24. J. H. Sheldon and Nuffield Foundation, *The Social Medicine of Old Age: Report of an Inquiry in Wolverhampton* (London: Oxford University Press, 1948), 13–14, 48.
25. Ibid., 46, 48.
26. Ibid., 3.
27. Ibid., 140–48.
28. Ibid., 150.
29. Townsend, *Family Life of Old People*, v.
30. T. Parsons, "Kinship System," 22–38.
31. Land and Rose, "Peter Townsend," 67.
32. Townsend, *Family Life of Old People*, 210.
33. Land and Rose, "Peter Townsend," 68.
34. Townsend, *Family Life of Old People*, 194.
35. Ibid., 199.
36. Nine of the fifteen photographs featured family groups. List headed "Photos," box 35, file B9, SN 4723 The Family Life of Old People, 1865–1955, Townsend Collection.

37. Ibid.

38. Peter Townsend to Cecil A. Franklin, 11 March 1957, box 35, file B9, Family Life of Old People, Townsend Collection.

39. Letters between Cecil A. Franklin and Peter Townsend, 7, 11, and 12 March 1957, box 35, file B9, The Family Life of Old People, Townsend Collection; Peter Townsend interviewed by Paul Thompson, part 1, 30 June 1997, Pioneers of Social Research, UKDA.

40. Peter Townsend interviewed by Paul Thompson, part 1, 30 June 1997, Pioneers of Social Research, UKDA.

41. Interviews with Sarah Agombar (aged seventy-six), 20 November 1954, 23 December 1954, 15 January 1955, 3 February 1955, 2 March 1955, 20 September 1955, 10 and 23 December 1955, 4 January 1956, 2 and 14 February 1956, 12 March 1956, 20 May 1956, Family Life of Old People, Townsend Collection, UKDA.

42. Interview with Sarah Agombar, 3 February 1955, Family Life of Old People, Townsend Collection, UKDA.

43. Ben Jones, *The Working Class in Mid-Twentieth-Century England: Community, Identity and Social Memory* (Manchester: Manchester University Press, 2012), 77.

44. Ibid., 138.

45. Land and Rose, "Peter Townsend," 70.

46. Jones, *Working Class in Mid-Twentieth-Century England*, 198.

47. Ben Jones, "Surveying Slum Clearance in Post-war England" (paper presented at the Re-analysing Social Survey Data colloquium, Emmanuel College, University of Cambridge, September 8, 2012). See also John English, Ruth Madigan, and Peter C. Norman, *Slum Clearance: The Social and Administrative Context in England and Wales* (London: Croom Helm, 1976); and Ken Coates and Richard Silburn, *Beyond the Bulldozer* (Nottingham: Department of Adult Education, University of Nottingham, 1980), 92–94.

48. Interview with Florence Parsons (aged seventy-one), 25 January 1955, Family Life of Old People, Townsend Collection, UKDA.

49. Land and Rose, "Peter Townsend," 70.

50. Interview with Sarah Agombar, 3 February 1955, Family Life of Old People, Townsend Collection, UKDA.

51. See Charles Vereker and John Barron Mays, *Urban Redevelopment and Social Change: A Study of Social Conditions in Central Liverpool, 1955–56* (Liverpool: Liverpool University Press, 1961); Great Britain Ministry of Housing and Local Government, *The Deeplish Study: Improvement Possibilities in a District of Rochdale* (London: Her Majesty's Stationery Office, 1966); R. K. Wilkinson and E. M. Sigsworth, "A Survey of Slum Clearance Areas in Leeds," *Yorkshire Bul-*

letin of Economic and Social Research 15, no. 1 (1963): 25–51; R.K. Wilkinson and E.M. Sigsworth, "Attitudes to the Housing Environment: An Analysis of Private and Local Authority Households in Batley, Leeds and York," *Urban Studies* 9, no. 2 (1972): 193–214; Norman Dennis, *People and Planning: The Sociology of Housing in Sunderland* (London: Faber, 1970); and Ken Coates et al., *Poverty, Deprivation and Morale in a Nottingham Community: St. Ann's; A Report of the Preliminary Findings of the St. Ann's Study Group* (Nottingham: Department of Adult Education, Nottingham University, 1967).

52. As Ben Jones has pointed out, the point was reinforced in studies that synthesized the results. Jones, "Surveying Slum Clearance in Post-war England." See also Ronald Frankenberg, *Communities in Britain: Social Life in Town and Country* (Harmondsworth: Penguin, 1966); and Josephine Klein, *Samples from English Cultures*, 2 vols. (London: Routledge and Kegan Paul, 1965).

53. Stefan Ramsden, "Remaking Working-Class Community: Sociability, Belonging and 'Affluence' in a Small Town, 1930–80," *Contemporary British History* 29, no. 1 (2015): 2.

54. See John H. Goldthorpe, *The Affluent Worker in the Class Structure* (London: Cambridge University Press, 1969).

55. Ramsden, "Remaking Working-Class Community," 6.

56. Jones, *Working Class in Mid-Twentieth-Century England*; Ramsden, "Remaking Working-Class Community," 1–26.

57. Jones, *Working Class in Mid-Twentieth-Century England*, 140–42.

58. Ibid., 198.

59. Harper and Thane, "The Consolidation of 'Old Age,'" 43–61.

60. Andrzej Olechnowicz, "Unemployed Workers, 'Enforced Leisure' and Education for 'the Right Use of Leisure' in Britain in the 1930s," *Labour History Review* 70, no. 1 (2005): 27. This problem was emphasized in interwar social surveys such as D. Caradog Jones and University of Liverpool, *The Social Survey of Merseyside*, 3 vols. (Liverpool: University Press of Liverpool, 1934); Hubert Llewellyn Smith, *The New Survey of London Life and Labour*, 9 vols. (London: P.S. King and Son, 1930); and Gwynne Meara, *Juvenile Unemployment in South Wales* (Cardiff, 1936).

61. Olechnowicz, "Unemployed Workers," 29. For an English translation of the Marienthal study, see Marie Jahoda et al., *Marienthal: The Sociography of an Unemployed Community* (London: Tavistock, 1972).

62. Walter Brierley, *Means Test Man* (London: Methuen, 1935); Walter Greenwood, *Love on the Dole: A Tale of the Two Cities* (London: J. Cape, 1933).

63. Thane, *Old Age in English History*, 283.

64. Mass Observation directive (author 3653, aged sixty-seven), reply to October/November 1948 directive, MOA.

65. Mass Observation directive (author 686, aged ninety), reply to October/November 1948 directive, MOA.

66. Mass Observation directives (author 2719, aged sixty-seven, and author 2885, aged sixty-two), replies to March 1943 directive, MOA.

67. Mass Observation directives (author 3330, aged sixty-three, and author 2142, aged sixty-one), replies to March 1943 directive, MOA.

68. Thane, *Old Age in English History*, 344–45.

69. National Association for the Care of Old People, *The Interests of the Aged* (London: National Council of Social Service, 1950), 20–32.

70. A. T. Welford, *Skill and Age: An Experimental Approach* (London: Published for the Trustees of the Nuffield Foundation by the Oxford University Press, 1951), 9.

71. Thane, *Old Age in English History*, 396.

72. Townsend, *Family Life of Old People*, 137.

73. Ibid., 140.

74. Interview with Harriet Allen (aged seventy-one), 23 August 1955, Family Life of Old People, Townsend Collection, UKDA.

75. Interview with John Williams Regelous (aged eighty), 26 October 1954, Family Life of Old People, Townsend Collection, UKDA.

76. Interview with Sarah Agombar, 20 November 1954, Family Life of Old People, Townsend Collection, UKDA.

77. Mass Observation directive "Do you consider you have any 'aims in life' clearly enough formulated to put in writing? If so, please say what they are and indicate their relative importance to you. If you haven't do you think it matters, or not?" August 1944, MOA.

78. Mass Observation directive, author 2058, reply to August 1944 directive, MOA.

79. Mass Observation directive, author 2251/1015, reply to August 1944 directive, MOA.

80. Mass Observation directive, author 1095, reply to August 1944 directive, MOA.

81. Mass Observation directive, author 1980, reply to August 1944 directive, MOA.

82. Mass Observation directives (author 1099, aged sixty-six, and author 1098, aged sixty-four), replies to August 1944 directive, MOA.

83. Thane, *Old Age in English History*, 284.

84. Pat Thane, "Old Women in Twentieth-Century Britain," in *Women and Ageing in British Society since 1500*, ed. L. A. Botelho and Pat Thane (Harlow: Longman, 2001), 212.

85. Interview with Ellen Nash (aged sixty), 12 August 1955, Family Life of Old People, Townsend Collection, UKDA.

86. Interview with Florence Parsons, 25 January 1955, Family Life of Old People, Townsend Collection, UKDA.

87. Mass Observation directive (author 1751, aged seventy-three), reply to March/April 1948 directive, MOA.

88. See Gail Wilson, "'I'm the Eyes and She's the Arms': Changes in Gender Roles in Advanced Old Age," in *Connecting Gender and Ageing: A Sociological Approach*, ed. Sara Arber and Jay Ginn (Buckingham: Open University Press, 1995), 104; Julia Twigg, "The Body and Bathing: Help with Personal Care at Home," in *Aging Bodies: Images and Everyday Experience*, ed. Christopher A. Faircloth (Walnut Creek, CA: AltaMira, 2003), 143–69.

89. Townsend, *Family Life of Old People*, 71–75.

90. Charlotte Greenhalgh, "Love in Later Life: Old Age, Marriage and Social Research in Mid-Twentieth-Century Britain," in *Love and Romance in Britain, 1918–1970*, ed. Alana Harris and Timothy Willem Jones (Basingstoke: Palgrave Macmillan, 2015), 144–60.

91. Land and Rose, "Peter Townsend," 62–63.

92. Subsequent research in homes for children, people with disabilities, and the aged, which was completed shortly after Townsend's work, found that two thirds of the staff of these institutions were unmarried women who were mostly over the age of fifty. See ibid., 71.

93. Savage, *Identities and Social Change*, 170.

94. Ibid.

95. Land and Rose, "Peter Townsend," 72.

96. Ibid., 63, 71.

97. Ibid., 74.

98. Townsend, *Family Life of Old People*, 50.

99. Ibid., 52.

100. Ibid., 56.

101. Ibid., 58–59.

102. Interviews with Sarah Hubbard (aged seventy-three), 29 August 1955; Daniel Sparks (aged seventy-eight), 21 June 1954; and Sophie Simmons (aged sixty-seven), 17 August 1955, Family Life of Old People, Townsend Collection, UKDA.

103. See Dorothy Jerrome, *Good Company: An Anthropological Study of Old People in Groups* (Edinburgh: Edinburgh University Press, 1992), 94.

104. Interview with Daniel Yeo (aged seventy-four), 8 September 1955, Family Life of Old People, Townsend Collection, UKDA.

105. See Jerrome, *Good Company*, 98.

106. Interviews with Florence Holborn (aged sixty-eight), 15 and 23 November 1954, 7 December 1954, Family Life of Old People, Townsend Collection, UKDA.

107. Interviews with Mary Pheby (aged sixty), 1 February 1955, 29 March 1955, Family Life of Old People, Townsend Collection, UKDA.

108. Interviews with Thomas Kempley (aged eighty-two), 31 August 1955, 15 October 1955, Family Life of Old People, Townsend Collection, UKDA.

109. Interview with Sarah Agombar, 20 November 1954, Family Life of Old People, Townsend Collection, UKDA.

110. See Cumming and Henry, *Growing Old*; and Michael Mulkay, "Social Death in Britain," in *The Sociology of Death*, ed. David Clark (Oxford: Blackwell Publishers, 1993), 31–49.

111. See Sheila Adams, "A Gendered History of the Social Management of Death in Folehill, Coventry, During the Interwar Years,"in *The Sociology of Death*, ed. David Clark (Oxford: Blackwell Publishers, 1993), 149–68.

112. Mass Observation directive (author 1056, aged sixty), reply to May 1942 directive, MOA.

113. Mass Observation directive (author 1622, aged sixty-five), reply to May 1942 directive, MOA.

114. Mulkay, "Social Death in Britain," 34.

115. Interview with Alfred Harvey (aged eighty-three), 3 January 1955, Family Life of Old People, Townsend Collection, UKDA.

116. Geoffrey Gorer, *Death, Grief, and Mourning in Contemporary Britain* (London: Cresset Press, 1965).

117. Peter Mandler, "Being His Own Rabbit: Geoffrey Gorer and English Culture," in *Cultures, Classes, and Politics: Essays on British History for Ross Mckibbin*, ed. C. V. J. Griffiths, James J. Nott, and William Whyte (Oxford: Oxford University Press, 2011), 193.

118. Ibid., 193–94.

119. Gorer, *Death, Grief, and Mourning*, 157.

120. Ibid., 160.

121. Ibid., 131.

122. Interview notes from interview 36 (aged seventy-three) in Gateshead; and interview 34 (aged sixty-six) in Middlesbrough, 1H, Death, Grief, and Mourning, Gorer Archive.

123. Interview notes from interview 34 with Mr. W.T. Rawlings (aged sixty-six) in Middlesbrough, 1H, Death, Grief, and Mourning, Gorer Archive.

124. Interview notes from interview 67 (aged sixty-one) in Birmingham, 1H, Death, Grief, and Mourning, Gorer Archive.

125. See Mihaly Csikszentmihalyi and Eugene Rochberg-Halton, *The Meaning of Things: Domestic Symbols and the Self* (Cambridge: Cambridge University Press, 1981), 174.

126. Interview notes from interview 43 (aged sixty-one) in Preston; interview 34 (aged sixty-six) in Middlesbrough, 1H, and interview 25 (aged sixty-four) in Ipswich, 1J, Death, Grief, and Mourning, Gorer Archive.

127. Interview 61 (aged seventy) in Dundee, 1H; and interview 25 (aged sixty-four), in Ipswich, 1J, Death, Grief, and Mourning, Gorer Archive.

128. Interview 67 (aged sixty-one), in Birmingham, 1H, Death, Grief, and Mourning, Gorer Archive.

129. Interview 72 (aged seventy-two) in West Bromwich, 1H, Death, Grief, and Mourning, Gorer Archive.

130. Interview 32 (aged sixty-seven) in Sunderland, 1H; interview 37 (aged 66) in Gateshead, 1H; interview 67 (aged sixty-seven) in Birmingham, 1H; interview 14 (aged sixty) in Bath; interview 21 (aged sixty-seven) in Torquay, 1I; interview 44 (aged seventy-four) in Lancaster, 1H; interview 15 (aged eighty-five) in Bath, 1I; and interview 20 (aged sixty-four) in Exeter, 1I, Death, Grief, and Mourning, Gorer Archive.

131. Interview 15 (aged eighty-five), in Bath, 1I, Death, Grief, and Mourning, Gorer Archive.

132. Michael Saler, "'Clap If You Believe in Sherlock Holmes': Mass Culture and the Re-enchantment of Modernity, c. 1890–c. 1940," *Historical Journal* 46, no. 3 (2003): 599–622.

133. Interview with Alice Bentley (aged sixty-seven), 13 January 1955, Family Life of Old People, UKDA.

134. Interview with Sarah Ware (aged seventy-two), 8 August 1955, Family Life of Old People, Townsend Collection, UKDA.

135. Interview with James Allford (aged eighty-one), 24 August 1955, Family Life of Old People, Townsend Collection, UKDA.

136. Interview with Sarah Ware, 8 August 1955, Family Life of Old People, Townsend Collection, UKDA.

137. Interview with Charles Ellwood (aged seventy-one), 15 June 1954, Family Life of Old People, Townsend Collection, UKDA.

138. Michael Roper, *The Secret Battle: Emotional Survival in the Great War* (Manchester: Manchester University Press, 2009); Elaine Scarry, *The Body in Pain: The Making and Unmaking of the World* (New York: Oxford University Press, 1985), 29.

3. INTO THE INSTITUTION

1. Lilian Chamberlain, *Mrs. C. in Residence* (Edinburgh: Pentland, 1997), 6.
2. N. Roberts, *Our Future Selves*, 31–33, 38–39.
3. Chamberlain, *Mrs. C. in Residence*, 6–7.
4. Ibid., 52, 54.
5. Ibid., 10, 75.
6. Ibid., 2–3, 6–7.
7. Ibid., 54.
8. *The Last Refuge* interview and observation notes did not include the names of authors. I therefore refer to the views of the research team rather than of individuals.
9. Townsend, *The Last Refuge*, 7–8.
10. Savage, *Identities and Social Change*, 129; Julia Johnson, Sheena Rolph, and Randall Smith, "Revisiting 'The Last Refuge': Present Day Methodological Challenges," in *Critical Perspectives on Ageing Societies*, ed. Miriam Bernard and Thomas Scharf (Bristol: Policy, 2007), 89–104; Thane, *Old Age in English History*; Robert Holman, *Champions for Children: The Lives of Modern Child Care Pioneers* (Bristol: Policy, 2001), 127–56; Alan Walker, Adrian Sinfield, and Carol Walker, *Fighting Poverty, Inequality and Injustice: A Manifesto Inspired by Peter Townsend* (Bristol: Policy, 2011).
11. Johnson, Rolph, and Smith, *Residential Care Transformed*, 65.
12. Peter Townsend interviewed by Paul Thompson, part 3, 24 November 1997, Pioneers of Social Research, UKDA, http://dx.doi.org/10.5255/UKDA-SN-4750–1.
13. Thane, *Old Age in English History*, 165–66.
14. Ibid., 291.
15. Alison Ravetz and Richard Turkington, *The Place of Home: English Domestic Environments, 1914–2000* (London: E. and F. N. Spon, 1995), 81.

16. Hussey, "An Inheritance of Fear," 187, 96–98.
17. Ibid., 202.
18. Roger E. Blackhouse and Tamotsu Nishizawa, *No Wealth but Life: Welfare Economics and the Welfare State in Britain, 1880–1945* (New York: Cambridge University Press, 2010), 1.
19. Means and Smith, *From Poor Law to Community Care*, 18.
20. Ibid., 29.
21. N. Roberts, *Our Future Selves*, 26–27.
22. Townsend, *The Last Refuge*, 378.
23. Means and Smith, *From Poor Law to Community Care*, 21.
24. Townsend, *The Last Refuge*, 377–78.
25. Ibid., 378.
26. Johnson, Rolph, and Smith, *Residential Care Transformed*, 24.
27. Ibid., 26.
28. Ibid., 7.
29. Townsend, *The Last Refuge*, 32.
30. Johnson, Rolph, and Smith, *Residential Care Transformed*, 38.
31. Ravetz and Turkington, *The Place of Home*, 81.
32. Townsend, *The Last Refuge*, 35.
33. Johnson, Rolph, and Smith, *Residential Care Transformed*, 25–26.
34. John Adams, "The Last Years of the Workhouse, 1930–1965," in *Oral History, Health and Welfare*, ed. Joanna Bornat (London: Routledge, 2000), 98–99.
35. Townsend, *The Last Refuge*, 40.
36. Ibid., 205, 174.
37. Ibid., 174.
38. Ibid., 88.
39. Means and Smith, *From Poor Law to Community Care*, 196.
40. Ibid., 198.
41. N. Roberts, *Our Future Selves*, 86–87.
42. Barbara N. Rodgers and June Stevenson, *A New Portrait of Social Work: A Study of the Social Services in a Northern Town from Younghusband to Seebohm* (London: Heinemann Educational, 1973), 19–21; National Council of Social Service, *Caring for People: Staffing Residential Homes; The Reports of the Committee of Enquiry Set Up by the National Council of Social Service,* National Institute for Social Work Training Series (London: Allen and Unwin, 1967).
43. N. Roberts, *Our Future Selves*, 87.
44. See, for example, National Council of Social Service, *Caring for People*, 27–28.

45. Townsend, *The Last Refuge*, 87–88.

46. Peter Townsend and Sheila Benson, notes on ward interviews, 14, 20–21, box 38, file 3, SN 4758 Old People in Long-Stay Institutions, 1965–1970, Townsend Collection.

47. Peter Townsend and Sheila Benson, Chapter 7: Social Relations in Institutions, February 1967, 20–21, file 14, Old People in Long-Stay Institutions, Townsend Collection.

48. Johnson, Rolph, and Smith, *Residential Care Transformed*, 11.

49. Townsend, *The Last Refuge*, 222.

50. Ibid., 192–93.

51. Peter Townsend interviewed by Paul Thompson, part 3, 24 November 1997, Pioneers of Social Research, UKDA.

52. Johnson, Rolph, and Smith, *Residential Care* Transformed, 7.

53. Townsend, *The Last Refuge,* following p. 241.

54. Claire Langhamer, "The Meanings of Home in Postwar Britain," *Journal of Contemporary History* 40, no. 2 (2005): 341–62.

55. Townsend, *The Last Refuge*, 152.

56. Ibid., 152–53, 61.

57. Ibid., 154, 56–57.

58. Ibid., 166.

59. Visits with welfare officers in Eastleigh, N.2, pilot two, The Last Refuge Collection, SN 4750 The Last Refuge, 1958–1959, Townsend Collection, UKDA, http://doi.org/10.5255/UKDA-SN-4750-1.

60. Visits with the welfare officer for South London, week ending 30 May 1958, Pilot three, Last Refuge Collection, Townsend Collection, UKDA.

61. Visits with the welfare officer for South London, week ending 30 May 1958, Pilot three, Last Refuge Collection, Townsend Collection, UKDA.

62. Visits with welfare officers for London County Council, 24 May 1958, Pilot three, Last Refuge Collection, Townsend Collection, UKDA.

63. Interview with the receiving ward officer at a home in London, January 1959, Home Interviews, Last Refuge Collection, Townsend Collection, UKDA.

64. Visits with the welfare officer for London County Council, 24 May 1958, Pilot three, Last Refuge Collection, Townsend Collection, UKDA.

65. Interview with residents of a welfare home in Southend-on-Sea, 18 March 1959, Home Interviews, Last Refuge Collection, Townsend Collection, UKDA.

66. Interview with residents of a home in London, 8 January 1959, Home Interviews, Last Refuge Collection, Townsend Collection, UKDA.

67. Ibid.

68. Interview with the warden of a voluntary home in Cheltenham, 6 March 1959; and interview with the secretary of the Cornwall County Association for the Blind and the matron of a home for the blind in Truro, Cornwall, 20 July 1959, Home Interviews, Last Refuge Collection, Townsend Collection, UKDA.

69. Interview with the mother superior of a Little Sisters of the Poor home in London, 30 September 1959, Home Interviews, Last Refuge Collection, Townsend Collection, UKDA.

70. Ibid.

71. Interview with the superintendent of a home in Pontefract, West Riding, 13 May 1959, Home Interviews, Last Refuge Collection, Townsend Collection, UKDA.

72. Interview with the owner of a small private home in Beckenham, Ashurst, no date, Home Interviews, Last Refuge Collection, Townsend Collection, UKDA.

73. Interview with the sister superior and assistant sister superior of a Catholic home in Birkenhead, Cheshire, 21 May 1959, Home Interviews, Last Refuge Collection, Townsend Collection, UKDA.

74. Out of the 131 homes Townsend visited, 60 had been converted in this way.

75. National Old People's Welfare Committee, *Age Is Opportunity: A New Guide to Practical Work for the Welfare of Old People* (London: National Council of Social Service, 1949), 66, 74–76.

76. B. Seebohm Rowntree, *Old People: Report of a Survey Committee on the Problems of Ageing and the Care of Old People* (London: Oxford University Press, 1947); Johnson, Rolph, and Smith, *Residential Care Transformed*, 38.

77. Rowntree, *Old People*, 58–60, 150.

78. Ibid., 60.

79. Interview with the matron of a Methodist home in Aigburth, Liverpool, 28 April 1959, Home Interviews, Last Refuge Collection, Townsend Collection, UKDA.

80. Interview with the matron of a private home in Addlestone, Surrey, 18 March 1957, Home Interviews, Last Refuge Collection, Townsend Collection, UKDA.

81. See, for example, N. Roberts, *Our Future Selves*, 135.

82. Interview with the matron of a Methodist home in Aigburth, Liverpool, 28 April 1959, Home Interviews, Last Refuge Collection, Townsend Collection, UKDA.

83. Interview with the sister superior and assistant sister superior of a Little Sisters of the Poor home in Birkenhead, Cheshire, 21 May 1959, Home Interviews, Last Refuge Collection, Townsend Collection, UKDA.

84. Interview with the warden and matron of a local authority home in Gloucester, 7 March 1959; interview with the manager and supervisory manager of a former public assistance institution in London, 27 April 1959; and interview with the secretary of the home management committee and the matron of a home in Hansworth, Birmingham, 17 June 1959, Home Interviews, Last Refuge Collection, Townsend Collection, UKDA.

85. Means, Morbey, and Smith, *From Community Care to Market Care?*, 77.

86. Ibid., 78.

87. Ibid., 79.

88. Claire Hilton, "The Clinical Psychiatry of Late Life in Britain from 1950 to 1970: An Overview," *International Journal of Geriatric Psychiatry* 20, no. 5 (2005): 423–28.

89. Interview with the county welfare officer for the East Riding, 13 May 1959, Welfare Officers Interviews, Last Refuge Collection, Townsend Collection, UKDA.

90. Interview with the matron of a private home in Tunbridge Wells, 2 March 1959; interview with the proprietor of a home in Worthing, Sussex, 8 April 1959; and interview with the county welfare officer for Monmouthshire, 8 December 1958, Home Interviews, Last Refuge Collection, Townsend Collection, UKDA.

91. Rounds made with a welfare officer for Tooley Street, London, 24 June 1958, Pilot three, Last Refuge Collection, Townsend Collection, UKDA.

92. Interview with the medical officer of health for Preston, 20 April 1959, Welfare Officers Interviews, Last Refuge Collection, Townsend Collection, UKDA.

93. Townsend, *The Last Refuge*, 120.

94. Interview with the matron and superintendent of a home in Wolverhampton, 15 and 16 June 1959, Home Interviews, Last Refuge Collection, Townsend Collection, UKDA.

95. Interview with the matron of a home near Abergavenny, 8 December 1958; and interview with the sister superior of a voluntary home in Newbury, Berkshire, 18 February 1959, Home Interviews, Last Refuge Collection, Townsend Collection, UKDA.

96. Interview with the owner of a private home in Ashurst, Beckenham, no date, Home Interviews, Last Refuge Collection, Townsend Collection, UKDA.

97. Interview with the sister superior of a voluntary home in Newbury, Berkshire, 18 February, Home Interviews, Last Refuge Collection, Townsend Collection, UKDA.

98. Interview with the superintendent and matron of a home in Norfolk, 27 May 1959, Home Interviews, Last Refuge Collection, Townsend Collection, UKDA.

99. Interview with the warden of a home in Lancashire, 20 April 1959, Home Interviews, Last Refuge Collection, Townsend Collection, UKDA.

100. Interview with the owners of a private home in St. Leonards, 20 March 1959, Home Interviews, Last Refuge Collection, Townsend Collection, UKDA.

101. Ellen Ross, *Love and Toil: Motherhood in Outcast London, 1870–1918* (New York: Oxford University Press, 1993), 32, 55; Maud Pember Reeves, *Round about a Pound a Week* (London: Virago, 1979).

102. Interview with the Reverend and matron of a home in Midhurst, October 1958, Home Interviews, Last Refuge Collection, Townsend Collection, UKDA.

103. Interview with the warden of a local authority home in London, 25 February 1959, Home Interviews, Last Refuge Collection, Townsend Collection, UKDA.

104. Interview with the owner a private home in Skegness, Lincolnshire, 18 January 1959, Last Refuge Collection, Townsend Collection, UKDA.

105. Interview with the matron of a home in Oldham, 6 May 1959; and interview with the matron of a private home in Tunbridge Wells, 2 March 1959, Last Refuge Collection, Townsend Collection, UKDA.

106. Englander and O'Day, *Retrieved Riches*, 8.

107. Townsend, *The Last Refuge*, 11.

108. Peter Townsend's accounts of participant observation and questionnaires, box 37, file B10, SN 4750 The Last Refuge, 1958–1959, Townsend Collection.

109. Interview with the manager of a private home in Brighton, no date, Home Interviews, Last Refuge Collection, Townsend Collection, UKDA.

110. Interview with the sister in change of a House of Bethany home in Boscombe, Hants, 2 April 1959, Home Interviews, Last Refuge Collection, Townsend Collection, UKDA.

111. Interview with the warden of a local authority home in Bury, 6 May 1959, Home Interviews, Last Refuge Collection, Townsend Collection, UKDA.

112. Ibid.

113. Mulkay, "Social Death in Britain," 47.

114. Notes on visits with a London County Council admitting officer for Victoria London, 22 May 1958, Pilot three, Last Refuge Collection, Townsend Collection, UKDA.

115. Interview with the superintendent of a home in Salisbury, 2 September 1959, Home Interviews, Last Refuge Collection, Townsend Collection, UKDA.

116. Letter from Emma to Peter Townsend, 30 June 1960, Box 37, folder B9: diaries/ correspondence, The Last Refuge, ASL.

117. Letter from Emma to Peter Townsend, 1 June 1960, box 37, folder B9, diaries and correspondence, The Last Refuge, Townsend Collection.

118. Letter from Emma to Peter Townsend, 30 June 1960, box 37, folder B9, diaries and correspondence, The Last Refuge, Townsend Collection.

119. "My Diary from the 1st of February," box 37, folder B9, diaries and correspondence, The Last Refuge, Townsend Collection.

120. Model diary entry and "My Diary from the 1st of February," box 37, folder B9, diaries and correspondence, The Last Refuge, Townsend Collection.

121. There are 218 quotes from "those in charge" and 31 from lower-ranking staff or administrators.

122. Townsend, *The Last Refuge*, 91–92.

123. Ibid., chapter 14.

124. Peter Townsend interviewed by Paul Thompson, part 1, 30 June 1997, Pioneers of Social Research, UKDA.

4. "MAKING THE BEST OF MY APPEARANCE"

1. Catherine Horwood, *Keeping Up Appearances: Fashion and Class between the Wars* (Stroud: Sutton, 2005), 50, 64.

2. Observation notes, 1 August 1940, Stepney and District, London, Topic Collection 18, Personal Appearances—Observations and On the Street Interviews, 1/E Observations and Overheards, MOA.

3. Interviews, 25 July 1940, Stepney, London, Topic Collection 18, 1/E Observations and Overheards, MOA.

4. "Colour Count" notes, 1941, Topic Collection 18, 1/H Colour Counts, MOA.

5. *Vogue* (UK), January 1950, 56.

6. Mass Observation directive (author 3910, aged sixty-four), reply to July 1950 directive, MOA.

7. Öberg, "Images versus Experience of the Aging Body," 15.

8. Frida Kerner Furman, *Facing the Mirror: Older Women and Beauty Shop Culture* (New York: Routledge, 1997), 30; Jaber F. Gubrium and James A. Holstein, "The Everyday Visibility of the Aging Body," in *Aging Bodies: Images and Everyday Experience*, ed. Christopher A. Faircloth (Walnut Creek, CA: AltaMira, 2003), 211.

9. Furman, *Facing the Mirror*, 106; Gubrium and Holstein, "Everyday Visibility," 210–12; Lois W. Banner, *In Full Flower: Aging Women, Power, and Sexuality; A History* (New York: Knopf, 1992), 15; Bill Bytheway and Julia Johnson, "The Sight of Old Age," in *The Body in Everyday Life*, ed. Sarah Nettleton and Jonathan Watson (London: Routledge, 1998), 255.

10. Mike Featherstone and Andrew Wernick, *Images of Aging: Cultural Representations of Later Life* (London: Routledge, 1995), 32.

11. Öberg, "Images versus Experience of the Aging Body," 126.

12. Ibid., 125.

13. Callum G. Brown, *The Death of Christian Britain: Understanding Secularisation 1800–2000* (London: Routledge, 2001), 131–32.

14. Quoted in Callum G. Brown, "Women and Religion in Britain: The Autobiographical View of the Fifties and Sixties," in *Secularisation in the Christian World: Essays in Honour of Hugh McLeod*, ed. Callum G. Brown and M. F. Snape (Farnham: Ashgate, 2010), 163.

15. Becky E. Conekin, "From Haughty to Nice: How British Fashion Images Changed from the 1950s to the 1960s," *Photography and Culture* 3, no. 3 (2010): 285–94.

16. Catherine Horwood, "Housewives' Choice: Women as Consumers between the Wars," *History Today* 47, no. 3 (1997): 24.

17. Ibid., 26.

18. *Good Housekeeping* (UK), March 1934, 74; *Good Housekeeping* (UK), August 1934, 74.

19. Ross McKibbin, *Classes and Cultures: England, 1918–1951* (Oxford: Oxford University Press, 1998), 508.

20. *Women's Weekly*, June 7, 1930, 989.

21. *Women's Weekly*, February 2, 1935, 172.

22. Christopher Breward, *The Culture of Fashion: A New History of Fashionable Dress* (Manchester: Manchester University Press, 1995), 185.

23. Ibid., 185–86, 91.

24. Jill Greenfield and Chris Reid, "Women's Magazines and the Commercial Orchestration of Femininity in the 1930s: Evidence from Woman's Own," *Media History* 4, no. 2 (1998): 163.

25. Ibid., 164.

26. Cynthia Leslie White, *Women's Magazines, 1693–1968* (London: M. Joseph, 1970), 118.

27. Greenfield and Reid, "Women's Magazines," 164–66.

28. On youth and beauty, see Cynthia Port, "'Ages Are the Stuff': The Traffic in Ages in Interwar Britain," *National Women's Studies Association* 18, no. 1 (2006): 138–61.

29. McKibbin, *Classes and Cultures*, 508.

30. Howard Cox and Simon Mowatt, "Vogue in Britain: Authenticity and the Creation of Competitive Advantage in the UK Magazine Industry," *Business History* 54, no. 1 (2012): 67.

31. Ibid., 72.

32. *Vogue* (UK), February/March 1937, 30–31, 48.

33. Ibid., 49.

34. Both outfits cost nine and a half guineas. *Vogue* (UK), July 21, 1937, 60–61.

35. Christopher Breward, Becky Conekin, and Caroline Cox, "Introduction: 'Dyed in the Wool English?,'" in *The Englishness of English Dress*, ed. Becky Conekin and Caroline Cox (Oxford: Berg, 2002), 5.

36. *Vogue* (UK), February 2, 1938, 52–53; *Vogue* (UK), February 16, 1938, 42, 52.

37. Cally Blackman, *100 Years of Fashion Illustration* (London: Laurence King, 2007), 71.

38. McKibbin, *Classes and Cultures*, 508.

39. Ina Zweiniger-Bargielowska, *Austerity in Britain: Rationing, Controls, and Consumption, 1939–1955* (Oxford: Oxford University Press, 2000), 91.

40. Zillah Halls, "Mrs Exeter: The Rise and Fall of the Older Woman," *Costume* 34 (2000): 106; Breward, *Culture of Fashion*, 191.

41. Ina Zweiniger-Bargielowska, "The Body and Consumer Culture," in *Women in Twentieth-Century Britain*, ed. Ina Zweiniger-Bargielowska (Harlow: Pearson Education, 2001), 188; Breward, *Culture of Fashion*, 191.

42. Linda Grant, *The Thoughtful Dresser: The Art of Adornment, the Pleasures of Shopping, and Why Clothes Matter,* (New York: Scribner, 2010), 34.

43. Halls, "Mrs Exeter," 106.

44. *Vogue* (UK), March 1949, 72. Mrs. Exeter advised older women how to present themselves with grace and style in a column that appeared about every two months until 1965.

45. *Vogue* (UK), June 1949, 63.

46. *Vogue* (UK), September 1949, 104.

47. *Vogue* (UK), June 1949, 63.

48. *Vogue* (UK), March 1949, 72.
49. *Vogue* (UK), August 1952, 65.
50. Mrs. Eastley's first name was not given by the magazine. Sheelagh Southwell Eastley was a justice of the peace who lived in Devon, like the competition winner. If this was the same Mrs. Eastley who appeared in Vogue, then she was aged fifty-six when she was named the real-life Mrs. Exeter. "Five Women in List of New Devon J.P.s," *Western Times,* November 12, 1937, 10.
51. Halls, "Mrs Exeter," 108.
52. *Vogue* (UK), October 1953, 84.
53. *Vogue* (UK), February 1959, 62–75.
54. Carol Dyhouse, *Glamour: Women, History, Feminism* (London: Zed, 2010), 3.
55. *Vogue* (UK), February 1951, 48–51; *Vogue* (UK), August 1951, 12.
56. Veronica Horwell, "Obituary: Barbara Goalen," *Guardian,* June 22, 2002, www.guardian.co.uk/news/2002/jun/22/guardianobituaries.veronicahorwell.
57. See Conekin, "From Haughty to Nice," 285; Linda M. Scott, *Fresh Lipstick: Redressing Fashion and Feminism* (New York: Palgrave Macmillan, 2005), 256–57.
58. Rebecca Arnold, "Goalen, Barbara Kathleen (1921–2002)," in *Oxford Dictionary of National Biography* (Oxford University Press, 2004; online ed., 2006), https://doi.org/10.1093/ref:odnb/76961.
59. Horwell, "Obituary: Barbara Goalen."
60. Diana Athill, *Somewhere towards the End* (London: Granta Books, 2008), 14.
61. Conekin, "From Haughty to Nice," 289.
62. *Vogue* (UK), February 1956, 54–55.
63. See, for example, the "Dressing for Committee Work / a Garden Party / Dinner/ the Theatre/ a Wedding" spread, *Vogue* (UK), February 1959, 62–75.
64. Christopher Breward, *The Hidden Consumer: Masculinities, Fashion and City Life 1860–1914* (Manchester: Manchester University Press, 1999), 39.
65. Ibid., 30–31.
66. Matt Houlbrook, "The Man with the Powder Puff in Interwar London," *Historical Journal* 50, no. 1 (2007): 145–71.
67. Ina Zweiniger-Bargielowska, *Managing the Body: Beauty, Health, and Fitness in Britain, 1880–1939* (Oxford: Oxford University Press, 2010); Caroline Daley, *Leisure and Pleasure: Reshaping and Revealing the New Zealand Body 1900–1960* (Auckland: Auckland University Press, 2003).
68. Jill Greenfield, Sean O'Connell, and Chris Reid, "Fashioning Masculinity: Men Only, Consumption and the Development of Marketing in the 1930s," *Twentieth Century British History* 10, no. 4 (1999): 470.

69. Breward, *Hidden Consumer*, 245, 49, 52.

70. Frank Mort, *Cultures of Consumption: Masculinities and Social Space in Late Twentieth-Century Britain* (London: Routledge, 1996), 137.

71. Ibid., 138.

72. Mass Observation directive (author 1124, aged seventy-three), reply to July 1950 directive, MOA.

73. The Aristoc advertisement appeared on the inside cover of British *Vogue* in June, July, August, September, October, and December 1954 and January, February, and March 1955.

74. Advertisement for Saint Joseph French jersey, *Vogue* (UK), March 1, 1962, 30.

75. Horwood, *Keeping Up Appearances*, 64, 124, 29, 32, 38.

76. Greenfield, O'Connell, and Reid, "Fashioning Masculinity," 122; Frank Mort and Peter Thompson, "Retailing, Commercial Culture and Masculinity in 1950s Britain: The Case of Montague Burton, the 'Tailor of Taste,'" *History Workshop Journal* 38, no. 1 (1994): 122.

77. Kathy Lee Peiss, *Hope in a Jar: The Making of America's Beauty Culture* (New York: Metropolitan Books, 1998), 44–46.

78. Liz Conor, *The Spectacular Modern Woman: Feminine Visibility in the 1920s* (Bloomington: Indiana University Press, 2004), 2.

79. Ibid., 48.

80. Peiss, *Hope in a Jar*, 16–17.

81. Ibid., 24, 144, 55.

82. Mass Observation directive (author 2895, aged sixty-three), reply to July 1950 directive, MOA.

83. Mass Observation directive (author 1099, aged sixty-one), reply to April 1939 directive, MOA.

84. Mass Observation directive (author 1016, aged sixty-three), reply to July 1950 directive, MOA.

85. Mass Observation directive (author 1015, aged sixty-four), reply to May 1939 directive, MOA.

86. Mass Observation directive (author 1099, aged sixty-one), reply to May 1939 directive, MOA.

87. Mass Observation directive (author 1041, aged sixty-two), reply to July 1950 directive, MOA.

88. Mass Observation directives, authors 631, 4693, and 914, replies to July 1950 directive, MOA.

89. Mass Observation directives (author 1538, aged sixty-five and author 1069, aged sixty), replies to April 1939 directive, MOA.

90. Mass Observation directives (author 1538, aged sixty-five, author 1069, aged sixty, and (author 1544 aged sixty-six), replies to April 1939 directive, MOA.

91. Mass Observation directive, author 3035, reply to July 1950 directive, MOA.

92. *Vogue* (UK), March 17, 1937, 17; *Vogue* (UK), October 1, 1964, 70.

93. Mass Observation directive (author 914, aged eighty-six), reply to July 1950 directive, MOA.

94. Mass Observation directive, author 1061, reply to July 1950 directive, MOA.

95. Mass Observation directive (author 1762, aged sixty-nine), reply to July 1950 directive, MOA.

96. Mass Observation directive (author 4564, aged seventy), reply to July 1950 directive, MOA.

97. Mass Observation directive (author 3204, aged seventy-four), reply to July 1950 directive, MOA.

98. Mass Observation directive (author 1095, aged sixty-three), reply to April 1939 directive, MOA.

99. Mass Observation directive (author 1015, aged sixty-three), reply to April 1939 directive, MOA.

100. Mass Observation directive (author 1916, aged sixty-eight), reply to July 1950 directive, MOA.

101. Mass Observation directive, author 3981, reply to June 1950 directive, MOA.

102. Mass Observation directive (author 2252, aged sixty-three), reply to July 1950 directive, MOA.

103. Mass Observation directive (author 1061, aged sixty), reply to July 1950 directive, MOA.

104. Mass Observation directive (author 1971, aged sixty-four), reply to July 1950 directive, MOA.

105. Mass Observation directives (author 631, aged sixty-three, and author 1061, aged sixty), replies to July 1950 directive, MOA.

106. Horwood, *Keeping Up Appearances*, 69.

107. There were seventeen respondents in total.

108. Kathy Peiss, "Making Up, Making Over: Cosmetics, Consumer Culture, and Women's Identity," in *The Sex of Things: Gender and Consumption in*

Historical Perspective, ed. Victoria de Grazia (Berkeley: University of California Press, 1996), 245; Zweiniger-Bargielowska, "Body and Consumer Culture," 187.

109. Mass Observation directive (author 3981, aged sixty), reply to July 1950 directive, MOA.

110. Mass Observation directive (author 1015, aged sixty-three), reply to April 1939 directive, MOA.

111. Mass Observation directive (author 1069, aged sixty), reply to April 1939 directive, MOA.

112. Peiss, *Hope in a Jar,* 132.

113. Ibid., 6.

114. Ibid., 175–76.

115. Mass Observation directive (author 1061, aged sixty), reply to July 1950 directive, MOA.

116. Peiss, *Hope in a Jar,* 6.

117. Mass Observation directive (author 9141, aged sixty-three), reply to July 1950 directive, MOA.

118. Lucy Delap, "Conservative Values, Anglicans, and the Gender Order in Interwar Britain," in *Brave New World: Imperial and Democratic Nation Building in Britain between the Wars,* ed. Laura Beers and Geraint Thomas (London: Institute of Historical Research Publications, 2012), 149–68.

119. Angus Calder et al., *Speak for Yourself: A Mass-Observation Anthology, 1937–1949* (Oxford: Oxford University Press, 1985), 74.

120. Mass Observation directive (author 4693, aged sixty-five), reply to July 1950 directive, MOA.

121. Graham Dawson, "The Blonde Bedouin," in *Manful Assertions: Masculinities in Britain since 1800,* ed. Michael Roper and John Tosh (London: Routledge, 1991), 118–19.

122. Mass Observation directive (author 1074, aged seventy-three), reply to April 1939 directive, MOA.

5. GAMES WITH TIME

1. Storm Jameson published forty-five novels and was the wartime president of English PEN (Poets, Essayists and Novelists) from 1938 to 1944.

2. Storm Jameson, *Journey from the North: Autobiography of Storm Jameson,* 2 vols. (London: Virago, 1984), 2:28. *Journey from the North* was first published in 1969.

3. Ibid., 2:17.

4. Ibid., 2:325.
5. Ibid., 1:91.
6. Ibid., 2:114.
7. Ibid., 2:355.
8. Michael Roper, "Splitting in Unsent Letters: Writing as a Social Practice and a Psychological Activity," *Social History* 26, no. 3 (2001): 318–39.
9. Jameson, *Journey from the North*, 2:71; Catherine Cookson, *Our Kate* (London: Macdonald, 1990), 8.
10. Cohen, *Family Secrets*, 182, 225.
11. Jameson, *Journey from the North*, 2:371; Cookson, *Our Kate*, 8.
12. Jameson, *Journey from the North*, 2:371.
13. Cookson, *Our Kate*, 7–8.
14. On the history of confessional culture in Britain, see Cohen, *Family Secrets*, 181–211, 41–53.
15. Arthur Quiller-Couch, *The Oxford Book of English Verse, 1250–1900* (Oxford: Clarendon, 1919).
16. Carolyn Steedman, *Strange Dislocations: Childhood and the Idea of Human Interiority, 1780–1930* (London: Virago, 1995), 12, 77; Graham Richards, "Britain on the Couch: The Popularization of Psychoanalysis in Britain 1918–1940," *Science in Context* 13, no. 2 (2000): 183–230.
17. Steedman, *Strange Dislocations*, 74, 12.
18. Hendrik Hartog, *Someday All This Will Be Yours: A History of Inheritance and Old Age* (Cambridge, MA: Harvard University Press, 2012), 149–50; Jenny Hockey and Allison James, "Back to Our Futures: Imagining Second Childhood," in *Images of Aging: Cultural Representations of Later Life*, ed. Mike Featherstone and Andrew Wernick (London: Routledge, 1995), 135–48.
19. Augustus John, *Chiaroscuro: Fragments of Autobiography; First Series* (London: J. Cape, 1952), 276.
20. Herbert Read, *The Contrary Experience: Autobiographies* (London: Faber and Faber, 1973), 54–55.
21. Evelyn Waugh, *A Little Learning: The First Volume of an Autobiography* (London: Chapman and Hall, 1964), 28.
22. Richard Church, *The Voyage Home* (London: Heinemann, 1964), 4.
23. V. S. Pritchett, *A Cab at the Door and Midnight Oil* (Harmondsworth: Penguin Books, 1979), 217.
24. Ibid.
25. Church, *Voyage Home*, 104.
26. Ibid.

27. Hannah Maria Webster Mitchell, *The Hard Way Up: The Autobiography of Hannah Mitchell, Suffragette and Rebel* (London: Faber, 1968), 37; E. Denison Ross and Alick Denison Ross, *Both Ends of the Candle: The Autobiography of Sir E. Denison Ross* (London: Faber and Faber, 1943), 15.

28. John, *Chiaroscuro,* 277.

29. Winifred Peck, *Home for the Holidays* (London: Faber and Faber, 1955), 127.

30. Church, *Voyage Home,* 160.

31. See George Gusdorf, "Conditions and Limits of Autobiography," in *Autobiography: Essays Theoretical and Critical,* ed. James Olney (Princeton: Princeton University Press, 1980); Philippe Lejeune and Paul John Eakin, *On Autobiography* (Minneapolis: University of Minnesota Press, 1989); and Karl Joachim Weintraub, *The Value of the Individual: Self and Circumstance in Autobiography* (Chicago: University of Chicago Press, 1978).

32. Lejeune and Eakin, *On Autobiography,* ix.

33. Donna Loftus, "The Self in Society: Middle-Class Men and Autobiography," in *Life Writing and Victorian Culture,* ed. David Amigoni (Aldershot: Ashgate, 2006), 67–69.

34. Mary G. Mason, "The Other Voice: Autobiographies of Women Writers," in *Autobiography: Essays Theoretical and Critical,* ed. James Olney (Princeton: Princeton University Press, 1980), 207–35.

35. Matt Houlbrook, "Commodifying the Self Within: Ghosts, Libels, and the Crook Life Story in Interwar Britain," *Journal of Modern History* 85, no. 2 (2013): 321–63.

36. Matt Houlbrook, *Prince of Tricksters: The Incredible True Story of Netley Lucas, Gentleman Crook* (Chicago: University of Chicago Press, 2016).

37. Steedman, *Strange Dislocations,* 4.

38. Susan Brown, Patricia Clements, and Isobel Grundy, eds., "Marie Belloc Lowndes," in In *Orlando: Women's Writing in the British Isles from the Beginnings to the Present* (Cambridge: Cambrigde University Press Online, 2006), http://orlando.cambridge.org/public/svPeople?person_id=lownma; C.R. Methol, "Arcadian Days," *Times Literary Supplement,* October 11, 1941, p. 509.

39. "Horace Horsnell," *Manchester Guardian,* February 12, 1949, p. 4.

40. "The Album by Horace Horsnell" (advertisement), *Observer,* April 1, 1945, p. 3.

41. Selina Todd, *The People: The Rise and Fall of the Working Class, 1910–2010* (London: John Murray, 2014), 152.

42. Ibid., 200–203.

43. Ibid., 236–46. See also Stephen Brooke, "Revisiting Southam Street: Class, Generation, Gender, and Race in the Photography of Roger Mayne," *Journal of British Studies* 53, no. 2 (2014): 453–96.

44. Todd, "Affluence, Class and Crown Street," 502.

45. Christopher Hilliard, *To Exercise Our Talents: The Democratization of Writing in Britain* (Cambridge, MA: Harvard University Press, 2006). This built on a much longer tradition. See John Burnett, David Vincent, and David Mayall, *The Autobiography of the Working Class: An Annotated, Critical Bibliography: 1790–1900*, vol. 1 (Brighton: Harvester, 1984).

46. Matt Houlbrook, "'A Pin to See the Peepshow': Culture, Fiction and Selfhood in Edith Thompson's Letters, 1921–1922," *Past and Present* 207, no. 1 (2010): 215–49. See also Sharon Marcus, *Between Women: Friendship, Desire, and Marriage in Victorian England* (Princeton: Princeton University Press, 2007).

47. Carolyn Steedman, "State-Sponsored Autobiography," in *Moments of Modernity: Reconstructing Britain 1945–1964*, ed. Becky Conekin, Frank Mort, and Chris Waters (London: Rivers Oram, 1999), 41–54.

48. Carolyn Steedman, "Enforced Narratives: Stories of Another Self," in *Feminism and Autobiography: Texts, Theories, Methods*, ed. Tess Casslett, Celia Lury, and Penny Summerfield (London: Routledge 2000), 25–39.

49. The autobiographies of Storm Jameson and Catherine Cookson are examples of this new style.

50. Paul Bailey, "Pritchett, Sir Victor Sawdon (1900–1997)," in *Oxford Dictionary of National Biography* (Oxford: Oxford University Press, 2004; online ed., 2014) https://doi.org/10.1093/ref:odnb/65704; V. S. Pritchett, *A Cab at the Door: An Autobiography; Early Years* (London: Chatto and Windus, 1968).

51. Chris Waters, "Autobiography, Nostalgia, and the Changing Practices of Working-Class Selfhood," in *Singular Continuities: Tradition, Nostalgia, and Identity in Modern British Culture*, ed. George K. Behlmer and F. M. Leventhal (Stanford: Stanford University Press, 2000), 179.

52. John Feather, *A History of British Publishing*, 2nd ed. (London: Routledge, 2006), 214.

53. Ibid., 215.

54. Waters, "Autobiography," 180.

55. Ibid., 184. See also Paddy Maguire, David Morley, and Ken Worpole, *The Republic of Letters: Working Class Writing and Local Publishing* (London: Comedia Publishing Group, 1982). Such groups were also active in the early 1970s in Peckham and Stepney. Other examples include the Aberdeen People's Press, Bristol Broadsides, Commonword (Manchester), and QueenSpark (Brighton).

56. Waters, "Autobiography," 184.
57. Ibid., 190.
58. L. Hulmes to Walter Greenwood, 13 October 1967, 2/15/9, Walter Greenwood Collection, Clifford Whitworth Library, University of Salford, Manchester (hereafter cited as Walter Greenwood Collection).
59. Priscilla Pagden to Walter Greenwood, c. 1970–1971, 2/15/39, Walter Greenwood Collection.
60. See Correspondence, WGC/2; and Newspaper Cuttings, WGC/3 Walter Greenwood Collection.
61. Alistair Thomson, *Anzac Memories: Living with the Legend* (Melbourne: Oxford University Press, 1994), 185.
62. Ibid., 8–11.
63. Paul John Eakin, *Fictions in Autobiography: Studies in the Art of Self-Invention* (Princeton: Princeton University Press, 1985), 55; Alessandro Portelli, "'The Time of My Life': Functions of Time in Oral History," *International Journal of Oral History* 2, no. 3 (1981): 162–80.
64. Burnett, Vincent, and Mayall, *Autobiography of the Working Class*, xx.
65. Brian Boyd, *On the Origin of Stories: Evolution, Cognition, and Fiction* (Cambridge, MA: Belknap Press of Harvard University Press, 2009), 153; Alan Collins, "The Psychology of Memory," in *Psychology in Britain: Historical Essays and Personal Reflections,* ed. G. D. Bunn, A. D. Lovie, and G. D. Richards (Leicester: BPS Books, 2001), 160.
66. This is similar to the relationship that Eakin has identified between the self and its cultural influences. Eakin, *Fictions,* 100.
67. Ben Jones, "The Uses of Nostalgia: Autobiography, Community Publishing and Working Class Neighbourhoods in Post-war England," *Cultural and Social History* 7, no. 3 (2010): 356.
68. Waters, "Autobiography," 189.
69. Jones, "Uses of Nostalgia," 357, 61.
70. Waters, "Autobiography," 186–87.
71. Jones, "Uses of Nostalgia," 361.
72. Waters, "Autobiography," 188.
73. Jones, "Uses of Nostalgia," 356.
74. Elizabeth Sanderson Haldane, *From One Century to Another: The Reminiscences of Elizabeth S. Haldane* (London: A. Maclehose, 1937), vi.
75. Ibid., 170, 315–16.
76. Mitchell, *Hard Way Up,* 37.

77. Thomas Joy, *Mostly Joy: A Bookman's Story* (London: Joseph, 1971), 198.
78. Walter Greenwood, *There Was a Time* (London: J. Cape, 1967), 13.
79. Robert Roberts, *A Ragged Schooling: Growing Up in the Classic Slum* (Manchester: Manchester University Press, 1976), 1.
80. Haldane, *From One Century to Another*, 36–37.
81. For discussions of World War I, see Bertrand Russell, *The Autobiography of Bertrand Russell*, vol. 2 of 3 (New York: Bantam, 1968); Edith Hall, *Canary Girls and Stockpots* (Luton: Workers' Educational Association, Luton Branch, 1977); and Storm Jameson, *Journey from the North: Autobiography of Storm Jameson*, vol. 2 of 2 (London: Virago, 1984). For a discussion of World War II, see Robert Henrey, *The Golden Visit* (London: J. M. Dent, 1979).
82. H. M. Burton, *There Was a Young Man* (London: G. Bles, 1958), 9–10.
83. Ibid., 11.
84. James Hinton, *The Mass Observers: A History, 1937–1949* (Oxford: Oxford University Press, 2013), 375.
85. Marcus, *Between Women*, 37.
86. Robert Henrey, *Her April Days* (London: Dent, 1963); Henrey, *Golden Visit*.
87. Henrey, *Her April Days*, 18.
88. Ibid., 51, 150.
89. Ibid., 1–3.
90. Ibid., 54.
91. Ibid., 3–11.
92. Henrey, *Golden Visit*, 134–35.
93. Robery Henrey, *Winter Wild* (London: Dent, 1966), 182.
94. Henrey, *Golden Visit*, 135.
95. Henrey, *Winter Wild*, 2.
96. Ibid., 141; Henrey, *Her April Days*, 13.
97. Greenwood, *There Was a Time*, 250.
98. Ibid., 251.
99. Ibid., 351.
100. Albert Paul, *Poverty: Hardship but Happiness; Those Were the Days, 1903–1917*, 3rd ed. (Brighton: QueenSpark, 1981), 65–66.
101. Burton, *Young Man*, 46–47.
102. Ibid., 48.
103. Ibid., 54.
104. Waters, "Autobiography," 186.
105. Grace Foakes, *My Part of the River* (London: Futura, 1974), 61.

106. For more on the history of the movements of children in the twentieth century, see Mathew Thomson, *Lost Freedom: The Landscape of the Child and the British Post-war Settlement* (Oxford: Oxford University Press, 2013).

107. Grace Foakes, *Between High Walls: A London Childhood*, 2nd ed. (Oxford: Athena Books, 1972), 81–82.

108. Ibid., 17–18, 23–24, 30.

109. Foakes, *My Part of the River*, 1.

110. Ibid., 85.

111. Foakes, *Between High Walls*, 3, 9, 25, 30, 33.

112. Ibid., 58, 20, 28.

113. Jameson, *Journey from the North*, 2:371.

114. Ibid., 383.

115. Cookson, *Our Kate*, 5.

116. Ibid., 6.

117. Jameson, *Journey from the North*, 2:371.

EPILOGUE

1. "Global Ageing: A Billion Shades of Grey," *Economist*, April 26, 2014.

2. These quotations are taken from the film's trailer and from the title of a review in the *Guardian*. Invisible Woman [Helen Walmsley-Johnson], "Vintage Years Advanced Style: A Much More Joyous Way of Ageing," *Guardian*, May 7, 2014.

3. United Nations, Department of Economic and Social Affairs, Population Division, *World Population Ageing 2015* (New York: Department of Economic and Social Affairs United Nations, 2015), 1.

4. Michael Drexler, Head of Financial and Infrastructure Systems at the World Economic Forum, cited in Stella Papadopoulou, "Global Pension Timebomb: Funding Gap to Dwarf World GDP," *Modern Diplomacy*, May 29, 2017, www.moderndiplomacy.eu/2017/05/29/global-pension-timebomb-funding-gap-set-to-dwarf-world-gdp.

5. World Bank, *Live Long and Prosper: Aging in East Asia and Pacific*, World Bank East Asia and Pacific Regional Reports (Washington, DC: World Bank, 2016), 3, https://openknowledge.worldbank.org/bitstream/handle/10986/23133/9781464804694.pdf.

6. "Political Challenges Relating to the Ageing Population: Key Issues for the 2015 Parliament," UK Parliament website, Key Issues, May 2015, www

.parliament.uk/business/publications/research/key-issues-parliament-2015/social-change/ageing-population.

7. See Stephen Katz, *Disciplining Old Age: The Formation of Gerontological Knowledge,* Knowledge, Disciplinarity and Beyond (Charlottesville: University Press of Virginia, 1996).

8. Pat Thane, "The Debate on the Declining Birth-Rate in Britain: The 'Menace' of an Ageing Population, 1920s–1950s," *Continuity and Change* 5, no. 2 (1990): 285.

9. Ibid., 286.

10. Grace G. Leybourne White and Kenneth White, *Children for Britain, Target for Tomorrow* (London: Pilot Press, 1945).

11. Thane, "Declining Birth-Rate," 286–87.

12. Ibid., 289.

13. Patrice Bourdelais, "The Ageing of the Population: Relevant Question or Obsolete Notion?," in *Old Age from Antiquity to Post-modernity,* ed. Paul Johnson and Pat Thane (London: Routledge, 1998), 110–31.

14. Thane, *Old Age in English History,* 344–51.

15. Office for National Statistics, "Statistical Bulletin: Births in England and Wales; 2016," July 19, 2017, www.ons.gov.uk/peoplepopulationandcommunity/birthsdeathsandmarriages/livebirths/bulletins/birthsummarytablesenglandandwales/2016.

16. Pat Thane, "Population Politics in Post-war British Culture," in *Moments of Modernity: Reconstructing Britain 1945–1964,* ed. Becky Conekin, Frank Mort, and Chris Waters (London: Rivers Oram, 1999), 115, 292.

17. This is also a problem for predictions about fertility rates and immigration. See Pat Thane, *Demographic Futures: Addressing Inequality and Diversity among Older People* (London: British Academy, 2012), 29–31.

18. Office for National Statistics, "Overview of the UK Population; July 2017," July 21, 2017, www.ons.gov.uk/releases/overviewoftheukpopulationjuly2017.

19. Thane, *Old Age in English History,* 339–40.

20. Ellen M. Gee, "Population and Politics: Voodoo Demography, Population Aging, and Canadian Social Policy," in *The Overselling of Population Aging: Apocalyptic Demography, Intergenerational Challenges, and Social Policy,* ed. Ellen M. Gee and Gloria M. Gutman (Don Mills, ON: Oxford University Press, 2000), 5.

21. Ibid.; Brian Barry and Richard I. Sikora, *Obligations to Future Generations* (Philadelphia: Temple University Press, 1978).

22. Gee, "Population and Politics," 8. An alternative method is to count the number of people aged twenty to sixty-four in the labor force.

23. Spijker Jeroen and MacInnes John, "Population Ageing: The Time-bomb That Isn't?," *BMJ*, no. 347 (2013): 2.

24. The dependent population includes children as well as the elderly.

25. Gee, "Population and Politics," 17; Phil Mullan, *The Imaginary Time Bomb: Why an Ageing Population Is Not a Social Problem* (London: I.B. Tauris, 2000), 6.

26. Mullan, *Imaginary Time Bomb*, 6.

27. Ibid.

28. Jeroen and John, "Population Ageing," 1.

29. Ibid., 2.

30. Peter Townsend interviewed by Paul Thompson, part 1, 30 June 1997, Pioneers of Social Research, UKDA.

31. See, for example, the research of Joanna Bornat and Bill Bytheway on the Oldest Generation project, which used 24 life history interviews, 3873 daily diary entries, and 824 photographs: "The Oldest Generation: Events, Relationships and Identities in Later Life," Timescapes: An ESRC Qualitative Longitudinal Initiative, School of Sociology and Social Policy, University of Leeds, www.timescapes.leeds.ac.uk/research/oldest-generation.html.

32. Julia Johnson, Sheena Rolph, and Randall Smith, *Residential Care Transformed: Revisiting "The Last Refuge"* (Basingstoke: Palgrave Macmillan, 2010), 65.

33. Ibid., 84.

34. Ibid., 66. All but five of these fifty-three homes had closed.

35. Ibid., 70.

36. Ibid., 75.

37. Peter Townsend interviewed by Paul Thompson, part 3, November 24, 1997, Pioneers of Social Research, UKDA.

38. Ibid.

39. Means, Morbey, and Smith, *From Community Care to Market Care?*, 101.

40. Ibid., 32.

41. Ibid., 102–5.

42. Ibid., 79–82.

43. Ibid.

44. Ibid., 27.

45. Ibid., 36.

46. Ibid., 38.

47. Ibid., 54.

48. Tim Booth, *Home Truths: Old People's Homes and the Outcome of Care* (Aldershot: Gower, 1985), 27.

49. Means, Morbey, and Smith, *From Community Care to Market Care?*, 58.

50. Johnson, Rolph, and Smith, *Residential Care Transformed*, 21.

51. Ibid., 29.

52. Means, Morbey, and Smith, *From Community Care to Market Care?*, 62.

53. Ibid., 64–68.

54. Ibid., 4, 99, 112.

55. Johnson, Rolph, and Smith, *Residential Care Transformed*, 23.

56. Ibid., 78.

57. Means, Morbey, and Smith, *From Community Care to Market Care?*, 164.

58. Ibid.

59. Johnson, Rolph, and Smith, *Residential Care Transformed*, 211.

60. Ibid., 215–16.

61. Michael Marmot, "The Rise in Life Expectancy in the UK Is Slowing," *Huffington Post,* July 20, 2017, www.huffingtonpost.co.uk/michael-marmot/the-rise-in-life-expectancy_b_17535686.html.

62. Institute of Health Equity, "Marmot Indicators 2017: Institute of Health Equity Briefing," July 18, 2017, www.instituteofhealthequity.org/resources-reports/marmot-indicators-2017-institute-of-health-equity-briefing/marmot-indicators-briefing-2017-updated.pdf.

63. Denis Campbell, "Rise in Life Expectancy Has Stalled since 2010, Research Shows," *Guardian,* July 18, 2017, www.theguardian.com/society/2017/jul/18/rise-in-life-expectancy-has-stalled-since-2010-research-shows.

64. John Hills, *The Coalition's Record on Cash Transfers, Poverty and Inequality 2010–2015,* Social Policy in a Cold Climate (London: Centre for Analysis of Social Exclusion, London School of Economics, 2015), 32.

65. Tania Burchardt, Polina Obolenskaya, and Polly Vizard, *The Coalition's Record on Adult Social Care: Policy, Spending and Outcomes 2010–2015,* Social Policy in a Cold Climate (London: Centre for Analysis of Social Exclusion, London School of Economics, 2015).

66. Marmot, "Rise in Life Expectancy."

67. Johnson, Rolph, and Smith, *Residential Care Transformed*, 85.

68. Ibid., 90–94.

69. Townsend, *Last Refuge*, 72.

70. Johnson, Rolph, and Smith, *Residential Care Transformed*, 88.

71. Ibid., 101.

72. Ibid., 100.

73. Ibid., 102.
74. Ibid., 140.
75. Ibid., 156, 62.
76. Ibid., 139.
77. Ibid., 126.
78. Ibid., 146–50.
79. Ibid., 120–22.
80. Chris Phillipson, *The Family and Community Life of Older People: Social Networks and Social Support in Three Urban Areas* (London: Routledge, 2001), 42.
81. Ibid., 41–42.
82. Ibid., 189–90.
83. Ibid., 58, 61, 187.
84. Ibid., 254.
85. Ibid., 159.
86. Ibid., 158–59.
87. Ibid., 160.
88. Ibid., 251.
89. Thane, *Demographic Futures*, 34.
90. Hills, *Coalition's Record*, 18.
91. Johnson, Rolph, and Smith, *Residential Care Transformed*, 46.
92. Ibid., 47.
93. Dana Rosenfeld, *The Changing of the Guard: Lesbian and Gay Elders, Identity, and Social Change* (Philadelphia: Temple University Press, 2003); Dana Rosenfeld, Bernadette Bartlam, and Ruth D. Smith, "Out of the Closet and into the Trenches: Gay Male Baby Boomers, Aging, and HIV/AIDS," *Gerontologist* 52, no. 2 (2012): 255–64; Steven P. Wainwright and Bryan S. Turner, "Aging and the Dancing Body," in *Aging Bodies: Images and Everyday Experience*, ed. Christopher A. Faircloth (Walnut Creek, CA: AltaMira, 2003), 259–92; Emmanuelle Tulle, *Ageing, the Body and Social Change: Running in Later Life* (Basingstoke: Palgrave Macmillan, 2008).
94. Jo Spence, *Beyond the Perfect Image: Photography, Subjectivity, Antagonism*, ed. Museu d'Art Contemporani de Barcelona (Barcelona: Museu d'Art Contemporani de Barcelona, 2005), exhibition catalogue, 172.
95. Shirley Dex and Heather Joshi, eds., *Millennium Cohort Study First Survey: A User's Guide to Initial Findings* (London: Centre for Longitudinal Studies; Bedford Group for Lifecourse and Statistical Studies; and Institute of Education, University of London, 2004).

96. Jan Van Bavel and Tom De Winter, "Becoming a Grandparent and Early Retirement in Europe," *European Sociological Review* 29, no. 6 (2013): 1295–308.

97. Thane, *Demographic Futures*, 36.

98. Ibid., 37.

99. Fraser, "Contradictions of Capital and Care," 114.

100. Ibid., 115–16.

BIBLIOGRAPHY

ARCHIVAL COLLECTIONS

Charles Booth Archive. London School of Economics Library, London School of Economics. https://booth.lse.ac.uk.
Geoffrey Gorer Archive. University of Sussex.
Mass Observation Archive. University of Sussex.
Peter Townsend Collection. National Social Policy and Social Change Archive. Albert Sloman Library, University of Essex, Colchester.
Pioneers of Social Research Collection. United Kingdom Data Archives. University of Essex.
Walter Greenwood Collection. Clifford Whitworth Library, University of Salford, Manchester.

NEWSPAPERS, PERIODICALS, AND PARLIAMENTARY DEBATES

Good Housekeeping, 1934–65.
Hansard parliamentary debates, 1942–65.
Manchester Guardian, 1945–49.
Observer, 1945.
Vogue (UK), 1937–65.
Woman, 1939–70.
Woman's Own, 1937–62.
Women's Weekly, 1930–70.

PUBLISHED SOURCES

Abel-Smith, Brian. "The Beveridge Report: Its Origins and Outcomes." In *Beveridge and Social Security: An International Retrospective*, edited by John Hills, John Ditch, and Howard Glennerster, 10–22. Oxford: Clarendon Press, 1994.

Achenbaum, W. Andrew. "Toward a Pschohistory of Late-Life Emotionality." In *An Emotional History of the United States*, edited by Peter N. Stearns and Jan Lewis, 417–30. New York: New York University Press, 1998.

Ackerley, J. R. *My Father and Myself.* Harmondsworth: Penguin, 1971.

Adams, G. F., Eric Arthur Cheeseman, and Northern Ireland Hospitals Authority. *Old People in Northern Ireland: A Report to the Northern Ireland Hospitals Authority on the Medical Social Problems of Old Age*. Belfast: Northern Ireland Hospitals Authority, 1951.

Adams, John. "The Last Years of the Workhouse, 1930–1965." In *Oral History, Health and Welfare*, edited by Joanna Bornat, 98–118. London: Routledge, 2000.

Adams, Sheila. "A Gendered History of the Social Management of Death in Folehill, Coventry, During the Interwar Years." In *The Sociology of Death*, edited by David Clark, 149–68. Oxford: Blackwell, 1993.

Amulree, William Warrender Mackenzie. *Adding Life to Years*. London: National Council of Social Service, 1951.

Arnold, Rebecca. "Goalen, Barbara Kathleen (1921–2002)." In *Oxford Dictionary of National Biography*. Oxford University Press, 2004; online ed., 2006. https://doi.org/10.1093/ref:odnb/76961.

Athill, Diana. *Somewhere towards the End*. London: Granta Books, 2008.

Bailey, Paul. "Pritchett, Sir Victor Sawdon (1900–1997)." In *Oxford Dictionary of National Biography*. Oxford: Oxford University Press, 2004; online ed., 2014. https://doi.org/10.1093/ref:odnb/65704.

Bailkin, Jordanna. *The Afterlife of Empire*. Berkeley: University of California Press, 2012.

Bamlett, R. B., and H. C. Milligan. "Health and Welfare Services and the Over 75s: A Geriatric Survey at West Hartlepool." *Medical Officer* 109 (1963): 379–85.

Banner, Lois W. *In Full Flower: Aging Women, Power, and Sexuality; A History*. New York: Knopf, 1992.

Barr, Pat, and National Old People's Welfare Council. *The Elderly: Handbook on Care and Services*. London: National Council of Social Service, 1968.

Barry, Brian, and Richard I. Sikora. *Obligations to Future Generations.* Philadelphia: Temple University Press, 1978.

Benson, John. *Prime Time: A History of Middle Age in Twentieth-Century Britain.* London: Longman, 1997.

Blackhouse, Roger E., and Tamotsu Nishizawa. *No Wealth but Life: Welfare Economics and the Welfare State in Britain, 1880–1945.* New York: Cambridge University Press, 2010.

Blackman, Cally. *100 Years of Fashion Illustration.* London: Laurence King, 2007.

"Book Notes." *Public Administration* 41, no. 4 (1963): 427–33.

Booth, Charles. *Life and Labour of the People in London: 1st Series; Poverty.* 5 vols. London: Macmillan, 1902.

———. *Life and Labour of the People in London: 2nd Series; Industry.* 5 vols. London: Macmillan, 1903.

———. *Life and Labour of the People in London: 3rd Series; Religious Influences.* 8 vols. London: Macmillan, 1902.

———. *Old Age Pensions and the Aged Poor: A Proposal.* London: Macmillan, 1899.

———. *Pauperism, a Picture; And Endowment of Old Age, an Argument.* London: Macmillan, 1892.

Booth, Charles, Richard M. Elman, and Albert Fried. *Charles Booth's London: A Portrait of the Poor at the Turn of the Century, Drawn from "Life and Labour of the People in London."* London: Hutchinson, 1969.

Booth, Tim. *Home Truths: Old People's Homes and the Outcome of Care.* Aldershot: Gower, 1985.

Botelho, Lynn A. "'An Idle Youth Makes a Needy Old Age': The 17th Century." In *The Long History of Old Age,* edited by Pat Thane, 113–73. London: Thames and Hudson, 2005.

Bourdelais, Patrice. "The Ageing of the Population: Relevant Question or Obsolete Notion?" In *Old Age from Antiquity to Post-modernity,* edited by Paul Johnson and Pat Thane, 110–31. London: Routledge, 1998.

Bowley, A.L., and Alexander Robert Burnett-Hurst. *Livelihood and Poverty: A Study in the Economic Conditions of Working-Class Households in Northampton, Warrington, Stanley and Reading.* London: G. Bell and Sons, 1915.

Boyd, Brian. *On the Origin of Stories: Evolution, Cognition, and Fiction.* Cambridge, MA: Belknap Press of Harvard University Press, 2009.

Breward, Christopher. *The Culture of Fashion: A New History of Fashionable Dress.* Manchester: Manchester University Press, 1995.

———. *The Hidden Consumer: Masculinities, Fashion and City Life 1860–1914*. Manchester: Manchester University Press, 1999.

Breward, Christopher, Becky Conekin, and Caroline Cox. "Introduction: 'Dyed in the Wool English?'" In *The Englishness of English Dress*, edited by Becky Conekin and Caroline Cox, 1–12. Oxford: Berg, 2002.

Brierley, Walter. *Means Test Man*. London: Methuen, 1935.

Brockington, Fraser, and Susanne M. Lempert. *The Social Needs of the Over-80's: The Stockport Survey*. Manchester: Manchester University Press, 1966.

Brooke, Stephen. "Revisiting Southam Street: Class, Generation, Gender, and Race in the Photography of Roger Mayne." *Journal of British Studies* 53, no. 2 (2014): 453–96.

Brown, Callum G. *The Death of Christian Britain: Understanding Secularisation 1800–2000*. London: Routledge, 2001.

———. "Women and Religion in Britain: The Autobiographical View of the Fifties and Sixties." In *Secularisation in the Christian World: Essays in Honour of Hugh McLeod*, edited by Callum G. Brown and M. F. Snape, 159–73. Farnham: Ashgate, 2010.

Brown, Susan, Patricia Clements, and Isobel Grundy, eds. "Marie Belloc Lowndes." In *Orlando: Women's Writing in the British Isles from the Beginnings to the Present*. Cambridge: Cambrigde University Press Online, 2006. http://orlando.cambridge.org/public/svPeople?person_id=lownma.

Bulmer, Martin, Kevin Bales, and Kathryn Kish Sklar. Introduction to *The Social Survey in Historical Perspective, 1880–1940*, edited by Martin Bulmer, Kevin Bales, and Kathryn Kish Sklar, 1–48. Cambridge: Cambridge University Press, 1991.

Burchardt, Tania, Polina Obolenskaya, and Polly Vizard. *The Coalition's Record on Adult Social Care: Policy, Spending and Outcomes 2010–2015*. Social Policy in a Cold Climate. London: Centre for Analysis of Social Exclusion, London School of Economics, 2015.

Burgess, E. W. *Aging in Western Societies*. Chicago: University of Chicago Press, 1960.

Burnett, John, David Vincent, and David Mayall. *The Autobiography of the Working Class: An Annotated, Critical Bibliography: 1790–1900*. Vol. 1. Brighton: Harvester, 1984.

Burton, H. M. *There Was a Young Man*. London: G. Bles, 1958.

Bytheway, Bill, and Julia Johnson. "The Sight of Old Age." In *The Body in Everyday Life*, edited by Sarah Nettleton and Jonathan Watson, 243–57. London: Routledge, 1998.

Calder, Angus, Dorothy Sheridan, Tom Harrisson, and Mass-Observation Archive. *Speak for Yourself: A Mass-Observation Anthology, 1937–1949.* Oxford: Oxford University Press, 1985.
Campbell, Denis. "Rise in Life Expectancy Has Stalled since 2010, Research Shows." *Guardian,* July 18, 2017. www.theguardian.com/society/2017/jul/18/rise-in-life-expectancy-has-stalled-since-2010-research-shows.
Chamberlain, Lilian. *Mrs. C. in Residence.* Edinburgh: Pentland, 1997.
Chase, Karen. *The Victorians and Old Age.* Oxford: Oxford University Press, 2009.
Chinn, Carl. *Poverty amidst Prosperity: The Urban Poor in England, 1834–1914.* Lancaster: Carnegie, 2006.
Church, Richard. *The Voyage Home.* London: Heinemann, 1964.
Coates, Ken, and Richard Silburn. *Beyond the Bulldozer.* Nottingham: Department of Adult Education, University of Nottingham, 1980.
Coates, Ken, Richard Silburn, and St. Ann's Study Group. *Poverty, Deprivation and Morale in a Nottingham Community: St. Ann's; A Report of the Preliminary Findings of the St. Ann's Study Group.* Nottingham: Department of Adult Education, Nottingham University, 1967.
Cohen, Deborah. *Family Secrets: Living with Shame from the Victorians to the Present Day.* London: Viking, 2013.
Cole, Thomas R., and Claudia Edwards. "'Don't Complain about Old Age': The 19th Century." In *The Long History of Old Age,* edited by Pat Thane, 211–62. London: Thames and Hudson, 2005.
Collins, Alan. "The Psychology of Memory." In *Psychology in Britain: Historical Essays and Personal Reflections,* edited by G.D. Bunn, A.D. Lovie, and G.D. Richards, 150–68. Leicester: BPS Books, 2001.
Conekin, Becky E. "From Haughty to Nice: How British Fashion Images Changed from the 1950s to the 1960s." *Photography and Culture* 3, no. 3 (2010): 283–96.
Conekin, Becky, Frank Mort, and Chris Waters. Introduction to *Moments of Modernity: Reconstructing Britain 1945–1964,* edited by Becky Conekin, Frank Mort, and Chris Waters, 1–21. London: Rivers Oram, 1999.
Conor, Liz. *The Spectacular Modern Woman: Feminine Visibility in the 1920s.* Bloomington: Indiana University Press, 2004.
Conrad, Christopher. "Old Age and the Health Care System in the Nineteenth and Twentieth Centuries." In *Old Age from Antiquity to Post-Modernity,* edited by Paul Johnson and Pat Thane, 132–45. London: Routledge, 1998.
Cookson, Catherine. *Our Kate.* London: Macdonald, 1990.

Corti, Louise. "Recent Developments in Archiving Social Research." *International Journal of Social Research Methodology* 15, no. 4 (2012): 281–90.

Corti, Louise, and Paul Thompson. "Secondary Analysis of Archive Data." In *Qualitative Research Practice,* edited by Clive Seale, Giampietro Gobo, Jaber F Gubrium, and David Silverman, 327–43. London: Sage Publications, 2004.

Cox, Howard, and Simon Mowatt. "Vogue in Britain: Authenticity and the Creation of Competitive Advantage in the UK Magazine Industry." *Business History* 54, no. 1 (2012): 67–87.

Csikszentmihalyi, Mihaly, and Eugene Rochberg-Halton. *The Meaning of Things: Domestic Symbols and the Self.* Cambridge: Cambridge University Press, 1981.

Cumming, Elaine, and William Earl Henry. *Growing Old: The Process of Disengagement.* New York: Basic Books, 1961.

Daley, Caroline. *Leisure and Pleasure: Reshaping and Revealing the New Zealand Body 1900–1960.* Auckland: Auckland University Press, 2003.

Dawson, Graham. "The Blonde Bedouin." In *Manful Assertions: Masculinities in Britain since 1800,* edited by Michael Roper and John Tosh, 113–44. London: Routledge, 1991.

Delap, Lucy. "Conservative Values, Anglicans, and the Gender Order in Interwar Britain." In *Brave New World: Imperial and Democratic Nation Building in Britain between the Wars,* edited by Laura Beers and Geraint Thomas, 149–68. London: Institute of Historical Research Publications, 2012.

Dennis, Norman. *People and Planning: The Sociology of Housing in Sunderland.* London: Faber, 1970.

Dex, Shirley, and Heather Joshi, eds. *Millennium Cohort Study First Survey: A User's Guide to Initial Findings.* London: Centre for Longitudinal Studies; Bedford Group for Lifecourse and Statistical Studies; and Institute of Education, University of London, 2004.

Dyhouse, Carol. *Glamour: Women, History, Feminism.* London: Zed, 2010.

Eakin, Paul John. *Fictions in Autobiography: Studies in the Art of Self-Invention.* Princeton: Princeton University Press, 1985.

Edge, J.R., and I.D.M. Nelson. "Survey of Arrangements for the Elderly in Barrow-in-Furness." *Medical Care* 1, no. 4 (1963): 202–18.

Englander, David, and Rosemary O'Day. *Retrieved Riches: Social Investigation in Britain 1840–1914.* Aldershot: Scolar, 1995.

English, John, Ruth Madigan, and Peter C. Norman. *Slum Clearance: The Social and Administrative Context in England and Wales.* London: Croom Helm, 1976.

Feather, John. *A History of British Publishing*. 2nd ed. London: Routledge, 2006.
Featherstone, Mike, and Andrew Wernick. *Images of Aging: Cultural Representations of Later Life*. London: Routledge, 1995.
Fielding, Nigel. "Getting the Most from Archived Qualitative Data: Epistemological, Practical and Professional Obstacles." *International Journal of Social Research Methodology* 7, no. 1 (2004): 97–104.
Foakes, Grace. *Between High Walls: A London Childhood*. 2nd ed. Oxford: Athena Books, 1972.
———. *My Part of the River*. London: Futura, 1974.
Frankenberg, Ronald. *Communities in Britain: Social Life in Town and Country*. Harmondsworth: Penguin, 1966.
Fraser, Nancy. "Contradictions of Capital and Care." *New Left Review* 100 (2016): 99–117.
Furman, Frida Kerner. *Facing the Mirror: Older Women and Beauty Shop Culture*. New York: Routledge, 1997.
Gee, Ellen M. "Population and Politics: Voodoo Demography, Population Aging, and Canadian Social Policy." In *The Overselling of Population Aging: Apocalyptic Demography, Intergenerational Challenges, and Social Policy*, edited by Ellen M. Gee and Gloria M. Gutman, 5–25. Don Mills, ON: Oxford University Press, 2000.
Gidley, Ben. *The Proletarian Other: Charles Booth and the Politics of Representation*. London: Goldsmiths University of London, 2000.
Gillies, Val, and Rosalind Edwards. "Working with Archived Classic Family and Community Studies: Illuminating Past and Present Conventions around Acceptable Research Practice." *International Journal of Social Research Methodology* 15, no. 4 (2012): 321–30.
Goldthorpe, John H. *The Affluent Worker in the Class Structure*. Cambridge Studies in Sociology. London: Cambridge University Press, 1969.
Gorer, Geoffrey. *Death, Grief, and Mourning in Contemporary Britain*. London: Cresset Press, 1965.
Grant, Linda. *The Thoughtful Dresser: The Art of Adornment, the Pleasures of Shopping, and Why Clothes Matter*. New York: Scribner, 2010.
Great Britain Ministry of Housing and Local Government. *The Deeplish Study: Improvement Possibilities in a District of Rochdale*. London: Her Majesty's Stationery Office, 1966.
Greenfield, Jill, Sean O'Connell, and Chris Reid. "Fashioning Masculinity: Men Only, Consumption and the Development of Marketing in the 1930s." *Twentieth Century British History* 10, no. 4 (1999): 457–76.

Greenfield, Jill, and Chris Reid. "Women's Magazines and the Commercial Orchestration of Femininity in the 1930s: Evidence from Woman's Own." *Media History* 4, no. 2 (1998): 161–74.

Greenhalgh, Charlotte. "Love in Later Life: Old Age, Marriage and Social Research in Mid-Twentieth-Century Britain." In *Love and Romance in Britain, 1918–1970*, edited by Alana Harris and Timothy Willem Jones, 144–60. Basingstoke: Palgrave Macmillan, 2015.

Greenwood, Walter. *Love on the Dole: A Tale of the Two Cities*. London: J. Cape, 1933.

———. *There Was a Time*. London: J. Cape, 1967.

Gubrium, Jaber F., and James A. Holstein. "The Everyday Visibility of the Aging Body." In *Aging Bodies: Images and Everyday Experience*, edited by Christopher A. Faircloth, 205–27. Walnut Creek, CA: AltaMira, 2003.

Gusdorf, George. "Conditions and Limits of Autobiography." In *Autobiography: Essays Theoretical and Critical*, edited by James Olney, 28–48. Princeton: Princeton University Press, 1980.

Haldane, Elizabeth Sanderson. *From One Century to Another: The Reminiscences of Elizabeth S. Haldane*. London: A. Maclehose, 1937.

Hall, Edith. *Canary Girls and Stockpots*. Luton: Workers' Educational Association, Luton Branch, 1977.

Hall, G. Stanley. *Senescence, the Last Half of Life*. New York: D. Appleton, 1922.

Halls, Zillah. "Mrs Exeter: The Rise and Fall of the Older Woman." *Costume* 34 (2000): 105–12.

Halsey, A.H. *A History of Sociology in Britain: Science, Literature, and Society*. Oxford: Oxford University Press, 2004.

Harper, Sarah, and Pat Thane. "The Consolidation of 'Old Age' as a Phase of Life, 1945–1965." In *Growing Old in the Twentieth Century*, edited by Margot Jefferys, 43–61. London: Routledge, 1989.

Harris, Amelia I., Rosemary Clausen, National Corporation for the Care of Old Peole, and Great Britain Scottish Home and Health Department. *Social Welfare for the Elderly: A Study in Thirteen Local Authority Areas in England, Wales and Scotland*. London: Her Majesty's Stationery Office, 1968.

Hartog, Hendrik. *Someday All This Will Be Yours: A History of Inheritance and Old Age*. Cambridge, MA: Harvard University Press, 2012.

Hazell, Kenneth. *Social and Medical Problems of the Elderly*. London: Hutchinson Medical Publications, 1960.

Heath, Kay. *Aging by the Book: The Emergence of Midlife in Victorian Britain*. Albany: SUNY Press, 2009.

Henrey, Robert. *The Golden Visit*. London: J. M. Dent, 1979.
———. *Her April Days*. London: Dent, 1963.
———. *Winter Wild*. London: Dent, 1966.
Hilliard, Christopher. *To Exercise Our Talents: The Democratization of Writing in Britain*. Harvard Historical Studies. Cambridge, MA: Harvard University Press, 2006.
Hills, John. *The Coalition's Record on Cash Transfers, Poverty and Inequality 2010–2015*. Social Policy in a Cold Climate. London: Centre for Analysis of Social Exclusion, London School of Economics, 2015.
Hilton, Claire. "The Clinical Psychiatry of Late Life in Britain from 1950 to 1970: An Overview." *International Journal of Geriatric Psychiatry* 20, no. 5 (2005): 423–28.
———. "The Origins of Old Age Psychiatry in Britain in the 1940s." *History of Psychiatry* 16, no. 3 (2005): 267–89.
Hinton, James. "'The "Class" Complex': Mass-Observation and Cultural Distinction in Pre-War Britain." *Past and Present* 199, no. 1 (2008): 207–36.
———. *The Mass Observers: A History, 1937–1949*. Oxford: Oxford University Press, 2013.
Hobson, Will, and John Pemberton. *The Health of the Elderly at Home: A Medical, Social and Dietary Study of Elderly People Living at Home in Sheffield*. London: Butterworth, 1955.
Hockey, Jenny, and Allison James. "Back to Our Futures: Imagining Second Childhood." In *Images of Aging: Cultural Representations of Later Life*, edited by Mike Featherstone and Andrew Wernick, 135–48. London: Routledge, 1995.
Holman, Robert. *Champions for Children: The Lives of Modern Child Care Pioneers*. Bristol: Policy, 2001.
"Horace Horsnell." *Manchester Guardian*, February 12, 1949, p. 4.
Horwell, Veronica. "Obituary: Barbara Goalen." *Guardian*, June 22, 2002. www.guardian.co.uk/news/2002/jun/22/guardianobituaries.veronicahorwell.
Horwood, Catherine. "Housewives' Choice: Women as Consumers between the Wars." *History Today* 47, no. 3 (1997): 23–28.
———. *Keeping Up Appearances: Fashion and Class between the Wars*. Stroud: Sutton, 2005.
Houlbrook, Matt. "Commodifying the Self Within: Ghosts, Libels, and the Crook Life Story in Interwar Britain." *Journal of Modern History* 85, no. 2 (2013): 321–63.
———. "The Man with the Powder Puff in Interwar London." *Historical Journal* 50, no. 1 (2007): 145–71.

———. "'A Pin to See the Peepshow': Culture, Fiction and Selfhood in Edith Thompson's Letters, 1921–1922." *Past and Present* 207, no. 1 (2010): 215–49.

———. *Prince of Tricksters: The Incredible True Story of Netley Lucas, Gentleman Crook*. Chicago: University of Chicago Press, 2016.

Howell, Trevor Henry. *Our Advancing Years: An Essay on Modern Problems of Old Age*. London: Phoenix House, 1953.

Hussey, Stephen. "'An Inheritance of Fear': Older Women in the Twentieth-Century Countryside." In *Women and Ageing in British Society since 1500*, edited by Lynn Botelho and Pat Thane, 186–206. Harlow: Longman, 2001.

Invisible Woman [Helen Walmsley-Johnson]. "Vintage Years Advanced Style: A Much More Joyous Way of Ageing." *Guardian*, May 7, 2014.

Jahoda, Marie, Thomas Elsaesser, Paul Felix Lazarsfeld, John Reginall, and Hans Zeisel. *Marienthal: The Sociography of an Unemployed Community*. London: Tavistock, 1972.

Jameson, Storm. *Journey from the North: Autobiography of Storm Jameson*. 2 vols. London: Virago, 1984.

Jeffery, Tom. *Mass-Observation: A Short History*. 2nd ed. Brighton: Mass-Observation Archive, 1999.

Jeroen, Spijker, and MacInnes John. "Population Ageing: The Timebomb That Isn't?" *BMJ*, no. 347 (2013): 1–5.

Jerrome, Dorothy. *Good Company: An Anthropological Study of Old People in Groups*. Edinburgh: Edinburgh University Press, 1992.

John, Augustus. *Chiaroscuro: Fragments of Autobiography; First Series*. London: J. Cape, 1952.

Johnson, Julia, Sheena Rolph, and Randall Smith. *Residential Care Transformed: Revisiting "The Last Refuge."* Basingstoke: Palgrave Macmillan, 2010.

———. "Revisiting 'The Last Refuge': Present Day Methodological Challenges." In *Critical Perspectives on Ageing Societies*, edited by Miriam Bernard and Thomas Scharf, 89–104. Bristol: Policy, 2007.

Johnson, Paul. "Historical Readings of Old Age and Ageing." In *Old Age from Antiquity to Post-Modernity*, edited by Paul Johnson and Pat Thane, 1–18. London: Routledge, 1998.

———. "Parallel Histories of Retirement in Modern Britain." In *Old Age from Antiquity to Post-Modernity*, edited by Paul Johnson and Pat Thane, 211–25. London: Routledge, 1998.

Jones, Ben. "Surveying Slum Clearance in Post-war England." Paper presented at the Re-analysing Social Survey Data colloquium, Emmanuel College, University of Cambridge, September 8, 2012.

———. "The Uses of Nostalgia: Autobiography, Community Publishing and Working Class Neighbourhoods in Post-war England." *Cultural and Social History* 7, no. 3 (2010): 355–74.

———. *The Working Class in Mid-Twentieth-Century England: Community, Identity and Social Memory*. Manchester: Manchester University Press, 2012.

Jones, D. Caradog, and University of Liverpool. *The Social Survey of Merseyside*. 3 vols. Liverpool: University Press of Liverpool, 1934.

Joy, Thomas. *Mostly Joy: A Bookman's Story*. London: Joseph, 1971.

Katz, Stephen. *Disciplining Old Age: The Formation of Gerontological Knowledge*. Charlottesville: University Press of Virginia, 1996.

Klein, Josephine. *Samples from English Cultures*. 2 vols. London: Routledge and Kegan Paul, 1965.

Koven, Seth. "The Dangers of Castle Building: Surveying the Social Survey." In *The Social Survey in Historical Perspective, 1880–1940*, edited by Martin Bulmer, Kevin Bales, and Kathryn Kish Sklar, 368–76. Cambridge: Cambridge University Press, 1991.

Land, Hilary, and Hilary Rose. "Peter Townsend, a Man ahead of His Time: Re-Reading *The Family Life of Old People* and *The Last Refuge*." In *Fighting Poverty, Inequality and Injustice: A Manifesto Inspired by Peter Townsend*, edited by Alan Walker, Adrian Sinfield, and Carol Walker, 59–78. Bristol: Policy, 2011.

Langhamer, Claire. *The English in Love: The Intimate Story of an Emotional Revolution*. Oxford: Oxford University Press, 2013.

———. "The Meanings of Home in Postwar Britain." *Journal of Contemporary History* 40, no. 2 (2005): 341–62.

———. "'Who the Hell Are Ordinary People?': Ordinariness as a Category of Historical Analysis." Paper presented at the Royal Historical Society Lecture, University College London, February 10, 2017.

———. *Women's Leisure in England, 1920–60*. Studies in Popular Culture. Manchester: Manchester University Press, 2000.

Laslett, Peter. *A Fresh Map of Life: The Emergence of the Third Age*. 2nd ed. Basingstoke: Macmillan, 1996.

———. "Necessary Knowledge: Age and Aging in the Societies of the Past." In *Aging in the Past: Demography, Society, and Old Age*, edited by David I. Kertzer and Peter Laslett, 3–77. Berkeley: University of California Press, 1995.

Lawrence, Jon. "Paternalism, Class, and the British Path to Modernity." In *The Peculiarities of Liberal Modernity in Imperial Britain,* edited by Simon Gunn and James Vernon, 147–64. Berkeley: University of California Press, 2011.

———. "Social-Science Encounters and the Negotiation of Difference in Early 1960s England." *History Workshop Journal* 77, no. 1 (2014): 215–39.

Lejeune, Philippe, and Paul John Eakin. *On Autobiography.* Theory and History of Literature 52. Minneapolis: University of Minnesota Press, 1989.

Light, Alison. *Common People: The History of an English Family.* London: Fig Tree, 2014.

Loftus, Donna. "The Self in Society: Middle-Class Men and Autobiography." In *Life Writing and Victorian Culture,* edited by David Amigoni, 67–85. Aldershot: Ashgate, 2006.

Macnicol, John. *The Politics of Retirement in Britain, 1878–1948.* Cambridge: Cambridge University Press, 1998.

Maguire, Paddy, David Morley, and Ken Worpole. *The Republic of Letters: Working Class Writing and Local Publishing.* London: Comedia Publishing Group, 1982.

Mandler, Peter. "Being His Own Rabbit: Geoffrey Gorer and English Culture." In *Cultures, Classes, and Politics: Essays on British History for Ross McKibbin,* edited by C. V. J. Griffiths, James J. Nott, and William Whyte, 192–208. Oxford: Oxford University Press, 2011.

———. *The Uses of Charity: The Poor on Relief in the Nineteenth-Century Metropolis.* Philadelphia: University of Pennsylvania Press, 1990.

Marcus, Sharon. *Between Women: Friendship, Desire, and Marriage in Victorian England.* Princeton: Princeton University Press, 2007.

Marmot, Michael. "The Rise in Life Expectancy in the UK Is Slowing." *Huffington Post,* July 20, 2017. www.huffingtonpost.co.uk/michael-marmot/the-rise-in-life-expectancy_b_17535686.html.

Mason, Mary G. "The Other Voice: Autobiographies of Women Writers." In *Autobiography: Essays Theoretical and Critical,* edited by James Olney, 207–35. Princeton: Princeton University Press, 1980.

Matthews, Dale A. "Dr. Marjory Warren and the Origin of British Geriatrics." *Journal of the American Geriatrics Society* 32, no. 4 (1984): 253–58.

Mayhew, Henry, and William Tuckniss. *London Labour and the London Poor: A Cyclopædia of the Condition and Earnings of Those That Will Work, Those That Cannot Work, and Those That Will Not Work.* 4 vols. London: Griffin, Bohn, and Company, 1861.

McKibbin, Ross. *Classes and Cultures: England, 1918–1951.* Oxford: Oxford University Press, 1998.

Means, Robin, Hazel Morbey, and Randall Smith. *From Community Care to Market Care? The Development of Welfare Services for Older People.* Bristol: Policy, 2002.

Means, Robin, and Randall Smith. *From Poor Law to Community Care: The Development of Welfare Services for Elderly People 1939–1971.* 2nd ed. Bristol: Policy, 1998.

Meara, Gwynne. *Juvenile Unemployment in South Wales.* Cardiff, 1936.

Methol, C.R. "Arcadian Days." *Times Literary Supplement,* October 11, 1941, p. 509.

Miller, Herbert Crossley. *The Ageing Countryman: A Socio-Medical Report on Old Age in a Country Practice.* London: National Corporation for the Care of Old People, 1963.

Ministry of Health (UK). *Welfare of Old People.* Circular 11/50. London: Ministry of Health, 1950.

Mitchell, Hannah Maria Webster. *The Hard Way Up: The Autobiography of Hannah Mitchell, Suffragette and Rebel.* London: Faber, 1968.

Mort, Frank. *Cultures of Consumption: Masculinities and Social Space in Late Twentieth-Century Britain.* London: Routledge, 1996.

———. "Social and Symbolic Fathers and Sons in Postwar Britain." *Journal of British Studies* 38, no. 3 (1999): 353–84.

Mort, Frank, and Peter Thompson. "Retailing, Commercial Culture and Masculinity in 1950s Britain: The Case of Montague Burton, the 'Tailor of Taste.'" *History Workshop Journal* 38, no. 1 (1994): 106–28.

Moscoso, Javier. *Pain: A Cultural History.* Basingstoke: Palgrave Macmillan, 2012.

Muirhead, John H., and John W. Harvey. *Reflections by a Journeyman in Philosophy on the Movements of Thought and Practice in His Time.* London: George Allen and Unwin, 1942.

Mulkay, Michael. "Social Death in Britain." In *The Sociology of Death,* edited by David Clark, 31–49. Oxford: Blackwell Publishers, 1993.

Mullan, Phil. *The Imaginary Time Bomb: Why an Ageing Population Is Not a Social Problem.* London: I.B. Tauris, 2000.

National Association for the Care of Old People. *The Interests of the Aged.* London: National Council of Social Service, 1950.

National Council of Social Service. *Caring for People: Staffing Residential Homes; The Reports of the Committee of Enquiry Set Up by the National Council of Social Service.* London: Allen and Unwin, 1967.

National Old People's Welfare Committee. *Age Is Opportunity: A New Guide to Practical Work for the Welfare of Old People*. London: National Council of Social Service, 1949.

———. *Old People's Welfare: A Guide to Practical Work for the Welfare of Old People*. London: National Council of Social Service, 1945.

———. *Report of the Conference on "The Care of Old People."* London: National Council of Social Service, 1947.

———. *The Welfare of Old People in Rural Areas*. London: National Council of Social Service, 1951.

———. *Welfare Problems of Old People*. London: National Council of Social Service, 1950.

———. *Working Together for Old People's Welfare*. London: National Council of Social Service, 1948.

Norman-Butler, Belinda. *Victorian Aspirations: The Life and Labour of Charles and Mary Booth*. London: Allen and Unwin, 1972.

Öberg, Peter. "Images versus Experience of the Aging Body." In *Aging Bodies: Images and Everyday Experience*, edited by Christopher A. Faircloth, 103–39. Walnut Creek, CA: AltaMira, 2003.

Olechnowicz, Andrzej. "Unemployed Workers, 'Enforced Leisure' and Education for 'the Right Use of Leisure' in Britain in the 1930s." *Labour History Review* 70, no. 1 (2005): 27–52.

Ortolano, Guy. *The Two Cultures Controversy: Science, Literature and Cultural Politics in Postwar Britain*. New York: Cambridge University Press, 2009.

Papadopoulou, Stella. "Global Pension Timebomb: Funding Gap to Dwarf World GDP." *Modern Diplomacy,* May 29, 2017. www.moderndiplomacy.eu/2017/05/29/global-pension-timebomb-funding-gap-set-to-dwarf-world-gdp.

Parkin, Tim. "'Old Age Has Always Been Revered': The Ancient Greek and Roman Worlds." In *The Long History of Old Age,* edited by Pat Thane, 31–70. London: Thames and Hudson, 2005.

Parsons, P. L. "Mental Health of Swansea's Old Folk." *British Journal of Preventive and Social Medicine* 19, no. 1 (1965): 43–47.

Parsons, Talcott. "The Kinship System of Contemporary United States." *American Anthropologist* 45 (1943): 22–38.

Paul, Albert. *Poverty: Hardship but Happiness; Those Were the Days, 1903–1917*. 3rd ed. Brighton: QueenSpark, 1981.

Peck, Winifred. *Home for the Holidays*. London: Faber and Faber, 1955.

Pedersen, Susan. *Family, Dependence, and the Origins of the Welfare State: Britain and France, 1914–1945*. Cambridge: Cambridge University Press, 1993.

Peiss, Kathy Lee. *Hope in a Jar: The Making of America's Beauty Culture*. New York: Metropolitan Books, 1998.

———. "Making Up, Making Over: Cosmetics, Consumer Culture, and Women's Identity." In *The Sex of Things: Gender and Consumption in Historical Perspective,* edited by Victoria de Grazia, 311–36. Berkeley: University of California Press, 1996.

Pember Reeves, Maud. *Round about a Pound a Week*. London: Virago, 1979.

Phillipson, Chris. *The Family and Community Life of Older People: Social Networks and Social Support in Three Urban Areas*. London: Routledge, 2001.

Political and Economic Planning. *The Exit from Industry*. London: Political and Economic Planning, 1935.

Port, Cynthia. "'Ages Are the Stuff': The Traffic in Ages in Interwar Britain." *National Women's Studies Association* 18, no. 1 (2006): 138–61.

Portelli, Alessandro. "'The Time of My Life': Functions of Time in Oral History." *International Journal of Oral History* 2, no. 3 (1981): 162–80.

Pratt, Henry J. *Gray Agendas: Interest Groups and Public Pensions in Canada, Britain, and the United States*. Ann Arbor: University of Michigan Press, 1993.

Pritchett, V. S. *A Cab at the Door: An Autobiography; Early Years*. London: Chatto and Windus, 1968.

———. *A Cab at the Door and Midnight Oil*. Harmondsworth: Penguin, 1979.

Quiller-Couch, Arthur. *The Oxford Book of English Verse, 1250–1900*. Oxford: Clarendon, 1919.

Ramsden, Stefan. "Remaking Working-Class Community: Sociability, Belonging and 'Affluence' in a Small Town, 1930–80." *Contemporary British History* 29, no. 1 (2015): 1–26.

Ravetz, Alison, and Richard Turkington. *The Place of Home: English Domestic Environments, 1914–2000*. London: E. and F. N. Spon, 1995.

Read, Herbert. *The Contrary Experience: Autobiographies*. London: Faber and Faber, 1973.

Reddy, William M. *The Navigation of Feeling: A Framework for the History of Emotions*. Cambridge: Cambridge University Press, 2001.

Richards, Graham. "Britain on the Couch: The Popularization of Psychoanalysis in Britain 1918–1940." *Science in Context* 13, no. 2 (2000): 183–230.

Richardson, I. M. *Age and Need: A Study of Older People in North-East Scotland*. Edinburgh: E. and S. Livingstone, 1964.

Roberts, Nesta. *Our Future Selves*. London: Allen and Unwin, 1970.

Roberts, Robert. *A Ragged Schooling: Growing Up in the Classic Slum*. Manchester: Manchester University Press, 1976.

Rodgers, Barbara N., and June Stevenson. *A New Portrait of Social Work: A Study of the Social Services in a Northern Town from Younghusband to Seebohm*. London: Heinemann Educational, 1973.

Roper, Michael. *The Secret Battle: Emotional Survival in the Great War*. Manchester: Manchester University Press, 2009.

———. "Splitting in Unsent Letters: Writing as a Social Practice and a Psychological Activity." *Social History* 26, no. 3 (2001): 318–39.

Rose, Nikolas S. *Inventing Our Selves: Psychology, Power and Personhood*. Cambridge: Cambridge University Press, 1996.

Rosenfeld, Dana. *The Changing of the Guard: Lesbian and Gay Elders, Identity, and Social Change*. Philadelphia: Temple University Press, 2003.

Rosenfeld, Dana, Bernadette Bartlam, and Ruth D. Smith. "Out of the Closet and into the Trenches: Gay Male Baby Boomers, Aging, and HIV/AIDS." *Gerontologist* 52, no. 2 (2012): 255–64.

Ross, E. Denison, and Alick Denison Ross. *Both Ends of the Candle: The Autobiography of Sir E. Denison Ross*. London: Faber and Faber, 1943.

Ross, Ellen. *Love and Toil: Motherhood in Outcast London, 1870–1918*. New York: Oxford University Press, 1993.

Rowntree, B. Seebohm. *Old People: Report of a Survey Committee on the Problems of Ageing and the Care of Old People*. London: Oxford University Press, 1947.

———. *Poverty: A Study of Town Life*. London: Macmillan, 1901.

Rowntree, B. Seebohm, and G. R. Lavers. *Poverty and the Welfare State: A Third Social Survey of York Dealing Only with Economic Questions*. London: Longmans Green, 1951.

Russell, Bertrand. *The Autobiography of Bertrand Russell*. 3 vols. New York: Bantam, 1968.

Saler, Michael. "'Clap If You Believe in Sherlock Holmes': Mass Culture and the Re-enchantment of Modernity, c. 1890–c. 1940." *Historical Journal* 46, no. 3 (2003): 599–622.

Salter, Tony. *100 Years of State Pension: Learning from the Past*. London: Faculty of Actuaries and Institute of Actuaries, 2009.

Savage, Mike. *Identities and Social Change in Britain since 1940: The Politics of Method*. Oxford: Oxford University Press, 2010.

———. "Working-Class Identities in the 1960s: Revisiting the Affluent Worker Study." *Sociology* 39, no. 5 (2005): 929–46.

Scarry, Elaine. *The Body in Pain: The Making and Unmaking of the World*. New York: Oxford University Press, 1985.

Scheer, Monique. "Are Emotions a Kind of Practice (and Is That What Makes Them Have a History)? A Bourdieuian Approach to Understanding Emotion." *History and Theory* 51, no. 2 (2012): 193–220.

Scott, Linda M. *Fresh Lipstick: Redressing Fashion and Feminism*. New York: Palgrave Macmillan, 2005.

Shahar, Shulamith. "'All Want to Reach Old Age but Nobody Wants to Be Old': The Middle Ages and Renaissance." In *The Long History of Old Age*, edited by Pat Thane, 71–112. London: Thames and Hudson, 2005.

———. *Growing Old in the Middle Ages: "Winter Clothes Us in Shadow and Pain."* London: Routledge, 1997.

Sheldon, J. H., and Nuffield Foundation. *The Social Medicine of Old Age: Report of an Inquiry in Wolverhampton*. London: Oxford University Press, 1948.

Slack, Kathleen M. *Councils, Committees, and Concern for the Old: A Study of the Provision, Extent, and Co-ordination of Certain Services for the Old People in the County of London*. Welwyn: Codicote Press, 1960.

Small, Helen. *The Long Life*. Oxford: Oxford University Press, 2007.

Smith, Hubert Llewellyn. *The New Survey of London Life and Labour*. 9 vols. London: P. S. King and Son, 1930.

Snellgrove, Douglas R. *Elderly Housebound: A Report on Elderly People Who Are Incapacitated*. Luton: White Crescent, 1963.

Spence, Jo. *Beyond the Perfect Image: Photography, Subjectivity, Antagonism*. Edited by Museu d'Art Contemporani de Barcelona. Barcelona: Museu d'Art Contemporani de Barcelona, 2005. Exhibition catalogue.

Steedman, Carolyn. "Enforced Narratives: Stories of Another Self." In *Feminism and Autobiography: Texts, Theories, Methods*, edited by Tess Casslett, Celia Lury, and Penny Summerfield, 25–39. London: Routledge, 2000.

———. *Landscape for a Good Woman*. London: Virago, 1986.

———. "State-Sponsored Autobiography." In *Moments of Modernity: Reconstructing Britain 1945–1964*, edited by Becky Conekin, Frank Mort, and Chris Waters, 41–54. London: Rivers Oram, 1999.

———. *Strange Dislocations: Childhood and the Idea of Human Interiority, 1780–1930*. London: Virago, 1995.

Szreter, Simon, and Kate Fisher. *Sex before the Sexual Revolution: Intimate Life in England 1918–1963*. Cambridge: Cambridge University Press, 2010.

Taylor, Jennie. "Mass Observation as Cultural Critic: The Problem of Leisure in the Worktown Study, 1937–1940." PhD diss., University of Sydney, 2012.

Thane, Pat. "The Debate on the Declining Birth-Rate in Britain: The 'Menace' of an Ageing Population, 1920s–1950s." *Continuity and Change* 5, no. 2 (1990): 283–305.

———. *Demographic Futures: Addressing Inequality and Diversity among Older People*. London: British Academy, 2012.

———, ed. *The Long History of Old Age*. London: Thames and Hudson, 2005.

———. "'My Age Is a Lusty Winter': The Age of Old Age." In *The Long History of Old Age*, edited by Pat Thane, 9–30. London: Thames and Hudson, 2005.

———. *Old Age in English History: Past Experiences, Present Issues*. Oxford: Oxford University Press, 2000.

———. "Older People and Equality." In *Unequal Britain: Equalities in Britain since 1945*, edited by Pat Thane, 7–28. London: Continuum UK, 2010.

———. "Old Women in Twentieth-Century Britain." In *Women and Ageing in British Society since 1500*, edited by L. A. Botelho and Pat Thane, 207–31. Harlow: Longman, 2001.

———. "Population Politics in Post-war British Culture." In *Moments of Modernity: Reconstructing Britain 1945–1964*, edited by Becky Conekin, Frank Mort, and Chris Waters, 114–33. London: Rivers Oram, 1999.

Thompson, Paul. "The Making of a Pioneer Researcher: Reflections from Peter Townsend's Life Story." In *Fighting Poverty, Inequality and Injustice: A Manifesto Inspired by Peter Townsend*, edited by Alan Walker, Adrian Sinfield, and Carol Walker, 29–58. Bristol: Policy, 2011.

Thomson, Alistair. *Anzac Memories: Living with the Legend*. Melbourne: Oxford University Press, 1994.

Thomson, Mathew. *Lost Freedom: The Landscape of the Child and the British Postwar Settlement*. Oxford: Oxford University Press, 2013.

———. *Psychological Subjects: Identity, Culture, and Health in Twentieth-Century Britain*. Oxford: Oxford University Press, 2006.

Todd, Selina. "Affluence, Class and Crown Street: Reinvestigating the Post-War Working Class." *Contemporary British History* 22, no. 4 (2008): 501–18.

———. *The People: The Rise and Fall of the Working Class, 1910–2010*. London: John Murray, 2014.

———. *Young Women, Work, and Family in England, 1918–1950*. Oxford: Oxford University Press, 2005.

Townsend, Peter. *The Family Life of Old People: An Inquiry in East London*. London: Routledge and Kegan Paul, 1957.

———. *The Last Refuge: A Survey of Residential Institutions and Homes for the Aged in England and Wales*. London: Routledge and Paul, 1962.
———. "Reflections on Becoming a Researcher." *International Journal of Social Research Methodology* 7, no. 1 (2004): 85–95.
Townsend, Peter, Dorothy Wedderburn, Sheila Benson, and Sylvia Korte. *The Aged in the Welfare State: The Interim Report of a Survey of Persons Aged 65 and over in Britain, 1962 and 1963*. London: G. Bell, 1965.
Troyansky, David G. "'Long Live the Republic where Old Men Preside': The 18th Century." In *The Long History of Old Age*, edited by Pat Thane, 175–210. London: Thames and Hudson, 2005.
Tulle, Emmanuelle. *Ageing, the Body and Social Change: Running in Later Life*. Basingstoke: Palgrave Macmillan, 2008.
Tunstall, Jeremy. *Old and Alone: A Sociological Study of Old People*. London: Routledge and Kegan Paul, 1966.
Twigg, Julia. "The Body and Bathing: Help with Personal Care at Home." In *Aging Bodies: Images and Everyday Experience*, edited by Christopher A. Faircloth, 143–69. Walnut Creek, CA: AltaMira, 2003.
United Nations, Department of Economic and Social Affairs, Population Division. *World Population Ageing 2015*. New York: Department of Economic and Social Affairs United Nations, 2015.
Van Bavel, Jan, and Tom De Winter. "Becoming a Grandparent and Early Retirement in Europe." *European Sociological Review* 29, no. 6 (2013): 1295–308.
Vereker, Charles, and John Barron Mays. *Urban Redevelopment and Social Change: A Study of Social Conditions in Central Liverpool, 1955–56*. Social Research Series. Liverpool: Liverpool University Press, 1961.
Vernon, James. *Hunger: A Modern History*. Cambridge, MA: Belknap Press of Harvard University Press, 2007.
Wainwright, Steven P., and Bryan S. Turner. "Aging and the Dancing Body." In *Aging Bodies: Images and Everyday Experience*, edited by Christopher A. Faircloth, 259–92. Walnut Creek, CA: AltaMira, 2003.
Walker, Alan. "Professor Peter Townsend: Campaigner for Social Justice Who Co-founded the Child Poverty Action Group." *Independent*, June 12, 2009.
Walker, Alan, Adrian Sinfield, and Carol Walker. *Fighting Poverty, Inequality and Injustice: A Manifesto Inspired by Peter Townsend*. Bristol: Policy, 2011.
Walkowitz, Judith R. *City of Dreadful Delight: Narratives of Sexual Danger in Late-Victorian London*. London: Virago, 1992.

Waters, Chris. "Autobiography, Nostalgia, and the Changing Practices of Working-Class Selfhood." In *Singular Continuities: Tradition, Nostalgia, and Identity in Modern British Culture*, edited by George K. Behlmer and F. M. Leventhal, 178–95. Stanford: Stanford University Press, 2000.

Waugh, Evelyn. *A Little Learning: The First Volume of an Autobiography*. London: Chapman and Hall, 1964.

Wedderburn, Dorothy. "Old People in Britain." *American Behavioral Scientist* 14, no. 1 (1970): 97–110.

Weintraub, Karl Joachim. *The Value of the Individual: Self and Circumstance in Autobiography*. Chicago: University of Chicago Press, 1978.

Welford, A. T. *Skill and Age: An Experimental Approach*. London: Published for the Trustees of the Nuffield Foundation by the Oxford University Press, 1951.

White, Cynthia Leslie. *Women's Magazines, 1693–1968*. London: M. Joseph, 1970.

White, Grace G. Leybourne, and Kenneth White. *Children for Britain*. Target for Tomorrow. London: Pilot Press, 1945.

Wilkinson, R. K., and E. M. Sigsworth. "Attitudes to the Housing Environment: An Analysis of Private and Local Authority Households in Batley, Leeds and York." *Urban Studies* 9, no. 2 (1972): 193–214.

———. "A Survey of Slum Clearance Areas in Leeds." *Yorkshire Bulletin of Economic and Social Research* 15, no. 1 (1963): 25–51.

Williams, Leonard Llewelyn Bulkeley. *Middle Age and Old Age*. Oxford Medical Publications. London: Oxford University Press, 1925.

Wills, Abigail. "Delinquency, Masculinity and Citizenship in England 1950–1970." *Past and Present* 187, no. 1 (2005): 157–85.

Wilson, Gail. "'I'm the Eyes and She's the Arms': Changes in Gender Roles in Advanced Old Age." In *Connecting Gender and Ageing: A Sociological Approach*, edited by Sara Arber and Jay Ginn, 98–113. Buckingham: Open University Press, 1995.

World Bank. *Live Long and Prosper: Aging in East Asia and Pacific*. World Bank East Asia and Pacific Regional Reports. Washington, DC: World Bank, 2016. https://openknowledge.worldbank.org/bitstream/handle/10986/23133/9781464804694.pdf.

Younghusband, Eileen Louise. *The Newest Profession: A Short History of Social Work*. Sutton: Community Care, 1981.

Zweiniger-Bargielowska, Ina. *Austerity in Britain: Rationing, Controls, and Consumption, 1939–1955*. Oxford: Oxford University Press, 2000.

———. "The Body and Consumer Culture." In *Women in Twentieth-Century Britain*, edited by Ina Zweiniger-Bargielowska, 183–97. Harlow: Pearson Education, 2001.

———. *Managing the Body: Beauty, Health, and Fitness in Britain, 1880–1939*. Oxford: Oxford University Press, 2010.

INDEX

Page numbers in *italics* denote illustrations.

Achenbaum, W. Andrew, 13
Adams, John, 82
Admiralty, 29
Advanced Style (Ari Seth Cohen, film), *156*
advertising: cosmetics use and, 128–29; fashion magazines and, 107, 108, 116, 117, 119, 121; and older women's fashion decisions, 123
advocacy groups for elderly: as collating messages from variety of sources, 33–34; conference proceedings and guidelines by, 34; WWII and funding of, 29–30
African-descent population, 166
ageism, 105
aging. *See* "aging population" concerns; old age as category; personal experiences of aging; physical aging; social research participants
"aging population" concerns, 157–58; assumption of older population as inferior in, 158; birth rates and, 11, 158–59; continued salience of, 159; contributions of older people as ignored in, 158; dependency ratio measurement and, 159–60, 214nn22,24; forecasts of demographers, as not borne out in reality, 158–60; as justification for cutbacks to welfare state, 157–58, 159, 160; life expectancy and, 160; and migrants entering workforce, 158–59; and perception of old age as uncommon prior to 20th century, 7; regional variation in, 157; as scapegoat for economic difficulties, 160; social anxiety produced by concerns about, 11, 157; and women entering workforce, 158–60
Allen, Adrianne, 117
Alzheimer's disease, 6, 11. *See also* dementia
Anderson, William Ferguson, 11
anomie/disengagement theories, 34
anthropological immersion in local culture, as research method, 28, 40–41, 58
anthropology, social, 40–41
art projects on aging, 169

Ashby-de-la-Zouch, 23
Athill, Diana, 117
Atlee, Clement, 39
autobiographies of aging authors, 5–6; and aging as relative, 154; as "cure," 134, 153–54; and emotional qualities of aging, 135, 147; experience and perspective as interest of, 138, 154; and fashion, 106; and gap between past and present, 148–49, 153; and gentleness with self and others, 154; iconic public events as boundaries in, 145–46, 147–48; landscape changes in, 147, 148–49, 151–52; memories as changed by act of writing, 134, 143; multiple versions drafted for, 134; and narrative and frame of childhood vs. middle and old age, 137–38, 144; and past as intruding on present, 133–34; preconceived ideas and prejudices and, 137, 138; and psychoanalysis/psychology, 134, 136, 153–54. *See also* autobiography as genre; memory/memories
autobiography as genre: and allegiance to truth telling, 138; "autobiographical pact," 138–39; conventions of, 138; iconic public events as boundaries in, 145–46, 147–48; and identity formation, 138, 139; individual achievements as focus, 138, 139; and lifelong significance of childhood, 135–36; literary traditions and, 135, 139–40; memories as changed/reconstructed in writing of, 134, 143; men as default of, 135; and modernist memoir style, 146; and personal coherence of a life history, 143; and popular culture, changes in, 135; psychological reckoning and, 134; and rise of human-interest journalism, 139; and romantic tradition, 135–37; and self-reflection, celebration of, 139, 141; and social change, 135, 139–41, 144–46, 147–53; and social class, changes in hierarchies of, 139, 146; status conferred by writing of, 143; upper class as traditional focus of, 139–40; women as eschewing individualistic model of, 139; and women's lives, new interest in confessional writing about, 135
—WORKING-CLASS AUTOBIOGRAPHY: ambivalence expressed in, 149–50, 151–53, 154; community presses and, 5–6, 135, 142, 149, 210n55; and end of postwar economic boom, 143–44; interest in working-class lives and development of, 135, 140; and joys of reminiscence, 142–43; mandatory education and, 141; and narrative and frame of childhood and young adulthood vs. middle and old age, 144; as new style, 141, 209n49; nostalgia and, 144, 150–53, 151–52; romanticization of past in, 143–44; social change and, 140–41, 144, 148–50; storytelling and, 144; technologies of printing and development of, 135, 141–42; transforming moment of conclusion in, 144
Ayers, Ruth M., 107

Bailkin, Jordanna, 19, 39
Bangladeshi population, 166
Bartlett, Frederic, 143
bereavement: clothing and, 103; death as taboo subject, 73; home decoration and memorials honoring, 74; loneliness and, 48; personal experiences of, 72–75; privacy sought for, 73; public rituals of, 73; stoicism in, 4, 73–74; visions and dreams of loved ones, 74–75. *See also* death
Bethnal Green, East London: changes evident in 1990s, 167; community

(in-home) care recipients in, 33; density of families and social connection in, 48–49; ethnicity of population of, 167; proportion of population over eighty-five in, 167; terraced cottages of, 48, 61–62. *See also* council estates; East London; *Family Life of Old People, The* (Townsend); slum clearance
Bevan, Aneurin, 32, 81, 94
Beveridge Report, 30–31
Beveridge, William, 30, 39
birth rates, and "aging population," 11, 158–59
Blackpool, life expectancy in, 165
Board of Trade, 109
bodybuilder culture, 119
body. *See* health; ill health and debility; mobility; physical aging; self-identity
books, large-print, 44
Booth, Charles, 10, 19, 21–27, 25–26, 49, 50
Booth, General William, 21
Boucher Report (1957), 94
Bowlby, John, 83
Bowley, A. L., 49, 51
Brierley, Walter, 63–64
Brighton, council estates and, 63
Brown, Callum, 106
Burnett-Hurst, Alexander Robert, 49, 51
Burton, Harry, 146, 149–50
Burton, House of, 119–20

Camberwell Reception Centre, 82
capitalism: contradictions of care and, 170; persistence of poverty and questioning of, 80; privatization of care, 79, 162, 164
care homes. *See* residential homes (institutions)
Caribbean-descent population, 166
Carter, Angela, 106

cell theory, 136
Centerprise, 142
Chamberlain, Joseph, 27
Chamberlain, Lilian, 77–78
charitable groups. *See* voluntary organizations (charitable groups)
charity: narratives utilized by working class to obtain, 23, 141; nineteenth-century working-class families and application for, 23; workhouse dissuasion of applications for, 23
—DESERVING/NOT DESERVING: and Booth's support for able-bodied, 24; local authority homes and, 95–96; seventeenth century and "discriminating relief," 7–8; voluntary and religious residential care homes and, 91
Charles, Enid, 158
childbirth, 9
child care: by grandparents, 56, 57, 169–70; and workhouse as destroying valued social roles, 80
childhood: lifelong significance of, 135–36; old age as "second childhood," 136
child mortality rates, 7
Child Poverty Action Group, 40
children: mortality rates for, 7; residential care for, 83. *See also* child care; childhood; families; grandchildren; youth
Chinese population, 166
Church, Richard, 137, 138
church services, tape recordings of, 44. *See also* religion
citizenship: care for elderly and, 32, 45; inner lives of aged as right of, 32, 45; material comfort as right of, 45; residential care as right of, 91, 94; retirement during WWII experienced as exclusion from, 64; state pensions as right of, 9–10

clothing: care of, 126; and "color divide" between older and younger women, 103–4; and colors for older women, 104; favorite color of women, 103; and men, 119–21, 125–26; for mourning, 103; as symbol of generational conflict, 106–7; white gloves, 106. *See also* fashion and beauty culture
Cohen, Ari Seth, 156
Cohen, Deborah, 134
collective subconscious, 28
community (at-home) care: access narrowed to "crisis situations," 163; Conservative governments and discouragement of, 164; cost of services of, 33, 163; establishment of right to, 163, 164; late-twentieth century return to midcentury policies for, 164–65, 170; local authorities providing, 32–33, 163; number of recipients of, 33; oil and sterling crises and cuts to, 163; Peter Townsend as recommending, 84, 89, 162, 164; Townsend on lack of good planning for, 162; voluntary organizations providing, 32. *See also* independent living of aged; meal services; welfare services for aged
community presses, 5–6, 135, 142, 149, 210n55
Conekin, Becky, 106
Conservative Party and governments: and austerity of twenty-first century, 165, 170; deindustrialization and denigration of working class by, 143–44; and national insurance, 30–31; and privatization of residential care, 164; and state pensions, 27, 168; undermining care of elderly, 12
consumer culture: extension of credit to working class and, 140; and feminine "techniques of appearing," 122; men's fashion and stances on, 119, 120. *See also* advertising; capitalism
Cookson, Catherine, 134–35, 154, 209n49
cosmetics: generational differences in use of, 127–28; marketing of, 128–29; numbers of women using, 127; older women and use of, 124, 126, 127–30
cost of living: national insurance pensions as not keeping up with, 31; and overstatement of transformation of working class, 140–41
council estates: allocation of, location of kin not factor in, 61; in autobiographies, 148, 152–53; establishment of, 61; family assistance persisting in move to, 62–63; neighbors and multigenerational families moved to, 63; nuclear family as requirement for allocation of, 61, 89–90; pragmatic decision to move to, 61, 152–53; public spaces in, lack of, 62; resistance to moving to, 61–62; and social researchers on effects of family dispersal, 62–63; as symbol of "affluence" of working class, 62, 140
Council for Training in Social Work, 83
credit, working-class participation in consumer culture and, 140

daily domestic tasks, Joseph Sheldon study of, 53–54
Dawson, Graham, 131
death: cell theory and, 136; child mortality rates, 7; expressions of fear of dying, 72; regrets about trouble one's death might cause others, 71–72; religious residential homes as most likely to care for elders until, 94; residential care homes and handling of, as terrifying residents, 94; "social

death" viewed as preceding, 71, 72. *See also* bereavement; life expectancy

deindustrialization, 143–44, 151–52, 168

dementia: closure of long-stay hospitals for, 163; judged to be part of aging process, 95; loneliness viewed as cause of, 53; mental health distinguished from, 11; as not inevitable part of aging, 6; residential care homes mandated to care for residents with, 94–95. *See also* ill health and debility

demographics. *See* "aging population" concerns; population

dependency of aged: dependency ratio, 159–60, 214nn22,24; state policy as strengthening perception of, 157. *See also* "aging population" concerns; independent living of aged

Depression: memories of, 72; questioning of capitalism and, 80; unemployment and, 63–64

diet. *See* food and diet

dignity: social researchers' perception of, 12–13, 161; workhouse and destruction of, 80

Dior, Christian, "New Look," 107, 109, 111

domestic help/care. *See* community (at-home) care

domiciliary care. *See* community (at-home) care

Eakin, Paul John, 210n66

East Asia, aging of population in, 157

Eastley, Mrs., 111, 203n50

East London: changing nature of poverty in, 18–19; community (at-home) care recipients in, 33; deindustrialization and, 143–44, 151–52, 168; density of families and social connection in, 48–49; nineteenth-century poverty in, 18, 20–21; terraced cottages of, 48, 61–62. *See also* council estates; *Family Life of Old People, The* (Townsend); residential homes (institutions); slum clearance; working class

education: expansion of, and increased opportunities, 146; mandatory, and encouragement of autobiographical and expressive writing, 141; mandatory, and increase of opportunities, 145; residential care worker training, 77, 83–84; of social workers/researchers, 33, 77, 169; volunteer training, 33

Education Act (1870), 80, 145

Education Act (1902), 146

egalitarianism: performance of, by residential home staff, 97–98; social researchers and difficulty of balancing dignity with, 161; social researchers and hierarchy as coexisting with, 41

"emotionology," 177n69

emotions: of aging, autobiography as revealing, 135, 147; aging body as source of suffering, 104–5; Booth survey and limitation of, 23; and fashion, 125, 129–31, 161; history of, 13–14, 177n69; and importance of home, 48, 51; and life in residential homes (institutions), 90–92, 99; love and sexuality histories as focused on young, 14; marriage and bonds of, 67–68, 72–73; and Herbert Miller's study, 34; and mobility, 36; repression of, as social researcher view of Britons, 73–74; residential homes (institutions) and focus on, 98–100; storytelling and, 161. *See also* inner lives of aged; loneliness; stoicism

England: aging of population in, 158; reduction of local authority homes in, 164; slum clearance in, 61; and state pensions, 27

ethnic groups: among community (at-home) care workers, 166; among residents of care homes, 166; among staff of care homes, 166; and multigenerational families in East London, 167. *See also* immigration
Europe, percentage of population over sixty, 7
European Commission Observatory on Ageing and Old People, 10
European Social Survey, 169

Fabian Society, 20–21
false teeth, 9, 44
families: and assistance to elderly on council estates, 62–63; bonds of, viewed as loosening, 51, 53, 56; density of, within Bethnal Green, 48–49; dispersal of, without access to greater resources, 167–68; ethnic makeup of East London and multigenerational households of, 167; extended family networks of reciprocal care, 56–58, 57, 61–63, 67–69, 72–73, 167–68, 169–70; and financial support for elderly, 51, 53, 56, 62; ill health and increased dependence on, 69, 70–71; lack of, 69, 80, 89; state payments to, for care of elderly, 68–69, 170; as support for elderly living alone, 54, 56; workhouses and separation of, 23, 80. *See also* children; grandchildren; nuclear family
Family Life of Old People, The (Townsend), 3–5, 38; bereavement in, 72–73; bond between marriage partners as unrecognized in, 67–68, 72–73; and changing nature of poverty, 18–19; communal chats as evaluation of self with others, 69–70; enthusiasm of participants in, 3; extended family networks of reciprocal care, 56–58, 57, 61–63, 67–69, 72–73, 168; family members living nearby, 48; and ill health, 69–71, 75–76; and importance of home, 47–49; interview conditions as revealing information, 42–43; interviewee desire to represent their own lives, 49, 76; interview method and, 38–39, 43, 58; interviews with audience of family and friends, 42, 43, 47; "kinship maps" and, 48–49; replication of aspects of study, 4–5, 167; and retirement, 63, 65–68; and segregated gender roles, 66–67; selection of participants in, 3, 46, 68; self-identity of participants in, 19; sex as subject in, 47; silence and, 75–76; storytelling and, 3, 49, 66, 71, 160–61; unpublished photographs in, 58, 59–60; violence and abuse as unrecognized in, 68; women in foreground as participants in, 68–69
fascism. *See* World War II
fashion and beauty culture: Dior's "New Look," 107, 109, 111; generational differences, 106–7, 127–28; inner/outer body relation and, 122; "knowledge of self" required by, 122; men's, 119–21, 120; and performance of "seeing and being seen," 122; respectability and, 107, 121; social researchers' views of, 103–4, 105, 121, 130; WWII restrictions on, 109, 111. *See also* grooming
—EXPERIENCE OF OLDER MEN AND WOMEN IN, 5; advertising and markets and, 123, 124; age as no barrier to attractiveness, 124; and attention, attraction of, 121–22; body confidence in aging and, 105, 131–32; care of clothing, 126; class-based standards and, 106, 130, 131; cosmetics, use of, 124, 126, 127–30; emotional stakes of getting appearance right, 125, 129–31, 161; expression of inner self/character

and, 104, 121, 122–23, 126–27, 131; fads and trends, flexible approach to, 5, 121–22, 123–25, 130, 161; and family and friends, influence of, 123, 125, 128, 129; hair care and grooming, 122, 124, 126, 128; men and, 122, 125–26, 131; oppressiveness of, 123; reasons for engaging in, 130–31; resources and inclination to participate in, 5, 104, 122, 131, 161; skin care, 124, 128; as visual affirmation of belonging, 124

fashion and women's magazines, older men and women in, 5, 104; advertising in, 107, 108, 116, 117, 119, 121; age as no barrier to style, 108–9, 131; and age-conscious gaze of historians, 105; aspirational identities and, 131; class and, 107–8; colors of clothing and, 104; men's fashion and grooming, 104, 119, *120*, 121; *Vogue's* "Mrs. Exeter" character and older woman as focus, 104, 111–17, *112–16*, 118–19, *120*, 131, 203nn44,50; vs. youth focus, 107–8, 117–19, *118*, 131

Federation of Worker Writers and Community Publishers, 142

feet, care of, 36. *See also* mobility

Foakes, Grace, 150–53, *151–52*

food and diet: downgrading of older people's caloric needs, 24; in residential homes (institutions), 97, 99, 100; social status and, 97; in workhouses, 80. *See also* malnutrition; meal services

Fortes, Meyer, 40–41

Fraser, Nancy, 170

Freud, Sigmund, 73, 136

gardens: and importance of privacy, 48; loss of, and move to council estates, 62; volunteers caring for, 44

gender: and access to welfare state benefits, 10; autobiography and, 147–48; and domestic work, 66–67;

men's fashion and policing of, 119, 122; and paid work, 65; retirement and blurring of roles of, 67; segregated roles of, social researcher view of, 66–67; and sexual activity, 47; and social research as field, 68. *See also* men; women

generational perspectives: and "aging population" concerns, 159; in autobiography, 144–53; fashion and beauty culture and, 106–7, 127–28; physical aging and, 147, 148; social welfare and, 10

generation gap, 56

George Moore Lodge care home, 77, 78

George V (king), 145–46

geriatric medicine: defined, 11; establishment of, 11, 31; lowly position of, in hierarchy of medicine, 84; and mental health problems, 11–12

Gladstone, William, 13

Glass, David, 159

global care chains, 170

Goalen, Barbara, 116–17, *116*, 131

Good Housekeeping (magazine), 107, 127

Gordon Road Workhouse, 82

Gorer, Geoffrey, 73–74

grandchildren: assistance to adult grandchildren, 170; childcare by grandparents, 56, 57, 169–70; loss of contact with, 48; visits from, during social research interviews, 58; visits from, in autobiographies, 147

grandfathers, 57

grandmothers, Peter Townsend's focus on, 68

Greenwood, Walter, 63–64, 142, 145, 148–49

grooming, older men and women's, 5; public bathing in residential care, 90–91. *See also* clothing; cosmetics; fashion and beauty culture; hair care and grooming

hair care and grooming: for men, 122; in residential homes (institutions), 91; for women, 124, 126, 128
Haldane, Elizabeth Sanderson, 145–46
Hall, Granville Stanley, 27–28
Harrisson, Tom, 28–29
Hazell, Kenneth, 53
health, as ability to meet responsibilities and demonstrate character, 69, 70–71. *See also* ill health and debility; life expectancy; medical care; mental health and old age; mobility; physical aging
health departments, administering residential homes (institutions), 84
Health Services and Public Health Act (1968), 163
Henrey (née Gal), Madeleine, 147–48
Henrey, Robert, 147
Hilliard, Christopher, 141
Hill, Octavia, 13
history and historians: "affective turn" in history writing, 13–14; age-conscious gaze of, 105; and autobiography, 138; change as focus of, vs. continuity, 130; and fashion, 103–4, 105, 121, 130; love and sexuality histories as focused on young, 14; and "parallel" histories of old age, 12; priorities of policymakers and professionals as reflected by, 12, 19; secondary analysis of data by, 14–17; of subjectivity, 139; testimonies of older people as missing from history of old age, 170–71
home: bereavement memorials in, 74; and importance of privacy, 47, 48, 93; "kinship maps" of family surrounding, 48–49; psychological importance of, 47–49. *See also* community (at-home) care; household labor; household organization; independent living of aged

home help (domiciliary care). *See* community (at-home) care
homelessness, 89–90, 92, 153
Horsnell, Horace, 139–40
hospitals: long-stay, allegations of abuse in, 84; long-stay, closure of, 163; and lowly position of geriatric medicine, 84; personal experiences of, 70, 99; psychiatric, 84, 163; public, and pre-WWII care for aged, chronically ill, and mental health patients, 81; uneven distribution of care revealed after NHS takeover of, 81; voluntary, pre-WWII care for acutely ill, 81; WWII and mass discharge from, 29–30, 81. *See also* medical care; residential homes (institutions)
household labor: retired men assisting with, 67; and women's double workload, 66–67; and workhouse as destroying social roles, 80
household organization: and debates over ethics and efficacy of social welfare, 51, 53; limitations of, as measure of emotional well-being, 48; measurement of, by social researchers, 48–49. *See also* families; independent living of aged
housing policy: and extended family networks, 56, 58; local authorities and, 51; Joseph Sheldon's warning on need for correct information in forming, 56; specially designed homes for elderly, 51, 52. *See also* council estates; slum clearance
Howell, Trevor, 53
Hungarian population, 166
Hussey, Stephen, 80
Hyndman, Henry, 21

ill health and debility: and differential treatment of aged, 94–96; distress of sudden disruptive illnesses, 69, 71; health experienced as ability to meet responsibilities, 69, 70–71; and increased dependence on family support, 69, 70–71; loneliness viewed as cause of, 53; as not confined to old age, 6; percentages of older people in, 69; and residential and community access to care, 163, 166; residential care homes mandated to house those with, 94–95, 163; retreat of social researchers from distressing subjects, 75–76; social researcher worries of isolation and loneliness resulting from, 70–71; social researcher worries of "social death" resulting from, 71, 72; women as more susceptible to, 8–9, 69. *See also* death; dementia; mobility; physical aging

immigration, and "aging population" predictions, 158–59

income: downgrading of older people's need for, in early social research, 24; as factor in grooming habits, 5, 104, 122, 131, 161; financial support of adult children, 169–70; inequality of, and effects on life expectancy, 165; inequality of, and persistence of poverty, 141; loss of, vs. loss of occupation as cause of difficulties, 12–13; rise of working class, 140. *See also* consumer culture; cost of living; material comfort; pensions; poverty; social class

independent living of aged: conceived of as problem by social researchers, 53; family support and assistance for, 54, 56; and forced move to residential care, 90; interwar value of state pension and increase in, 51; as popular but problematic objective, 164–65; Peter Townsend recommendation for, 84, 164–65. *See also* community (at-home) care; meal services; mobility

Indian population, 166

individuality, residential care and need for, 78, 79, 93

industrialization: deindustrialization, 143–44, 151–52, 168; view of family bonds as weakened by, 51, 56

industry, Booth's survey of, 22

inequality. *See* income; poverty

inner lives of aged: connection between aging and childhood, 136; postwar welfare state and concern for, 31–32; as revealed in social research data, 3–4, 65–66, 69–75, 99–101, 124–27; as right of citizenship, 32, 45; shift to concern for, in residential home administration, 77–78, 84, 93–94, 98, 167; silences around, in social research data, 4, 75–76. *See also* emotions; psychology of aging

Institute of Community Studies, 40

institutions. *See* residential homes (institutions)

interwar period: and democratization of British culture, 141; economic turmoil of, and questioning of capitalism, 80; and employment of youth, encouragement of, 64; memories of, 72; and measurement of popular opinion, 28–29; and rising independent living of older people, 51; and shift from Victorian liberalism to social planning, 51

Ireland, and state pensions, 27

Jamaican population, 166
Jameson, Storm, 133–35, 153–54, 207n1, 209n49
Jewish population, 166
John, Augustus, 136–37, 138
Jones, Ben, 61, 143–44
Joy, Thomas, 145

Kensington and Chelsea, life expectancy in, 165

Keynes, John Maynard, 159
King, Geoffrey, 51, 53, 56

labor shortages, and encouragement of older workers, 64–65, 159
Labour Party and governments: and National Health Service, 81; and national insurance, 30–31; and National Insurance Act (1946), 31; and persistence of poverty, 40; and reform of residential care, 81; and state pensions, 30–31; and support for social science, 39–40; and Peter Townsend, 40; and undermining of care of elderly, 12; and workhouse, condemnation of, 79, 81
Langhamer, Claire, 13–14
Last Refuge, The (Townsend), 40, 78–79, 194n8; anti-institutional position of, 84–85, 85–88, 89, 93–94; brevity of time/attention spent with residents, 42, 101; and closure of residential homes, 162; community (at-home) welfare services as recommendation of, 84, 89, 162, 164; and differential treatment of residents by administrators and staff, 95–96; disagreement of social researchers with practices of staff, 96–98; ethnicity of residents in, 166; and inconvenience for participants, 96–97; and interview conditions as revealing information, 42–43, 98; interviews as focusing on administrators and staff, 42, 101; and lack of progress in reform of residential homes, 79; legacy of, on social research, 79, 96–97, 169; and medical priorities of staff, 84; method used in, 42, 78–79, 98–99, 101, 166; performance of egalitarianism by staff for social researchers, 97–98; and persistence of poverty, 40; photographs and, 58, 85, 85–88, 89;
replication of, 165–67, 168–69; resistance of participants to research methods in, 100–101; selection of participants in, 68. *See also* residential homes (institutions)
Lawrence, Jon, 15
Lazarsfeld, Paul, 63
leisure activities, planning for age-appropriate, 51
Lejeune, Philippe, 138–39
Leybourne, Grace, 158
Liberal government, state pension introduction by (1908), 8
libraries, mobile, 44
life expectancy: austerity as shortening, 165; and improvements in child mortality, 7; and improvements in health of older people, 7; in nineteenth century, 7; and recalibration of dependency ratio, 160; in twentieth century, 7; twenty-first century and slowing of rate of increase in, 165; of women, 8, 165
Light, Alison, 23
literary scene, midcentury, and connection between aging and childhood, 136
lithography, 141–42
local authorities: as "arrangers and purchasers" of care, 164; community (at-home) care provided by, 32–33, 163; forcing older people to move to residential care, 90; housing policy of, 51; meal services provided by, 32, 163; and private homes, use of, 81, 164. *See also* residential homes (institutions)—local authority homes
Local Government Act (1929), 80
London: Booth's maps quantifying poverty, 49, 50. *See also* East London
London County Council, 83

loneliness: bereavement and, 48; lack of behavioral norms as identifier of, 53; living alone seen as cause of, 53, *54*; mobility as measure of, 36; of residential care institution residents, 99–100; serious consequences for health of, 53; social connection prescribed as alleviation of, 53. *See also* social connection; social isolation
Lord Mayor's Air Raid Distress Fund, 30
love and sexuality histories, as focused on young, 14
Lowndes, Marie Belloc, 139–40
Luxborough Lodge, 82

Madge, Charles, 28–29
malnutrition and old age: mental health and, 6; working-class women and, 8–9
Manchester, life expectancy in, 165
Mandler, Peter, 23
Marmot, Michael, 165
marriage: and blurring of gender roles in later life, 67; and bonds of emotion in later life, 67–68, 72–73; pensions for women as dependent on marital status, 9
masculinity: policing of fashion and, 119, 122; work and, 65–66. *See also* gender; men
Mass Observation, as source, 2–3, 14, 29, 178n79
material comfort: as definition of home, 93; residential homes (institutions) and, 99; as right of citizenship, 45
Mayhew, Henry, 18–19
meal services: benefits beyond nutritional value of, 32; by family members, 56; by local authorities, 32, 163; voluntary organizations and provision of, 32, 44, 163. *See also* food and diet; welfare services for aged

Mearns, Andrew, 21
media and media coverage: and "aging populations" of developed nations, 156; human-interest journalism and autobiographical genre, 139; nineteenth-century exposés of poverty, 21; and perception of old age as uncommon prior to 20th century, 7; potential for mass manipulation by, 28. *See also* fashion and women's magazines, older men and women in; public opinion
medical care: advice for, rejection of, 4; overburdened system for, 44, 45; physiotherapy, 44; podiatry services, 36, 44; "social death" viewed as consequence of, 71, 72; technological advancements in, 9. *See also* geriatric medicine; hospitals; ill health and debility; mental health and old age; mobility; National Health Service; residential homes (institutions)—medical care in
memory/memories: autobiography as changing/constructing content of, 134, 143; childhood as most vivid type of, 136; as intruding on present, 133–34; joys of reminiscence, 142–43; as unpredictable and irregular, 133, 136–37
men: and autobiography, 139; and body confidence in aging, 105, 131–32; fashion and grooming culture, 119–21, *120*, 122, 125–26, 131; in ill health, 69; pensions for, as dependent on employment status, 9; and retirement, 65–66, 67; state pension age for, 8; widowed, increased chances of isolation of, 71. *See also* families; gender; masculinity; women
Men Only (magazine), 119

mental health and old age: and autobiography, 134; and closure of long-stay hospitals, 163; dementia distinguished from, 11; and differential treatment in residential care by administrators and staff, 94–96; identification and diagnosis of, 11–12; inability to discuss in interviews, 75; loneliness and, 53; lowly position of geriatrics in psychiatric hospitals, 84; malnutrition and, 6; suicide, 75. *See also* ill health and debility; medical care
methodology of text, 2
middle class: and death, regret over trouble it might cause others, 71–72; differential treatment of, in residential homes (institutions), 94–96; and participation in social research, 3; private pensions and, 27, 168; and resources for personal grooming, 104; retirement goals of, 66; topics raised with, vs. working-class or institutionalized participants, 10; women's magazines aimed toward, 107, 108
Miller, Herbert Crossley, 34–36, *35*
Ministry of Health: and residential care, 81–82; and training for care staff, 83
Ministry of Information, 29
Mitchell, Hannah, 145
mobility: as measurement of loneliness/social isolation, 36; podiatry services and, 36, 44; self-reliance/self-esteem and, 36; social researchers and focus on, *35*, 36–38, *37*; welfare services for lack of, 44. *See also* daily domestic tasks; ill health and debility; independent living of aged
morality, physical environmentalism theories of, 49, 51
motherhood, 61, 70

Nast, Condé, 108, 109. *See also Vogue*
National Assistance (Amendment) Act (1962), 32
National Assistance Act (1948), 31, 81, 94, 164
National Assistance Board, 81
National Corporation for the Care of Old People, 30
National Council of Social Services, 33, 83
National Health Service: and closure of long-stay hospitals, 163; cuts to, 163, 165; elder beneficiaries of, 9; and lengthening of later life, 9; and position of geriatric medicine in psychiatric hospitals, 84; responsibility for hospitals assumed by, 81; technological advancements and, 9; and workhouse, 82
national insurance: Beveridge Report in support of, 30–31; as cradle-to-grave insurance, 31; incomplete delivery of welfare via, and need for commercial and voluntary organizations, 31, 32; and privatization of residential care, 164
National Insurance Act (1946), 31
National Old People's Welfare Committee (Council), 30, 32, 36, 44, 52, 83, 182n62
New Liberalism, 20–21
North America. *See* United States
nuclear family: council estate allocation as dependent on, 61; extended family system as invisible due to research focus on, 56
Nuffield Foundation, 30, 78
nursing homes, 164
nutrition. *See* food and diet; malnutrition

Oak Tree home (London), 77–78
Öberg, Peter, 105
occupational therapists, 51
offset printing, 141–42

old age as category: as relative, subjective, and lifelong process, 6–7; Booth and creation of, 24; characteristics associated with, 6; chronological age determined by state, 6, 8, 63; establishment of, 19–20; historians' lack of analytical primacy given to, 11; history of legal and bureaucratic management of, 7–11; length of, as varying, 6; "old" old age, 6; as percentage of population, 7; as questioned by older people, 16–17; scholarly primacy given to, 11; social research publications on, 33–34; "young" old age, 6

old-age homes. *See* residential homes (institutions)

Pacific nations, aging of population in, 157
Parkinson, Norman, 117
Parsons, Talcott, 51, 56
Paul, Albert, 149
Peck, Winifred, 138
pensions: official age for (1898), 8, 27; establishment of public service pensions, 8; for women, as dependent on marital status, 9
—PRIVATE PENSIONS: cutbacks in, 168; and retirement age, 27
—STATE PENSIONS: acceptance as right of citizenship, 9–10; amount of, 27; Booth's case for, 22, 24, 27; decreasing value of, 31; effects on poverty of, 8; establishment of (1908), 8, 19, 27; government's triple guarantee of value of, 165; interwar value of, and rise in independent living of older people, 51; limitation to "thrifty," campaign for, 24, 27; number initially applying for, 9; and pension age, 27, 63, 168; personal experiences of, 9–10; Poor Law benefits as disqualification for, 27; regional variations in poverty and effects of establishment of, 27; social research as influence in establishing, 19. *See also* national insurance

People's History classes, 142
period of study, 1
personal discipline, health and healing attributed to, 4. *See also* stoicism
personal experiences of aging: bereavement, 72–75; ill health, 69–72, 74–75; pensions, 9–10; priorities of state as mismatch with, 156–57; and questioning of "old age" as category, 16–17; retirement, 12–13, 64, 65–68. *See also* autobiographies of aging authors; fashion and beauty culture—experience of older men and women in; residential homes (institutions)—interviewees/residents
physical aging: aging body perceived as source of emotional suffering, 104–5; body confidence and, 105, 131–32; expected difficulties of, stoicism and, 4, 69–71; gendered response to, 148; generational response to, 147, 148; as trauma, 75; women as "disappearing" as they age, 105; and women's roles in household, 66–67. *See also* death; health; ill health and debility
physical environmentalism, theory of homes and neighborhoods as revealing moral qualities of inhabitants, 49, 51
physiotherapy, 44
Pinker, Robert, 78, 101
Pioneers of Social Research, 43
podiatry services, 36, 44
Polish population, 166
Political and Economic Planning, 39–40, 51

Poor Law (1834), and Poor Law institutions and practices, 80; and able-bodied, 24; Booth and aim of releasing older people from, 24; legislation reforming, and unwillingness to assist older people, 80; marker of old age set by, 8; National Health Service takeover of responsibility for, 81; and persistence of poverty as casting doubt on laissez-faire ideology, 80; and residential care homes, 78, 91; state pension disqualification of those who received benefits of, 27; union restrictions on relief alternatives and standardization of, 23. *See also* residential homes (institutions); workhouses

popular culture: autobiography and changes in, 135; potential for mass manipulation by, 28

population: percentage of aged over eighty-five, 167; percentage of aged over sixty, 7; reduction of in 1990s East London, 167. *See also* "aging population" concerns; ethnic groups

postwar period: as "age of expert," 33; and end of economic boom, 143–44; and increase in welfare services for aged, 9–10, 44–45; labor shortages of, 64–65, 159; workforce expansion and, 158–60

poverty: autobiographical coverage of social change in, 145, 149–50, 153; Booth survey on (1886–1903), 21–27, 25–26, 49, 50; late nineteenth-century awareness of environmental and biological factors in, 20–21, 22, 80; lifecycle and patterns of, 22; maps of London (Booth), 49, 50; mid-nineteenth-century perspective of, 21; nineteenth-century rates of, 21, 22. *See also* charity; Poor Law (1834), and Poor Law institutions and practices; workhouses; working class

—IN OLD AGE: Booth survey and (1886–1903), 22, 23–24; and delivery of residential care, 95–96; effect of pensions on, 8; percentage living below poverty line, 10; persistence of, 10, 12, 40, 45; "rediscovery" of (1960s), 12; and reliance on National Assistance benefits, 31; women as more susceptible to, 9. *See also* charity—deserving/not deserving; pensions—state pensions

—PERSISTENCE OF: and family culture in move to council estates, 63; and income inequality, 141; in old age, 10, 12, 40, 45; and overstatement of working-class transformation, 140–41; and questioning of capitalism, 80

Pritchett, Victor, 137, 141

privacy: bereavement and need for, 73; home as defined by, 47, 48, 93; need for, 78, 79, 93, 95, 167; residential care homes and improvement in, 167; residential care homes and lack of, 78, 93–94, 95, 98; residential home interviews and lack of, 98

private pensions. *See* pensions—private pensions

private welfare services: national insurance gaps and need for, 31, 32. *See also* residential homes (institutions)—private homes

privatization of care, 79, 162, 164

psychiatric hospitals: closure of, 163; and lowly position of geriatric medicine, 84

psychoanalytical language and theories, 134, 136

psychological attachment theories, 83

psychology of aging: and European fascism and total war, 28–29; Granville Stanley Hall and disappointment in, 27–28; Leonard

Williams and wisdom of age, 28; work as beneficial in, 64–65
psychology of memories, 143
Public Assistance (Local Government Act, 1929), 80
public housing. *See* council estates
public opinion: of national insurance, 30–31; perception of dependency of elderly, 157; during period of fascism and total war, 28–29; of "population aging," 157, 158. *See also* media and media coverage
public service pensions, establishment of, 8

QueenSpark Books, 149

race, and access to welfare state benefits, 10. *See also* ethnic groups
Rathbone, Eleanor, 107
Read, Herbert, 137
Rees, Brian, 78
Relief Fund (London), 21
religion: Booth's survey of, 22–23; church services, tape recordings of, 44; and residential homes (institutions), 94. *See also* charity; residential homes (institutions)—voluntary and religious homes; voluntary organizations (charitable groups)
residential homes (institutions), 4–5; access narrowed to "crisis situations," 163; anti-institutional critique of, 84–85, 85–88, 89, 93–94; closures of, 162, 163; and inner lives of residents, focus on, 77–78, 84, 93–94, 98, 167; interviews in, as molded by public spaces and intrusions of staff, 42–43, 98; Labour Party and utopian vision of, 81–82; lack of progress in implementation of new legislation reforming, 79, 82–83, 84, 91–92; and mandated care of infirm and senile, 94–95, 163; numbers of people in, 81–82, 164; podiatry services and, 36; as right of citizenship, 91, 94; Townsend as living in, 4, 99; Townsend recommendations for at-home delivery of services, 84, 89, 162; waiting lists for, 90. *See also Last Refuge, The* (Townsend)
—FACILITIES AND OPERATIONS: food and diet, 97, 99, 100; home-like environments, 85, 86, 89, 93–94; intake practices, 90, 91; and lack of inspections, 83; and lack of government influence over, 83; and lack of material comfort, 99; priorities of efficiency and hierarchy in, 92; privacy and lack of independence, 78, 93–94, 95, 98; privacy improvements in, 167; privatization and cost-saving measures for, 79, 162, 164; public bathing practices, 90–91; recreational activities, 167; small homes, and preference for middle-class residents, 95–96; subservience of residents to staff, 96; workhouses, resemblance to, 4, 78, 79, 82, 85, 85, 87–88, 89, 91–92, 95–96, 96. *See also* residential homes (institutions)—medical care in
—INTERVIEWEES/RESIDENTS: confusion and fear experienced by, 90, 91, 94, 95; deaths of, 94; and desire for independence and privacy, 78, 79, 93, 95, 167; differential treatment of, by administrators and staff, 94–96; differential treatment of, by social researchers, 10–11, 101; disabled, interviews with, 98–99; disempowering treatment of, by administrators and staff, 96–98; emotional needs of, 98–100; ethnic groups among, 166; and family, lack of, 89; family relations and decision

—INTERVIEWEES/RESIDENTS *(continued)* to enter residential care, 90; forced to move to residential care, 90; homelessness and, 89–90, 92; loneliness of, 99–100; and privacy, improvements in, 167; and privacy, lack of, 78, 93–94, 95, 97, 98; silence of, in fear of punishment, 4, 98; testimony of, as ignored by social researchers and policymakers, 78, 79, 161; vocal complaints of, 4, 91; work in homes done by, 166–67

—LARGE INSTITUTIONS: closures/rebuilding of, 79, 82, 162; differential treatment of working-class and frail elderly in placement within, 94–96; ethnicity of residents in, 166; local authority homes as tending to be largest, 83; number of people housed in, 82; photographs portraying, 85, *85*, *87–88*, 89

—LOCAL AUTHORITY HOMES: closures of, 162, 164; and incomplete delivery of welfare, 32; as mandated by National Assistance Act, 81; material conditions of, 99; narrowing of access to, and frailty of residents, 163, 166; number of, 82–83; payment for, 81; photographs portraying, 85, *85*, *87–88*, 89; priorities of efficiency and hierarchy in, 92–93; private homes converted to, 93, 162; smaller purpose-built (postwar) homes, 82, 89, 93, 95; standards of care established for, 164. *See also* residential homes (institutions)—large institutions

—MEDICAL CARE IN: greater needs for, and narrowing of access to residential care, 163; medical priorities as focus of staff, 84, 167; private home conversions as unsuited for, 93

—PRIVATE HOMES: commercial interests of, 92; and death of residents, handling of, 94; ethics of care as compromised in, 92, 162, 164; and home-like atmosphere, 93; and lack of accountability, 164; and lack of privacy for interviews, 98; local authorities authorized to utilize, 81; local authorities required to utilize, 164; number of, 82–83; performance of egalitarianism for social researchers, 97; privatization of residential care, 79, 162, 164

—SOCIAL RESEARCHERS AND: differential treatment of residents by, 10–11; home-like atmosphere as value of, 93; independence of residents as value of, 92–93; and religious homes, admiration for, 94

—STAFF AND ADMINISTRATORS: conditions of employment for, 166; differential treatment of residents by, 94–96; disempowering treatment of residents by, 96–98; dismissing complaints of residents, 91; effects of education on, 77–78, 83; ethnic groups among, 166; *Last Refuge* study as focusing on, 42, 101; medical priorities of, 84; performance of egalitarianism for social researchers, 97–98; ratios of, 166; reluctance to change from previous ways of doing things, 78, 83; rushing intake of new residents, 90; and shift to focus on inner lives of residents, 77–78; training and qualifications of, 83–84, 166; women as majority of workers, 68, 191n92

—VOLUNTARY AND RELIGIOUS HOMES: charitable relief attitudes of, 91; closures of, 162; conditions of employment in, 166; material conditions of, 99; as most likely to house residents until death, 94; number of, 82–83; photographs portraying as home-like, 85, 86, 89; and privatization of care, 164; religious services and, 94; and workhouses, resemblance to, 91–92

respectability: fashion and grooming and, 107, 121; self-reliance as source of, for working class, 80

retirement: age of, formal, 27, 63, 168; age of, lowered to encourage employment of youth, 64; age of, rise in, 168; age of, to care for grandchildren, 169; average age of, 168; and bonds of affection in later life, 67–68; gender role blurring in, 67; goals of participants for, 65, 66; and marriage, 67–68; men viewed as causing friction in home following, 67; personal experience of, 12–13, 64, 65–68; and postwar labor shortages, 64–65, 159; sickness and death promoted by, as social researcher view, 12–13; viewed as tragic event for men, 65; from white-collar positions, 168. *See also* pensions; unemployment

Roberts, Nesta, 44–45

Roberts, Robert, 145

romantic tradition, 135–37

Roper, Michael, 134

Rowntree, Seebohm, 22, 24, 51, 55, 93

royal family events, autobiography and, 145–46

rural areas, Herbert Miller's study of, 34–36, *35*

St. Marylebone Workhouse, 82

St. Pancras, 23, 91

Sandow, Eugene, 119

Savage, Mike, 15

Scheer, Monique, 13

Scotland: and geriatric medicine, invention of, 11; and state pensions, 27

Seal, Elizabeth, 117

self-identity: autobiography and formation of, 138, 139; as family or workgroup member, vs. old, 19; grooming as expression of, 104, 121, 122–23, 126–27, 131; stability of, 160–61; state activity and, 13

self-reliance, 36, 80

senility. *See* dementia

Settle, Alison, 109

sex, Peter Townsend interviewees on, 47

sexual appeal: of older women and men in *Vogue* magazine, 113, *115*, 121; and pleasures of grooming, 130; and use of cosmetics, 128

Sheldon, Joseph, 12, 53–54, 56, 168

Sims, George, 21

slum clearance: in autobiographies as boundary event, 148; number of people displaced by, 61; resistance to displacement by, 61–62; social effects of, 62–63, 140. *See also* council estates

Smyly, Margot, 111, *113–15*

social anthropology, 40–41

social change: autobiography and, 135, 139–41, 144–46, 147–53; East London comparison with 1950s, 167–68

social class: and ability of older Britons to speak about their lives, 161; and access to welfare state benefits, 10; changes in hierarchies of, and autobiography as genre, 139, 146; and differential treatment of interviewees by social researchers, 10–11; and differential treatment of older people by residential home administrators and staff, 94–96; fashion and, 106, 107–8, 130, 131; and life expectancy, 165. *See also* autobiography as genre—working-class autobiography; middle class; working class

social clubs, 53, *55*, 163

social connection: "kinship maps" of, 48–49; loneliness as alleviated by, 53; radios and television as, 48; state support for, 32, 53. *See also* social isolation social isolation: bereavement viewed as cause of, 72; ill health viewed as cause of, 70, 71; incorrect clocks as sign of, 48; independent living as not a cause of, 53–54, 56; independent living viewed as cause of, 53; mobility (physical) as measurement of, 36; mobility of youth as contributing to, 51; as not a function of old age, 6; retirement viewed as time of, 63–64, 65; and weakening of family bonds, 51, 53, 56. *See also* loneliness; social connection

social movements, 170

social planning: conceptual shift from Victorian liberalism to, 51; specialized housing for aged, 51, 52; WWII and implementation of, 30

social researchers: biography of, as research influence, 39; differential treatment of older people by, 10–11; disagreement with practices of residential care institutions, 96–98; downgrading requirements of aged, 24; education of, 33, 77, 169; and fashion, views of, 103–4, 105, 121, 130; gender of, 68; and hierarchy as coexisting with egalitarianism, 41; historians as reflecting priorities of, 12; international comparisons by, 34; judgments by authorities as focus of, 23; literature produced by, 33–34; and norm of aging, 12–13; participants as learning about aging from, 15–16; retreat of from distressing subjects, 75–76; secondary analysis of findings of, 14–15; on slum clearance, social effects of, 62–63; working-class cultural findings by, as compared to workers' viewpoint, 14–15. *See also* residential homes (institutions)—social researchers and; testimony of aged—ignored by social researchers

social research methods, 19–20; anthropological immersion in local culture, 28, 40–41, 58; case studies, 36–38, *37*; demography, and "aging of population," 158–60; diaries, 100–101; and direct evidence vs. expert judgments, 38; and excision of mental, moral, and social side of human nature, 24; and experts, privileging of, 42, 101; inconveniencing participants, 96–97; as instructing participants about aging, 15–16; interview conditions as revealing information, 42–43; interviewees as having mixed experiences during, 43–44; interview format, shortcomings of, 43; interviewing, rise of "informal," 38; interviews done with audience of family members and friends, 42, 43, 47; interviews done with audience/presence of welfare workers in institutions, 42–43, 98; national panel for diary writing and monthly questionnaires, 28–29; note taking and, 41; nuclear family, focus on, 56; policy ends as served by, 34, 38, 41, 44; questionnaires, 22, 27–29, 34–38, *35*, *37*, 42, 73, 99; replication of Townsend's *Last Refuge* methods, 166; resistance of participants to, 100–101; sociomedical studies of elderly, 34–36, *35*, 53–56; Peter Townsend's interviews, 38–39, 40–42, 43–44, 46–47, 58; Townsend's *Last Refuge* study, 42, 78–79, 98–99, 100–101, 166

social research participants: as absorbed in their narrative, 161–62; continuities as stressed by, 63, 160–61; desire to represent their own lives, 49, 76; exerting control of conversation with researchers, 73, 74, 100–101; as learning about aging from researchers, 15–16; as

"ordinary" vs. "unusual" people, 2, 29; and progressive politics, identification with, 29; range of commitment to participation, 2; selection of, 3, 46; silences of, on ill health and bereavement, 73–74, 75–76; and skepticism for project of social research, 46; and sympathy for project of social research, 3, 29, 168–69. *See also* personal experiences of aging; residential homes (institutions)—interviewees/residents; testimony of aged
Social Science Research Council, 33
Social Survey, 29
spectacles and eye care, 9
Spence, Jo, 169
stages theory of unemployment, 63–64
standard of living, ambivalence of working-class autobiographers and, 149–50, 153
state pensions. *See* pensions—state pensions
Statistical Society (London), 21
statistics, and identification of "aging population," 158
Stead, W. T., 21
Stearns, Carol, 177n69
Stearns, Peter, 177n69
Steedman, Carolyn, 13
"Stepney Stories" (Booth), 23–24, 25–26
stoicism: bereavement and, 4, 73–74; expected difficulties of physical aging and, 4, 69–71; and institutional environment of care homes, 91
style. *See* fashion and beauty culture
suburbanization, 61, 168

technology: medical care advances in, 9; of printing, and rise of autobiography as genre, 135, 141–42; social change and, in autobiographies, 145

testimony of aged: as contributing to fuller picture of old age, 156, 170–71; social class and opportunities to express, 161; social researchers' enthusiasm for, 18–19, 36, 38, 40–41, 46–47, 58, 98, 161. *See also* social research participants
—IGNORED BY ADVOCACY GROUPS AND GOVERNMENT MINISTRIES: replication of Townsend study and, 4–5; residential home conditions, 78
—IGNORED BY SOCIAL RESEARCHERS, 19–20, 161–62; Booth survey poverty series and, 23–24; and difficulty of balancing dignity with egalitarianism, 161; and histories of old age, 170–71; of residential home residents, 78, 79, 161
Thane, Pat, 12
Thompson, Edith, 141
Thompson, Paul, 41, 43, 58
Thomson, Alistair, 143
Thomson, Mathew, 32
Titmuss, Richard, 40, 158
Todd, Selina, 13–14, 15, 140–41
Townsend, Peter: on absorption of older people into their narrative, 161; biography of, as influencing research, 39; on difficulties of aging, 69, 70; on enthusiasm for subjects and blindness to negative qualities in, 39; and focus on experts, 42; on interview format, shortcomings of, 43; interview technique of, 38–39, 40–42, 43–44, 46–47, 58; "kinship maps" of, 48–49; legacy of, 79, 169; and persistence of poverty, 40; photographs by, 58, 59–60, 85, 85–88, 89; and policy ends, 41, 44; and political parties, relationship to, 39–40; *Poverty in the United Kingdom*, 43; "rediscovery" of poverty and, 12; regrets on brevity of time spent with residential care interviewees, 42; regrets on not recognizing

Townsend, Peter *(continued)*
violence and abuse, 68; on retirement experience for men, 65; selection of participants, 3, 46, 68; skepticism about privatization and cost-saving measures, 79, 162; as source, 14; women in forefront of studies by, 68, 191n92. *See also Family Life of Old People, The* (Townsend); *Last Refuge, The* (Townsend)
Townsend, Ruth (neé Pearce), 68, 78, 91, 92, 96
trauma, histories of, 14
Tunstall, Jeremy, 36–38, *37*

unemployment: deindustrialization and, 143–44, 168; Depression and, 63–64; and effects on families, 64; as increasing with age, 66, 80; stages theory of, 63–64; white-collar positions and, 168; women and, 66. *See also* workhouses
unions, restriction of alternative forms of relief by, 23
United Nations, and aging of population, 157
United States: cosmetics sales and, 128–29; old age as subject of legal and bureaucratic management in, 7–8; percentage of population over sixty, 7
universal social safety net: Beveridge Report proposing, 30; perceived as solution for every problem, 44–45; popularity of, 30, 31
universities, social science education in, 33
University of the Third Age, 169

Vernon, June, 78
Victoria (queen), 145–46
violence and abuse: in autobiography, 153; Townsend on regrets for not recognizing, 68
Vogue (American edition), 108

Vogue (British edition), 5, 108–9; advertising and, 108, 116, 117, 121; and age as no barrier to good style, 108–9; line drawings in, 109, *110*, 117; men's fashion and grooming, 104, *120*, 121; older women as focus of, Mrs. Exeter character and, 104, 111–17, *112–16*, 118–19, *120*, 131, 203nn44,50; and photographs, switch to, 109, *110*; readership of, 109; WWII restrictions and, 109, 111; and youth market, 117–19, *118*
voluntary organizations (charitable groups): Grandfathers' Club, 53, *55*; limits to capacities of, 32; and mass discharge of elderly from hospitals in WWII, 30; national insurance gaps and need for, 31, 32; provision of welfare services by, 32–33, 163; training of volunteers, 33. *See also* charity; residential homes (institutions)—voluntary and religious homes

Wales: aging of population in, 158; local authority homes in, 164; slum clearance in, 61; and state pensions, 27. *See also Last Refuge, The* (Townsend)
Wapping, East London, 151–53
Warren, Marjory, 11, 31–32
Wartime Survey, 29
Waters, Chris, 143
Waugh, Evelyn, 137
Webb, Beatrice, 13, 107
welfare services for aged: inner life of aged, concern for, 31–32; local authorities providing, 32–33, 163; national insurance gaps in, and need for voluntary and commercial organizations, 31, 32; persistence of poverty despite, 45; postwar increases in, 9–10, 44–45; publicity for, as strengthening notion of dependency, 157; and rise of social

researchers, 1–2, 19, 34; skepticism about, by interviewees, 3–4; state payment to families for care, Townsend as advocating, 68–69; voluntary groups as providing, 32–33, 163; WWII and recognition of need for, 29–30. *See also* community (at-home) care; residential homes (institutions)

welfare state: achievements of, for elderly, 9; "aging of population" as justification for cutbacks in, 157–58, 159, 160; and care of elderly as social vs. individual problem, 32; as contested and unevenly provided, 10–11; as "damaging to character" of British people, 53; and deindustrialization, 143–44; and generation of information, 19; and loosening of family ties, 51, 53; monetary policies of, 160; as overburdened system, 44, 45; persistence of poverty despite, 45; symbolic significance of elder care and, 9–10; and tax revenues, reduction of, 160. *See also* universal social safety net

Wells, H. G., 140

white-collar positions, retirement from, 168

widowhood/widowerhood, 72–75. *See also* bereavement

Williams, Leonard, 28

Willmott, Peter, 168

Wilson, Harold, 39

Wolverhampton, 168

Woman (magazine), 108

Woman's Own (magazine), 108

women: autobiographies of, as eschewing individualistic model, 139; autobiographies of, new interest in, 135; and body confidence in aging, 105; bonds with adult children, 61, 70–71, 90; and childbirth, ramifications of, 9; as "disappearing" as they age, 105; fiction and selfhood, exploration of, 141; in forefront of Townsend's studies, 68, 191n92; life expectancy of, 8, 165; malnutrition of, 8–9; pensions dependent on marital status, 9; postwar workforce expansion and, 158–60; state pension age for, 8; and susceptibility to ill health, 8–9, 69; and susceptibility to poverty, 9; unemployment and, 66; voting rights of, 145. *See also* clothing; families; fashion and beauty culture; gender; household labor; men

Women's Royal Voluntary Service, 32, 163

Women's Weekly (magazine), 107, 108

Woodford, 168

Wordsworth, William, 135–36

work: importance of, and difficulties of retirement, 65–66; and masculinity, 65–66; outside formal employment, 64; postwar labor shortages and, 64–65, 159; by residents of care homes, 166–67; and storytelling, 65–66; and women, 9; WWII and full employment, 64. *See also* "aging population" concerns; household labor; retirement; unemployment

Workers' Education Association, 142

workhouses, 80; condemnation of, by Labour government, 79, 81; disciplining with physical labor in, 23, 80; hatred and fear of, in working classes, 23, 80; and judgments of authorities as priority of social researchers, 23; last years of, 82; and narratives utilized by working people, 23, 141; number of people in, 80; residential institutions as resembling, 4, 78, 79, 82, 85, 85, 87–88, 89, 91–92, 95–96, 96; and separation and destruction of families, 23, 80. *See also* residential homes (institutions) working class: and deindustrialization, 143–44; differential treatment of, by administrators and staff of residential homes, 94–96; differential treatment of, by social researchers, 10–11; and family life, 58–63; fashionability of culture of, 140; hatred and fear of workhouse among, 23, 80; and importance of self-reliance, 80; malnutrition of women in, 8–9; men's fashion marketed to, 119–20; social researchers' vs. workers' view of, 15; women's magazines aimed toward, 107–8. *See also* autobiography as genre—working-class; council estates; families; *Family Life of Old People, The* (Townsend); slum clearance

World Bank, and aging of population, 157

World Economic Forum, and aging of population, 157

World War I: in autobiographies as boundary event, 146; and social change, 139. *See also* interwar period

World War II: and advocacy groups for elderly, 29–30; in autobiographies as boundary event, 146, 147–48; baby booms following, 158–59; fashion restrictions and, 109, 111; mass discharge from hospitals due to mass civilian bombing victims, 29–30, 81; and need to measure public opinion, 28–29; and postwar labor shortages, 64–65, 159; and retirement experienced as exclusion, 64. *See also* national insurance; postwar period

Young, Michael, 12, 40, 168

youth: and "color divide" in clothing choices, 103–4; in fashion and women's magazines, 107–8, 117–19, *118*, 131; history of emotions of, 13–14; lowering of retirement age to encourage employment of, 64; mobility of, as contributing to social isolation, 51; preference of businesses to hire, 65; and use of cosmetics, 127–28. *See also* autobiographies of aging authors; generational perspectives

www.ingramcontent.com/pod-product-compliance
Lightning Source LLC
Chambersburg PA
CBHW030532230426
43665CB00010B/852